D1083715

THE SOCIOLOGY OF THE PROFESSIONS

OXFORD SOCIO-LEGAL STUDIES

General Editors: J. Maxwell Atkinson, Donald R. Harris, R. M. Hartwell

Oxford Socio-Legal Studies is a series of books published by the Centre for Socio-Legal Studies, Wolfson College, Oxford (a research unit of the Social Science Research Council). The series is concerned generally with the relationship between law and society, and is designed to reflect the increasing interest in this field of lawyers, social scientists and historians.

J. Maxwell Atkinson and Paul Drew: ORDER IN COURT: The Organization of Verbal Interaction in Judicial Settings
Ross Cranston: REGULATING BUSINESS: Law and Consumer Agencies
Robert Dingwall and Philip Lewis (*editors*): THE SOCIOLOGY OF THE PROFESSIONS: Lawyers, Doctors and Others
David P. Farrington, Keith Hawkins and Sally M. Lloyd-Bostock (*editors*): PSYCHOLOGY, LAW AND LEGAL PROCESSES
Sally M. Lloyd-Bostock: PSYCHOLOGY IN LEGAL CONTEXTS: Applications and Limitations
Mavis Maclean and Hazel Genn: METHODOLOGICAL ISSUES IN SOCIAL SURVEYS
Doreen J. McBarnet: CONVICTION: Law, the State and the Construction of Justice
Alan Paterson: THE LAW LORDS

THE SOCIOLOGY OF THE PROFESSIONS

Lawyers, Doctors and Others

Edited by

Robert Dingwall

Senior Research Officer, SSRC Centre for Socio-Legal Studies, Wolfson College, Oxford

and

Philip Lewis

Fellow, All Souls College, Oxford

First published 1983 by
THE MACMILLAN PRESS LTD
London and Basingstoke
Companies and representatives
throughout the world

ISBN 0 333 30961 8

Printed in Hong Kong

Contents

The Contributors

Paul Atkinson, Lecturer, Department of Sociology, University College, Cardiff.

Maureen Cain, Lecturer, Department of Law, London School of Economics and Political Science.

Celia Davies, Senior Research Fellow, Department of Sociology, University of Warwick.

Robert Dingwall, Senior Research Officer, SSRC Centre for Socio-Legal Studies, Wolfson College, Oxford.

John Eekelaar, Fellow of Pembroke College and part-time Research Fellow, SSRC Centre for Socio-Legal Studies, Wolfson College, Oxford.

Eliot Freidson, Professor, Department of Sociology, New York University.

Marc Galanter, Professor, Law School, University of Wisconsin-Madison.

Gordon Horobin, Deputy Director, MRC Medical Sociology Unit, Aberdeen.

Malcolm Johnson, Senior Fellow, Policy Studies Institute, London.

Philip Lewis, Fellow, All Souls College, Oxford.

Geoff Mungham, Senior Lecturer, Department of Sociology, University College, Cardiff.

Topsy Murray, Research Officer, SSRC Centre for Socio-Legal Studies, Wolfson College, Oxford.

Alan Paterson, Lecturer, Department of Scots Law, University of Edinburgh.

Dietrich Rueschemeyer, Professor, Department of Sociology, Brown University.

P. M. Strong, Research Officer, Department of Community Medicine, and General Practice, University of Oxford.

Philip Thomas, Senior Lecturer, Department of Law, University College, Cardiff.

Foreword

This collection of essays is the outcome of an attempt to take advantage of the editors' different intellectual backgrounds, in sociology and law, and research experience, among health and welfare organisations and occupations and on the legal profession and the provision of legal services. It seemed to us that the development of an adequate theoretical base for the analysis of the professions was being severely hindered by the lack of comparative inquiry.

Major advances had taken place as a result of the empirical work of medical sociologists on the division of labour in health and welfare services and its implications for organisational and occupational forms. This contribution, however, rested on an uncertain and even speculative foundation in the absence of comparable work on the organisation and practice of other service sectors. Which features of the category 'professions' were of general applicability and which related to the specific circumstances of medicine and its associated occupations? Did it, indeed, make any sense to talk about 'professions' as a discriminable and internally homogeneous category?

We felt, then, that a good deal might be gained from an attempt to reassess the current state of the sociology of the professions against a specific comparison of two occupations - medicine and law - which would, on any commonsense basis, be considered as such, if the category, 'professions', had any analytic significance at all. Moreover, a reassessment of this kind might provoke an awareness of new issues in the study of both medicine and law in the attempt to find common ground between two rather discrete intellectual enterprises.

With the help of the Centre for Socio-Legal Studies, a conference was arranged in Oxford at Easter 1979 to promote such a discussion. All the papers in this volume were first presented on that occasion, although they have been extensively revised for publication in the light of the debates which took place. We are grateful to the (British) Social Science Research Council for the funds which supported the conference and to the Trustees of the Nuffield Foundation, whose support made it possible for Lewis to take part in the preparations. Secretarial support was provided by Ginny Rosamond, Caroline Mason and Rosemary Stallan. Noël Harris, Beverly Roger and Jennifer Dix have also helped in the preparation of the typescript. We are particularly grateful to Chris Storrar for her meticulous work in editing the various drafts and in preparing the volume bibliography.

December 1980   ROBERT DINGWALL
PHILIP LEWIS

Introduction

ROBERT DINGWALL

Research in the sociology of the professions is, today, largely founded on the contributions of two people, Talcott Parsons and Everett Hughes. Although, as both Freidson and Rueschemeyer show, it is possible to identify earlier writings, these have, for the most part, been treated as of mainly antiquarian interest. Even when we come to the recent flourishing of neo-Marxist literature, we still tend to find the contributions of Parsons and Hughes taken as a starting-point.

Parsons's general work has suffered badly from an excess of critical zeal in which the complexity and development of his thought has been obscured in an overall lambasting of functionalism. His writings on the professions, however, belong, in the main, to a pre-functionalist period when Parsons's main intellectual stimulus came from Weber rather than Freud. Two statements are of particular interest: his introduction to a translation from Weber, *The Theory of Social and Economic Organisation*, published in 1947 but apparently written before the war, and a paper, 'The Professions and Social Structure', first published in 1939. Hughes's greatest legacy, by contrast, lies not in his own work but in that of his students, most notably Howard Becker and Blanche Geer, although Eliot Freidson, Erving Goffman and Anselm Strauss all passed through Chicago while he was on the staff. Like most of the major ethnographers in that department, Hughes had little sympathy for grand synthetic visions of the kind that Parsons aspired to. His sociology was transmitted almost as an oral culture which was available only at second-hand or in a rather heterogeneous assortment of papers, which were only collected in a substantial and readily available format with the publication of *The Sociological Eye* in 1971. Hughes too, drew from Weber but perhaps more crucially also from Simmel, whom Parsons disregarded as a microsociologist.[1] Hughes's interest in the professions also went back to the 1930s, but his thought was much less affected by the post-war intellectual fashion for Freud and displays much greater basic continuity.

The starting point for Parsons's discussion was his critique of utilitarian economics in *The Structure of Social Action*. One of the major themes of that work was the inadequacy of the economists' analysis of the social order of modern capitalist societies as the aggregate product of myriads of conceptually atomised unit acts, based on immediate calculations of maximal self-interest. How was an actor to recognise what was to count as maximising self-interest? Through the writings of Marshall, Pareto, Durkheim and Weber, Parsons sought to trace a concentration of social thought around this problem, eventually proposing his own solution, with a theoretical base in the sociology of knowledge, in terms of a socially-grounded normative order. The professions were an important empirical test for this proposition. Was their co-existence with a business economy an anachronism, given their apparent denial of self-interest as a motive for action, or was it an illustration of an alternative approach to a shared normative end?

The professions also presented a significant difficulty for Weber's rationalist account of order in modern society. Like most of the classic sociologists, Parsons was fascinated by the fragility of social order. For him, one of the most striking features of Weber's thought was its concern with the regulation and legitimation of the exercise of power. The selfish anarchy of the economists was held at bay by the recognition of authority, power normatively constrained and, thereby, rendered acceptable to its subjects. Weber argued that modern capitalist societies were characterised by the spread of rationality, what he termed the 'dis-enchantment of the modern world'. In such a society authority rested on a rational-legal foundation, where the exercise of power was limited and justified by appeals to an impersonal order of generalised rules. The social organisational counterpart of this mode of authority was the bureaucracy, whose disinterested stance was underwritten by a clear delimitation of its sphere of action and its separation from the private commitments of its employees. Internally, these were reinforced by a strict system of supervision and control. Weber's analysis offers no explicit treatment of the professions, an omission which is readily understandable in the light of Freidson's and Rueschemeyer's comments on the Anglo-American bias in the concept itself. One might, however, propose, as Horobin does in this volume, that the professions have significant charismatic elements to their authority and organisation. Many features of their relationship to society are mysterious, in the old sense of the word, and their mode of practice is highly individualised. On the Weberian model of social evolution they seem as anachronistic as on that of the classical economists.

Parsons, however, recognised what is by now a commonplace: the capitalist economy, the rational-legal social order *and* the modern professions are contemporary historical developments. What modifications did the accepted theories require in the light of this empirical observation? At the prompting of one of his principal Harvard mentors, L. J. Henderson, Parsons became involved in a study of medical practice in the Boston area in order to explore this question.[2] Tantalisingly few details of this research have ever been published. However, medicine offered a particularly useful testing-ground because of its relevance to a further disagreement between Parsons and Weber over the epistemological status of natural and social science. Weber tended to argue for a break between them but Parsons took the more radical position from the sociology of knowledge, arguing for their essential continuity.

In studying medical practice Parsons could demonstrate the social foundation of its knowledge and its translation into the impersonal normative order of science. Science provided an equivalent to the legal order and a similar foundation for rational action. However, that action took place through collegial forms of organisation. In fact, as Murray, Dingwall and Eekelaar argue later, these are less antithetical to the notion of a bureaucracy than Parsons supposed, since he tended to elide one manifestation - the monocratic type - with the underlying ideal.

Nevertheless, Parsons showed that the individualist collegial organisations of the professions and the hierarchical organisations of monocratic bureaucracy rested their authority on the same principles - functional specificity, the restriction of their domain of power, and the application of impersonal standards on a universalistic basis, without regard to the personal characteristics or circumstances of their subjects. The alleged distinction in terms of self-interested as opposed to altruistic motivation was of minor significance. What was more important was a shared orientation to 'success', whether material or non-material, as judged by the prevailing normative standards. These standards overrode the utilitarian calculus of the economists. The normative order was of course, a complex phenomenon. A variety of contributions might be counted as successful in ways which might or might not be merited. Other institutional spheres - family, friends, classes - might be founded on different values and embody other organisational forms with a diffuse and particularistic character, their authority spilling over an ill-defined territory in a selective and individually-responsive fashion. Social integration was always empirically problematic.

In his later writings, the professions became less central to Parsons's work, although *The Social System* proposes some interesting ideas about the relations between professions and deviance. Parsons himself became more interested in unravelling the nature of the normative order of modern capitalist societies and the ways in which it was transmitted, an enterprise in which he was deeply influenced by Freudian thought.[3]

Hughes, on the other hand, maintained his interest in the professions throughout his career. It is more difficult to present his contribution in a synthetic fashion: like most Chicago sociologists, as Rock (1979) has demonstrated, he had less grandiose preoccupations. However, there are certain consistent themes, which may relate in part to the different experiences of prewar Chicago and of prewar Europe. Parsons was writing in a European tradition of conservative sociology, developed in response to the turmoil of the nineteenth-century political, industrial and economic revolutions. American sociology was a sociology of progress. Where Parsons had a deep anxiety about the apparent disintegration of social order and the collapse of its normative foundations into fascism and chaos, Hughes saw the great melting-pot of Chicago where a bewildering variety of ethnic interests were being forged into a new social order.

The division of labour, then, lies at the heart of Hughes's interest in the professions; not in the pessimistic vision of Marx and Weber but in the optimistic spirit of Durkheim and Simmel who saw its possibilities for the extension of human freedom and cooperative interdependence. The world of work was treated as an analogue to the city of Chicago urban ecology. A given terrain of demands for goods and services was divided into blocks of tasks, which might be developed, redeveloped or extinguished. These blocks had successive occupiers, competing for access and struggling to improve their status by new acquisitions or the relinquishment of less attractive properties. Some occupiers were prestigious and powerful, others disregarded. All were caught up in a constant evolutionary process as demands and technology changed, either from clients or from internal attempts to influence the market.

Two concepts are particularly important in Hughes's thought: licence and mandate. All occupations have an implicit or explicit licence to carry out certain activities which are different from those of others, in exchange for money, goods and services. It is this formalised exchange-relationship which distinguishes work from non-work spheres. If the occupation members have any sense of community by virtue of their shared work experience, they are also likely to claim a mandate to define, for themselves and others, proper conduct in relation to their work, to influence its technical content, styles of delivery and, most crucially, the patterns of public demand and response. Hughes emphasises that both licence and mandate should be thought of in the broadest terms.

Nowhere is this more true than in the case of professions, which Hughes regards as the prime illustration of the possible legal, intellectual and moral scope of a mandate. Not only do professions presume to tell the rest of their society what is good and right for it: they can also set the very terms of thinking about problems which fall in their domain. They exemplify in an extreme form the role of trust in modern societies with an advanced division of labour. The professions are licensed to carry out some of the most dangerous tasks of our society - to intervene in our bodies, to intercede for our prospects of future salvation, to regulate the conflict of rights and obligations between social interests. Yet in order to do this, they must acquire guilty knowledge - the priest is an expert on sin, the doctor on disease, the lawyer on crime - and the ability to look at these matters in comparative and, hence, relative terms. This is the mystery of the professions. Their privileged status is an inducement to maintain their loyalty in concealing the darker sides of their society and in refraining from exploiting their knowledge for evil purposes.

It is important to emphasise that Hughes regards these features as differences of degree rather than kind, present in all occupations. In consequence, any occupation may aspire to similar privileges if it can reconstruct its licence and win acceptance of an enlarged mandate, just as, in fact, the urban sociologists recognised the potential mobility routes for ethnic groups. Professionalising occupations are a zone of transition, a point of change from which new social forms are emerging and, hence, a matter of particular interest for the sociologist.

Finally, we must note that, unlike Parsons, Hughes was offering a distinctive methodology. Chicago sociology had a central belief in the importance of first-hand experience of the social world. This was never dealt with in any very systematic written fashion but formed part of the oral tradition from which students acquired a sense of research practice in the quasi-anthropological fieldwork which dominated the chronicling of interwar Chicago.

This difference is important in understanding the legacies of the two men. Hughes's students went on to produce a series of detailed ethnographies within the department's tradition of concentrating on change as an everyday process. Parsons's more structural approach left few guidelines for its realisation in empirical study, particularly given his own failure to publish an adequate account of his research. The resulting intellectual vacuum was filled by the emergence of an empiricist methodology derived from the work of Lazarsfeld, whose old-fashioned scientism responded to the conservative climate of fifties America in its depoliticisation of debate and its pretensions to objectivity. In retrospect, the two seem uneasy intellectual bedfellows linked more by their scientistic than their philosophical coherence. One might, indeed, argue that C. Wright Mills's twin bogeys of Grand Theory and Abstracted Empiricism were able to co-exist mainly as a result of a tendency in American sociology to avoid internal conflict by a process of compartmentalisation. Neither sought to occupy the territory of the other and a superficial harmony reigned. The main opposition came from Chicago-trained students and faculty, themselves compartmentalised into the Society for the Study of Social Problems. One consequence, however, was that some of the most formative writings of Hughes's students were characterised by an explicitly oppositional stance, products of a group on the intellectual and organisational margins of the discipline. The effects on that work are discussed by a number of contributors to this volume, most particularly Atkinson.

Both traditions, then, left a series of open questions. How were we to know a profession when we saw one? Parsons took the category for granted, Hughes said it was merely a question of degree. What was the relationship between values, organisation and practice? Parsons had been very vague about the sources of values, their transmission and their internalisation as regulators of work standards. He tended to play down the significance of organisational forms in favour of their pervading spirit. Hughes, on the other hand, gave more attention to organisational features. Although his own writings contain considerable discussions of the relationship between professions and moral order, the work they inspired led to a downgrading of values in favour of an analysis which often owed more to a maximal self-interest model. Professional work and its collective forms were presented as the aggregate outcomes of everyday battles over the use of resources, the limits of task ownership and the delegation of 'dirty work'. Crudely, one might suggest it was economics with the money left out.

Finally, and most crucially, both traditions neglected the role of the marketplace and the professions' wider contract with their society. Parsons's repudiation of economic reasoning seems responsible for one of the most glaring omissions from his discussion of the relationship between professions and business: the monopoly power of the former. Similarly, Hughes's disdain for the unworldliness of neo-classical economics and his vision of sociology as a study of social forms undermines his own remarks on the importance of exchange relationships. Competition within and between occupations is drawn around status attributes rather than financial gain. The lack of attention to exchange relationships also affected both traditions' handling of the wider dimensions of the professions. Weber's discussion of bureaucracy emphasises control and supervision rather than accountability. It is, however, vital to ask where the impersonal rules come from. Insofar as they have some democratic foundation, for instance, then a bureaucracy is not just an engine of control in a necessarily oppressive sense but a device for ensuring that the popular sentiments expressed in the rules are respected by employees and clients alike. This weakness carries over to Parsons's work and is never directly resolved in relation to the professions. Hughes does offer a way of talking about such issues in his discussion of licence and mandate. It is, however, a theme which is subordinated in later empirical work in favour of the study of intra-occupational events, partly, one suspects, as a reaction against the abstracted macro-sociology of the fifties.

Empirical work on the professions has clustered around these questions. Hughes comments several times on the avid interest of graduate students in writing about their own occupations as a means of professionalisation. In some hands (e.g. Greenwood 1957) this turned into the trait approach, often mistakenly identified with Parsons, to the issue of definition. Could we list exhaustive criteria for distinguishing professions from other occupations? Other writers (e.g. Becker 1970) sought to defend profession as a non-evaluative term by identifying sociological and lay concepts. The former would be restricted to an analytic sense, while the latter would yield data on the rhetoric of justification current in some community. Interest in the relationship between values and institutional forms as determinants of occupational practice generated several major studies of professional socialisation and countless pieces of research, of various methodological persuasions, on professional work. (Merton *et al.* 1957; Becker *et al.* 1961; Strauss *et al.* 1964; etc.) Finally, the reawakening of interest in political economy has led to some notable discussions of the relationship between professions and the market for their services and of their wider societal context (Johnson 1972; Larson 1977).

However, the empirical base for such work has remained oddly skewed. In his recent review of work on American lawyers, Abel (1980, p.335) has pointed to the dearth of writing about lawyers in any critical or theoretical sense, compared with the wealth of literature on medicine. Similarly, Campbell *et al.* (1980, p.9) draw attention to the discrepancy between their original classificatory frame and the available work in preparing a bibliography on the British legal profession and its work. There is a lack of basic socio-demographic data on recruitment, training and career paths. Historical work is still dominated by biographies of great men and great firms. Relatively little work has been done on the formal and informal organisation of practice. How does the occupational community police itself? What is the impact of specialisation on the division of labour? Where, and in what fashion, does occupational socialisation occur? Where do paraprofessional workers and self-help fit? On the other hand, it must be recognised that in some respects the available work on lawyers goes well beyond traditional work on doctors. Medical sociology has had relatively little to say about the impact of the cash nexus and restrictive economic practices. It has also tended to underplay the political and community activities of doctors as topics for detailed study rather than polemic. Moreover, the concentration of sociologists on law rather than lawyers, knowledge rather than practice, has permitted a perspective on the former as a social product which medical sociologists still find difficult to sustain in relation to medicine (Dingwall 1977b). Nevertheless, one is forced to conclude that, despite a number of contributions which would be first class by any criteria, the sociology of lawyers is comparatively underdeveloped on both sides of the Atlantic.

The reasons for this are both social and intellectual. We have already alluded to the critical importance of medicine as a testing ground in Parsons's debates with Weber. It was similarly strategic for Hughes's thought. The proliferation of specialties within medicine, the explosive growth of new paramedical occupations, the aspirations of lower-status personnel to the rewards of doctors, all constitute a vast natural laboratory for the ecological concerns of the Chicago-influenced sociologist. We must also recognise that medicine is a matter of public concern in a way which most law is not. The development of the modern welfare state, even if it does not directly nationalise health service provision, creates a political stake in containing premature death, disease and disability as costs to social security schemes. There has then been an investment of research funding in medical sociology which has not been paralleled in the study of law. With the important exception of criminal law-enforcement and correction, legal matters are treated as a private or corporate rather than a collective problem. Such features have interacted with the organisation of academic work to create distinctive combinations of activity in the study of medicine and law on the two sides of the Atlantic.

I have discussed some of the features underlying these differences elsewhere (Dingwall et al. 1980; Payne et al. 1981) and cannot explore them in detail here. However, in brief, we can identify both empiricist and theoretical currents in both fields in both locations, the distinctions which Straus (1957) identifies as sociology in and sociology of medicine and Campbell and Wiles (1976) term 'socio-legal studies' and 'sociology of law'. The former concentrate on the application of research techniques to questions given by the allied discipline; the latter is a more theoretical enterprise which embraces the disciplinary perspective which poses those questions as part of its own problematic. It is a distinction between working within, if not actually serving, established interests and appropriating those same interests as the subject of one's research.

In the UK the sociologies of medicine and law both grew up in the shadow of existing interests in social medicine and criminology - pragmatic, utilitarian and atheoretical enterprises. Both of these interests owed more to traditions in social administration and social biology than to the likes of Hobhouse, Ginsberg or Marshall who shared the more fundamental orientations of Continental European sociology. With the increased professionalisation of British sociology in the 1960s, sociologists became less satisfied with the underlabourer role of 'social factors in ...' to which they had traditionally been consigned and eager to secure a share of the substantial funding resources available to their competitors. The ideas of the American sociology of deviance were imported as a spearhead in this revolution. There was, however a key difference between the two fields: criminology was a profoundly conservative discipline while social medicine's practitioners held a strong self-image of themselves as radicals. The sociology of law, then, emerged out of a highly politicised debate while the sociology of medicine tended to retain a political consensus with social medicine and to dispute with it on predominately intellectual grounds.

The American picture is rather different. From the earliest days of its establishment in the universities sociology was a strongly empirical discipline. In consequence the sociology/social administration split is not reproduced in North America and the terrains of criminology and, to a lesser extent, social medicine are occupied by sociologists. Moreover the sociology of medicine was at the heart of sociological development rather than being a fringe speciality, as in the UK, and there was a much weaker demarcation between the study of medicine and other areas such as deviance, work and organisations. The shape of research in the two fields, then, represents more clearly the effects of outside forces, largely the availability of funding, which in turn flows from the political visibility of health care and justice as social issues, upon which we have already commented. A good deal of this is profoundly empiricist in character, but there is also a substantial body of theoretically informed empirical work.

British medical sociology lies closer to this model, although periodically agonising about its lowered indigenous prestige resulting from its lack of abstracted theorising in the mainstream domestic tradition. After a short-lived flirtation with American writings on deviance, however, British sociologists of law gravitated towards European Marxism. Empirical concerns disappeared, particularly under the impress of Althusserianism, in favour of the armchair manipulation of closed deductive systems, where studies of historical or contemporary events entered only as vehicles for previously stipulated themes. In part this also reflects funding contingencies: medical sociology's accommodation with social medicine meant that substantial, by sociological standards, research funds were available. The sociologists of law, on the other hand, were largely forced back onto what might be worked on alongside teaching positions. It is only comparatively recently that Britain has begun to produce a sociology of law which is capable of seeing its subject matter as a human product rather than as given *a priori* by the needs of capitalism. Only with the work of Podmore (1980a, 1980b) and some of the contributors to this volume, for instance, have we begun to acquire any sense of what a lawyer's work might be like.

Coupled with the lack of American studies stemming from the funding market, this leaves a serious gap in our knowledge. The study of the professions is weakened by an inadequate foundation for its generalisations. The study of medicine suffers from a lack of challenge to its dominant problematic, neglecting, for instance, the study of medical knowledge. The sociology of law is biased towards the study of criminal justice, a minor part of the totality of legal activity, and decontextualised. Laws exist *in vacuo* without adequate appreciation of their everyday creation, recreation, translation and extension.

The sociology of the professions stands at some kind of a turning point. The 1970s were invigorated by a sequence of major theoretical contributions, most notably from Freidson (1970a), Johnson (1972; 1977) and Larson (1977). Established traditions were seen to have reached the limits of their original paradigm and the research problems given within it. While the present collection reflects the plurality of theoretical positions which have developed in the course of the subsequent debates, there does seem to be a broad consensus on the key issues. First, it is clear that we need to take a very much wider perspective in attending to the historical setting of both individuals and collectivities. Professional work must be studied not just in the context of a division of labour but as part of a network of social and economic relations. Second, the importance of knowledge is reaffirmed. The division of labour is also a division of knowledge, with consequential implications of reciprocal dependence and vulnerability between participants. That knowledge is, moreover, a social product, reproducing and constituting a particular order. Third, and most important, is the stress on comparative empirical work. Throughout this collection, contributors, explicitly or implicitly, suggest that the separation of a sociology of professions from a sociology of occupations has been a blind alley. Rather than presupposing the sociological significance of professions as a catgeory, we should be asking what kinds of occupations there are. Such a question can, of course, only be posed against detailed case studies of work settings, case studies, however, which, in adopting the preceding injunctions, must be grounded in a wider understanding of structural and cultural features than has previously been common. It is a time, perhaps, for paradigm evolution through research into recognised problems, rather than a continuing self-indulgence in revolutionary debate from the comfort of academic armchairs.

ACKNOWLEDGEMENTS

I am grateful to my co-editor, Philip Lewis, and to Phil Strong and Max Atkinson for their comments and criticisms on an earlier draft of this paper. Responsibility for the final contents and assessments is, however, mine alone.

NOTES

1.   '... the most important single figure neglected in *The Structure of Social Action* and to an important degree in my subsequent writings is probably Simmel. It may be of interest that I actually drafted a chapter on Simmel for *The Structure of Social Action* but partly for reasons of space finally decided not to include it. Simmel was more a micro- than a macro-sociologist; moreover he was not, in my opinion, a *theorist* on the same level as the others. He was much more a highly talented essayist in the tradition of Tocqueville than a theorist like Durkheim ...' (Parsons 1968, p.xiv, n.10.)

2.   Henderson (1935) had himself produced one of the first essays on the doctor/patient relationship.

3. Given Parsons's involvement with psychotherapist/patient interaction
    during his study of medical practice, it is tempting to wonder whether
    this represents a case of a researcher 'going native'.

Part I

Professions, Knowledge and Power

The first part of this collection presents three papers bearing on the theme of Professions, Knowledge and Power. Eliot Freidson and Dietrich Rueschemeyer have contributed reviews of the development of sociological thinking about the professions over the postwar period. Freidson returns to the definitional problem and the difficulties which this has led to in recent metatheoretical debates. He points to the ambiguities which have arisen between talking about professions as a social stratum and as a subcategory of occupations distinguished by specific criteria, as a folk concept and as a sociological concept. These relate to two different enterprises: the study of the peculiar historical development of a part of the social structure of Anglo-American societies and the development of a comparative sociology of occupations, based on case studies of particular groups of workers in an attempt to induce a socially meaningful taxonomy. Rueschemeyer reappraises the functionalist contribution and its treatment of the social control of expertise. The division of labour creates the possible use of knowledge as a source of power. How is that power to be regulated? Where the functionalist writers had adopted self-regulation as the answer, however, Rueschemeyer points to the broad range of historical solutions depending upon the characteristics of different national societies, the balance between professionals, consumers and the State, and the recognised cultural forms of knowledge.

Before presenting the results of sociologists writing about other occupations, however, Phil Strong's paper turns their analyses back on themselves. In a theme he has addressed elsewhere (most notably in his comparison of sociological and medical imperialism), Strong asks what the relevance of the sociology of professions is for sociology itself. On this occasion, Strong considers the relationship between sociology and its popular rivals in social analysis - journalism, literature and the arts. What is it that distinguishes our product from theirs? Strong argues that many of the differences are exaggerated in pursuit of our own ambitions and suggests that a more liberal attitude to our rivals might well open up new issues and sources of data, not least in the study of work and occupations.

This section is biassed somewhat by the lack of a representative of current neo-Marxist writing, although this is discussed by both Freidson and Rueschemeyer. The original conference included such a paper but, unfortunately, it became unavailable at a late stage and we were unable to replace it without delaying publication to a degree which would have been unfair to other contributors.

1 The Theory of Professions: State of the Art

ELIOT FREIDSON

While professions have never been among the core topics for sociological theorising, a surprising number of the most prominent English-language sociologists, from Herbert Spencer (1914, pp.179-324) to Talcott Parsons (1968), have paid them rather more than glancing attention. Until recently, most sociologists have been inclined to see professions as honoured servants of public need, conceiving of them as occupations especially distinguished from others by their orientation to serving the needs of the public through the schooled application of their unusually esoteric knowledge and complex skill. In contrast, representatives of the other social sciences have stressed quite different characteristics of the professions. Economists have been inclined to note the closed, monopolistic character of the professionalised labour market (Cairnes 1887, pp.66-7; Friedman 1962, pp.137-60). Political scientists have been inclined to concern about professions as privileged private governments (Gilb 1966). And policy-makers have been inclined to see professional experts as overnarrow and insular in their vision of what is good for the public (Laski 1931).

The 1960s marked a watershed in sociological writings on the professions. For one thing, the evaluative flavour of the literature has changed. Whereas most sociologists had earlier emphasised the positive functions and achievements of the professions (though they were not unaware of their deficiencies), recent writers have been consistently more critical. Furthermore, the substantive preoccupation of the literature changed. In the earlier literature, the major scholarly writers focussed primarily on the analysis of professional norms and role relations and on interaction in work settings. While they all acknowledged the importance of political and economic factors, they did not analyse them at any length. The more recent scholarly literature, on the other hand, focusses on the political influence of professions (Freidson 1970a), on the relation of professions to political and economic élites and the state (Johnson 1972), and on the relation of professions to the market and the class system (Larson 1977).

But while there have been significant changes in the evaluative and substantive emphasis of sociological writings on the professions, they reflect changes in the *content* of theorising while remaining unchanged in the *nature* of theorising. This has been the case even though some of the recent criticism of the traditional approach has been metatheoretical in character. Unfortunately, those metatheoretical critiques have either addressed false issues or issues which are essentially insoluble because of the very nature of the concept of profession itself. For this reason, there has not been any significant advance in developing a theory of professions over the past decade or so that does not have as many deficiencies as past theories.

This is the point of the present paper. In it, I shall examine several common metatheoretical issues addressed by recent writings on the professions, and evaluate both their validity and their utility for advancing a theory of professions. In doing so, it will be necessary to address the concept of profession itself. The very nature of that concept, I shall argue, plays a critical role in creating some of the problems addressed by metatheoretical writings and precludes their solution in abstract, theoretical terms. The nature of the concept of profession, I shall argue, provides us with a limited number of options. The option that can lead to a coherent and systematic method of analysis is one that requires forsaking the attempt to treat profession as a generic concept and turning instead to formulating a generic conception of occupations within which we can locate analytically the particular occupations that have been labelled professions. To advance a theory of professions, however, requires a rather different option, which treats the concept as an historical construction in a limited number of societies, and studies its development, use and consequences in those societies without attempting more than the most modest generalisations.

THE PROBLEM OF DEFINITION

Much debate, going back at least as far as Flexner (1915), has centred around how professions should be defined - which occupations should be called professions, and by what institutional criteria. But while most definitions overlap in the elements, traits or attributes they include, a number of tallies have demonstrated a persistent lack of consensus about which traits are to be emphasised in theorising (Millerson 1964, p.5). No small part of the criticism of the traditional literature on the professions has been devoted to pointing out a lack of consensus. Because we seem to be no nearer consensus than we were in 1915, and because usage varies substantively, logically and conceptually (Freidson 1977), some analysts have given the impression of condemning the very practice of seeking a definition. But surely such condemnation is inappropriate. In order to think clearly and systematically about anything, one must delimit the subject-matter to be addressed by empirical and intellectual analysis. We cannot develop theory if we are not certain what we are talking about.

One method of attempting to solve the problem of definition has been to deprecate the value of defining the characteristics of professions as 'inherently distinct from other occupations' (Klegon 1978, p.268) and to urge instead discussing the process by which occupations claim or gain professional status. The outcome of such a position, however, is to avoid entirely any *conscious* definition while in fact covertly advancing an implicit and unsatisfactorily vague definition of a profession as an occupation that has gained professional status. What is professional status? How does one determine when it does and when it does not exist? What are its characteristics?

A closely related suggestion is to shift focus from a 'static' conception of profession as a distinct type of occupation to the process by which occupations are professionalised (Vollmer and Mills 1966). However, as Turner and Hodge (1970, p.23) and Johnson (1972, p.31) have correctly noted, an emphasis on process rather than structure, on professionalisation rather than on the attributes of professions, does not really solve the problem of definition. To speak about the process of professionalisation requires one to define the direction of the process, and the end-state of professionalism toward which an occupation may be moving. Without *some* definition of profession the concept of professionalisation is virtually meaningless, as is the intention to study process rather than structure. One cannot study process without a definition guiding one's focus any more fruitfully than one can study structure without a definition.

In all, the issue of definition for a theory of professions cannot be dealt with profitably either by denial or by avoidance. A word with so many connotations and denotations cannot be employed in precise discourse without definition. One can avoid the issue of definition only if one adopts the patently anti-analytical position that all occupations - whether casual day-labour, assembly-line work, teaching, surgery or systems analysis - are so much alike that there is no point in making distinctions of any kind among them. That there are no differences of any analytic importance must be firmly denied.

Given the necessity of definition, one may note that the character of an adequate definition must be such as to specify a set of referents by which the phenomenon may be discriminated in the empirical world - that is, specifying attributes, traits or defining characteristics. Unfortunately, there has been a tendency in the recent critical literature to confuse the act of specifying defining characteristics with the particular characteristics specified by earlier writers. One can criticise a definition because of the analytically and empirically ambiguous traits it singles out (Freidson 1970a), or because its traits have no systematic interrelations and no theoretical rationale (Johnson 1972). But it is not the fact that a definition is composed of traits or attributes that can be justifiably criticised.

In all, then, it would seem that in the present state of the art of theorising about professions, recent comments on the issue of definition miss the mark. The definitional problem that has plagued the field for over half a century is not one created by squabbling pedants, to be solved by eschewing definition entirely. Nor is the problem created by the adoption of a static 'structural' or 'functional' approach, to be solved by a 'process' or 'conflict' approach. Nor is the problem created by including traits or attributes in a definition. The problem, I suggest, lies much deeper than that. It is created by attempting to treat profession as if it were a generic concept rather than a changing historic concept, with particular roots in an industrial nation strongly influenced by Anglo-American institutions.

THE PAROCHIALISM OF THE INSTITUTIONAL CONCEPT OF PROFESSION

In order to elaborate my argument about the nature of the concept of profession, it is necessary first of all to emphasise the difference between two very different usages which are sometimes confused. First, there is the concept of profession that refers to a broad stratum of relatively prestigious but quite varied occupations whose members have all had some kind of higher education and who are identified more by their educational status than by their specific occupational skills. Second, there is the concept of profession as a limited number of occupations which have particular institutional and ideological traits more or less in common. It is only this second concept which allows us to think of 'professionalism' as, in Johnson's terms, a way of organising an occupation (Johnson 1972, p.45). It represents much more than only a status, for it produces distinctive occupational identities and exclusionary market shelters (cf. Parkin 1979) which set each occupation apart from (and often in opposition to) the others.

Furthermore, the two differ markedly in their relevance to present-day industrial societies. The concept of profession as a very broad, educated stratum has been applied without much difficulty to all industrial nations (for example, Ben-David 1977, p.30). But it refers to a much more general and vague phenomenon than does the institutional concept of profession as a distinctive form of organised occupation. The major theoretical writings on the professions have all addressed themselves to professions in this second sense - as a fairly limited number of occupations which share characteristics of considerably greater specificity than higher education alone, and which are distinctive as separate occupations. Their members conceive of themselves by their occupation first and by their 'class', if at all, only second. It is precisely this institutional concept of profession which is very difficult to apply to the entire range of occupations in the 'professional stratum' of any industrial nation, or even to those middle-class occupations in Europe which would, in Anglo-American nations, be considered professions in the more narrow sense.

Occupations called professions in English have had a rather special history. As we all know, the medieval universities of Europe spawned the three original learned professions of medicine, law and the clergy (of which university teaching was part). Elliott (1972, pp.14, 32) has suggested the term 'status professions' for them, pointing out quite accurately their marked difference from the recent 'occupational professions'.

As the occupational structure of capitalist industrialism developed during the nineteenth century in England, and then later in the United States, terminological consensus became greatly confused by the efforts of newly reorganised or newly formed middle-class occupations to seek the title of 'profession' because it was connected with the gentlemanly status of the traditional learned professions (Reader 1967; Larson 1977). While there were very important differences between the two nations, they had in common a comparatively passive state apparatus with a strong but by no means unambivalent *laissez-faire* philosophy, and a small civil service.

Occupations seeking a secure and privileged place in the economy of those countries could not do more than seek state support for an exclusionary shelter in the open market where they had to compete with rival occupations. They had to organise their own training and credentialling institutions, since the state played a passive role in such affairs. Unlike other countries, the title 'profession' was used to establish the status of successful occupations; it became part of the official occupational classification scheme in the United States and in England, expanding its coverage slowly by including more occupations in the same category, with the same title, as the original status professions of the medieval universities (cf. Reader 1967, pp.146-66, 207-11). Gaining recognition as a 'profession' was important to occupations not only because it was associated with traditional gentry status, but also because its traditional connotations of disinterested dedication and learning legitimated the effort to gain protection from competition in the labour market. Given *laissez-faire* philosophy, only quite special excuses could justify the state-sanctioned creation of a market shelter. The ideologies of special expertise and moral probity provided by the traditional concept of status profession, sustained by ostensibly supportive occupational institutions, provided just such a basis for legitimating protection from the winds of occupational competition.

In England and the United States, the tendency was for each occupation to have to mount its own movement for recognition and protection. Its members' loyalties and identities were attached to their individual occupation and its institutions. The situation was rather different in Europe, where the state was much more active in organising both training and employment. The traditional status professions maintained their occupational distinctions as they reorganised their corporate bodies, but the new, middle-class occupations did not seek classification as 'professions' to gain status and justify a market shelter: such an umbrella title imputing special institutional characteristics to them is not employed to distinguish them (cf. Hughes 1971, pp.387-8). Rather, their status and security are gained by their attendance at state-controlled, élite institutions of higher education which assures them of élite positions in the civil service or other technical-managerial positions. In nineteenth-century Russia and Poland, merely to be a graduate of a *gymnasium* was what was important, not one's occupation (Gella 1976). In Germany, what was important was to be a university graduate, an *Akademiker* (Rueschemeyer 1973b, pp.63-122; Ringer 1979, p.411). In France, one's fortunes flowed from attending one of the *grandes écoles* (for example, Ben-David 1977, pp.38-46). Primary identity was not given by occupation, but by the status gained by élite education no matter what the particular specialty. As Ben-David noted for France,

> the technically competent ... whom the [*grandes écoles*] system was ... designed to produce ... do not primarily identify themselves by their professional qualifications, but by their employment. If they are in private practice, they tend to consider themselves part of the *bourgeois entrepreneur* class, and if they are salaried, they consider themselves officials of a certain rank, rather than chemists or engineers. (Ben-David 1977, p.46)

This is a far cry from Anglo-American professions, which gain their distinction and position in the marketplace less from the prestige of the institutions in which they were educated than from their training and identity as particular, corporately-organised occupations to which specialised knowledge, ethicality and importance to society are imputed, and for which privilege is claimed.[1]

It is thus not without justice that professionalism has been called 'the British disease' (Fores and Glover 1978, p.15), though I would prefer to call it an 'Anglo-American disease'. Nor is it an accident that the theoretical literature on the professions is almost wholly Anglo-American, European reviews and use of the Anglo-American literature notwithstanding (Maurice 1972, pp.213-25). All in all, I would argue that as an institutional concept, the term 'profession' is intrinsically bound up with a particular period of history and with only a limited number of nations in that period of history.

THE INEVITABILITY OF APOLOGETICS AND POLEMICS

If we grant the concrete, historically bound character of the term, we can better understand some of the other controversies surrounding definition in the recent literature. Metatheoretical critiques have frequently noted that earlier writings on the professions created definitions which were reflections of what spokesmen for Anglo-American occupations seeking social recognition as professions say about themselves (Freidson 1970a, pp.77-84; Gyarmati 1975, pp.629-54). Roth (1974, p.17) put this criticism very forcefully: 'Sociologists ... have become the dupe of established professions (helping them justify their dominant position and its payoff) and arbiters of occupations on the make'. The implication of such criticism is that theorisers should in some sense strive to create a definition which does not reflect the interests of the groups it attempts to delineate, that their definition should be more detached in its perspective. However, because of the very nature of the concept, one cannot avoid its intrinsic connection with the evaluative social processes which create it.

For the professions, the issues for commentary and analysis are determined more or less by the national history of the term itself, and by the usage of that term both by members of particular occupations and by members of other groups in Anglo-American society. Given the historical fact that the term is a socially valued label, with the possibility of social, economic, political or at the very least symbolic rewards accruing to those so labelled, it seems inevitable both that disagreement about its application to particular persons or occupations will exist, and that disagreement will exist about the propriety of the special rewards accruing to those to whom it is applied. Because of the nature of the concept, *any* enterprise of defining and analysing it is inevitably subject to the possibility of being employed to direct the assignment and justification of rewards to some, and the withholding of rewards from others.

It follows, therefore, that those whom Roth described as 'dupes' sustain the positions both of established professions and those attempting to gain their success by emulating them. It also follows, however, that those, including myself and Roth, who undertake highly critical evaluations of others' definitions and analyses, also serve as 'dupes', though of different agents - 'dupes' both of managerial programmes of deskilling and proletarianising professional work, and of working class movements aimed at reducing pay differentials and barriers to entry into 'professional' jobs. Both sets of writers, while differing in substance, do not differ in intellectual approach to the concept. The watershed of the scholarly literature that I noted as occurring in the 1960s was a watershed in changing social sympathy and substantive interest, but marked no break with the earlier preoccupation of adjudicating the application of the label and its rewards. Perhaps that is why there have not been any coherent advances in theorising in spite of the marked change in the tone of the literature - because the *basis* for theorising has not changed.

THE PHENOMENOLOGY OF PROFESSION

If 'profession' may be described as a folk concept, then the research strategy appropriate to it is phenomenological in character. One does not attempt to determine what profession is in an absolute sense so much as how people in a society determine who is a professional and who is not, how they 'make' or 'accomplish' professions by their activities, and what the consequences are for the way in which they see themselves and perform their work. This is not, however, a simple undertaking, for we cannot realistically assume that there is an holistic folk which produces only one folk concept of profession in societies as complex as ours. There must be a number of folk and thus a number of folk concepts. Surely it seems likely that rather different concepts of profession would be advanced by occupations seeking the rewards of a professional label than by other occupations attempting to preserve the rewards they have already won, or by sets of employers or clients seeking to control the terms, conditions and content of the jobs they wish done, or by government agencies seeking to create a systematic means by which to classify and account for the occupations of the labour force, or by the general public. Indeed, the very fact of such a variety of group interests and perspectives may be seen to be responsible for the variety of conceptions of profession advanced, each to its own appreciative audience, responsible for the dissensus characteristic of the usage and concrete occupational referents of the term. Is there, however, one of those perspectives which can be said to be authoritative? Are there others which can be said to be invalid or unimportant?

Many recent critics of the literature on professions seem to feel that it is somehow inappropriate for sociologists to make their own pronouncements about the essence of the concept of profession, and thus to serve as arbiters or dupes. Some urge that sociologists should instead study how other members of society employ the concept without projecting their own conceptions. In a well-reasoned statement, Dingwall (1976, pp.331-49) recently suggested that rather than define professions by fiat, sociologists would do better to devote themselves to the study and explication of the way ordinary members of particular occupations invoke and employ the term during the course of their everyday activities, to study how such members 'accomplish' profession independently of sociologists' definitions. However, unlike most critics, who are content with exhortation alone, Dingwall goes on to present data from an interesting study of his own which took that advice seriously. But my reading of his study indicates that such accomplishment on the part of the members of one occupation cannot fail to include taking into account the conceptions of members of other occupations with whom interaction takes place, and negotiating with them some workable agreement on usage and the activities and relationships it implies. Nonetheless, even that is not enough: among the groups which have to be taken into account are the very sociologists who define profession by fiat, since they, too, are members of the phenomenological world of occupations.

Sociologists are part of social life, and they produce some of the symbolic resources employed by other members of their society, most especially when they play the deliberately accessible role of commenting on and analysing contemporary social issues. In their way, serving in their special role of intellectual, sociologists accomplish profession as much as do the occupations they discuss. Even without efforts at disseminating their analyses widely by popularisation, the esoteric, specialised work of sociologists is sought out by others and, if not taken as authoritative, then at least considered worth thinking about. Perhaps most consequentially for the actual process of professionalisation, some sociological formations are employed in part as rationale and justification for the creation of the official occupational categories by which modern governmental and corporate agencies sort and classify occupations with an eye to justifying job requirements, perquisites and wage differentials (Scoville 1965; Désrosières n.d.; Davies 1980b). Those official categories, or titles, and the criteria by which they are constituted, pose critical contingencies for the rewards available to an occupation, including the status of 'profession'.

If they are to succeed in their attempt to gain the official title of profession, it is not enough that occupations accomplish profession interpersonally, negotiating their daily tasks with the others with whom they work. Both the limits and the substance of negotiation are in part given in advance. Only after getting jobs of a given character can the members of an occupation negotiate profession with other workers. In order to obtain the jobs which provide the resources for negotiation, both the institutional characteristics of an occupation, and such characteristics of its members as their formal education, must conform to official criteria of profession. Cosmetic changes on the institutional face which an occupation presents to the world may not be enough for official recognition. The everyday world of the ordinary members of a striving occupation may also have to change, taking on some of the appearances that sociologists have specified as intrinsically professional, albeit by fiat (Hughes 1971, p.339). Thus, how everyday members accomplish profession through their activities may be in part influenced by how sociologists accomplish profession as a concept, and by how official agencies accomplish profession as an administrative category.

What profession is phenomenologically, then, is not determined solely by members of occupations performing work in a way that leads others to respond to them as professionals. There are a number of different perspectives and performances, no one of which may be thought to be better grounded, phenomenologically, than any other. Some, however, are more consequential than others, if only because they are attached to positions in which it is possible to exercise substantial political and economic power of far-ranging significance. While these may not be authoritative in any epistemological sense, they might be taken to be authoritative in a pragmatic sense of setting the political and economic limits within which everyday professional work can go on, and of providing the political and economic resources without which some circumstances and opportunities for work cannot take place.[2] Though such pragmatically authoritative 'definitions' are themselves negotiated and changed by the efforts of organised occupational groups and other agencies, and thus are not so rigid and stable as the terms 'official' and 'formal' imply, they cannot be dismissed as somehow less legitimate than those of the participants in everyday work.

So, too, may the work of sociologists be viewed. As researchers and consultants in everyday work-settings, and as researchers and theorists whose work is examined and consulted by those formulating the legal and economic parameters of the marketplace, sociologists also are legitimate participants. They can no more avoid creating definitions, if only implicitly, than can other participants. The fact of advancing definitions cannot be much of an issue in comparison to the choice of particular interests to advance in the social process of definition. But even there, the diversity of emphases and interests in the sociological literature implies a variety of choices. It also implies that the prospects for unanimity in the future are rather poor. How, then, can the state of the art be advanced?

BEYOND THE FOLK CONCEPT

One way of attempting to resolve the problem of defining and theorising coherently about professions in institutional terms lies in asserting the role of the sociologist as an especially authoritative analyst who is free to forsake ordinary usage in favour of his own more precise and 'scientific' abstractions. Even though sociologists in such a role cannot claim to be independent of their time and place, they can nonetheless attempt to create abstract concepts which are applicable to more than what is to be found in their time and place. Such an attempt has in fact been made by some of the more theoretically inclined writers on the professions. Remaining concerned with analysing historic professions, they have abandoned the effort to delineate all the traits that professions have in common and attempted instead to emphasise a parsimonious set of circumstances which have analytic importance in themselves and with which other institutional characteristics can be connected systematically (Goode 1969, pp.266-313; Freidson 1970a, pp.71-84; Johnson 1972, pp.37-47).

Interesting as those efforts may be, however, they have been too compromised to be successful. They are, as Becker (1970, p.91) noted, no longer faithful to the folk concept insofar as they abstract and select from it. But at the same time they have stopped short of creating fully abstract concepts which go beyond the folk concept. If those efforts were to be really abstract and 'scientific', then their conceptualisation would have to be tested by examining all occupations known to have the postulated critical traits of trust, autonomy, collegial control or whatever, but instead, only the occupations called professions are referred to by such writers. Were they to go beyond the folk concept, no longer would they be addressing professions as such so much as occupations in general. That is the crux of the matter.

I do not believe that it is possible to move beyond the folk concept of profession without forsaking one's preoccupation with professions (Turner and Hodge 1970, p.33). In order really to move beyond the folk concept one must ask on the grounds of some reasoned theoretical stance what the features are by which one may usefully and consequentially distinguish among occupations in general and the processes through which they develop, maintain themselves, grow and decline. On the basis of such features one could distinguish theoretically significant groupings or types of occupations and occupational processes by which historically defined occupations, including professions, could be classified and understood. Since theoretical salience is the issue, and not the historic Anglo-American professions as such, no attempt would be made to create a class into which would fit all the occupations that are called professions. By the nature of the enterprise, no attempt *need* be made. The 'essence' of profession ceases to be an issue. One's conceptualisation would be evaluated for its capacity to order and guide the explanation of the circumstances of a variety of historical occupations, no matter how they happen to be labelled by one audience or another in a particular country and at a particular time.

Liberated from the concept of profession by such an approach, one is also liberated from the grotesque dichotomy, or continuum, by which an ideal type or model of 'profession' is used to order *all* occupations. Since virtually all occupations do not come close to conforming to that model, the whole rich variety is reduced to being merely non-professions, defined negatively and emptily as lacking professional characteristics. When one goes beyond the folk concept and attempts to conceptualise the variety of occupations *among* which are to be counted the historic professions, one is in a position to formulate a considerably more flexible set of concepts about occupations that would go far to remedy the present conceptual poverty that stems from the use of such a parochial and simplistic dichotomy or continuum.

PURSUING THE FOLK CONCEPT

The theoretical programme which takes us beyond the folk concept deliberately replaces the task of developing a theory of professions with the task of developing a more general and abstract theory of occupations by which one can analyse the historic professions as well as other occupations in the same conceptual terms, but without assuming that those professions necessarily represent a single, generic type of occupation. But this does not mean that there is no future at all for a theory of professions. The future of a theory of professions seems to lie in adopting a different strategy. Whereas a theory of occupations would be concerned with developing a genuinely abstract theory which attempts to be exhaustive in its applicability, a theory of professions, relieved of the task of broad generalisation, would attempt instead to develop better means of understanding and interpreting what is conceived of as a concrete, changing, historical and national phenomenon. The future of profession lies in embracing the concept as an intrinsically ambiguous, multifaceted folk concept, of which no single definition and no attempt at isolating its essence will ever be generally persuasive. Given the nature of the concept, such a theory is developed by recognising that there is no single, truly explanatory trait or characteristic - including such a recent candidate as 'power' - that can join together all occupations called professions beyond the actual fact of coming to be called professions. Thus, profession is treated as an empirical entity about which there is little ground for generalising as an homogeneous class or a logically exclusive conceptual category. The task for a theory of professions is to document the untidiness and inconsistency of the empirical phenomenon and to explain its character in those countries where it exists. Such a theory would have, I believe, two major tasks.

First, such a theory should be able to trace and explain the development and significance of the use of the title in Anglo-American societies. Such a task is aided, but not accomplished, by the chronology of usage which the invaluable *Oxford Unabridged Dictionary* provides. A chronology, however, does not tell us why usage developed as it did in English-speaking countries, as opposed to those which have the same root in their vocabularies, but which use the noun form to denote occupations in general and requires an adjective like 'liberal', 'free' or 'learned' to denote a particular type of occupation. Furthermore, a chronology of usage does not tell us how and why particular occupations came to be labelled professions by their members and recognised as such by others; how and why official classifications employing the term developed; why the occupations so classified changed over time; or what the consequences were of membership in such classifications for both the organised occupation and its members. Some small movement toward the development of a theory of occupational nomenclature has begun (Scoville 1965; Katz 1972; Désrosières n.d.; Sharlin 1979), as has some modest effort to analyse the development of the official title of profession in English-speaking countries (cf. Reader 1967; Davies 1980b) but a great deal more must be done before we are in a position to dignify what we know by calling it a theory.

In contrast to investigating the nature of the official title itself, a great deal has already been done to investigate the special privileges of organised occupations which have gained official recognition as professions. In addition, numerous field studies have investigated the problems that the members of those occupations have at work in negotiating with administrators, other occupations, and clients for the prerogatives of the title. The former body of studies tells us about the consequences of official, legal use of the title, while the latter tells us how the title is negotiated and accomplished in everyday work life. As a number of critics have noted correctly, however, a disproportionate number of those studies is addressed to health-related occupations that claim the title. Advances in theorising about the title and its use positively require the close study of many more occupations in other industries.

While the first task is concerned primarily with analysing the title 'profession' as a socio-political artefact, the second task is concerned primarily with analysing in some detail the occupations to which the title has been applied. In the spirit of the distinction between a sociology of occupations and a sociology of professions, it follows that the thrust of such a task is to be concerned with the role of the title in the aspirations and fortunes of those occupations claiming it, and not with some quality or trait that all occupations claiming the title may share. The strategy of analysis, therefore, is particular rather than general, studying occupations as individual empirical cases rather than as specimens of some more general, fixed concept.

As individual cases, the question becomes how the quest for the classification in official categories and, on occasion, for legal status as a profession interacts with the development of the occupation's corporate organisation and influences its position in the polity and the labour market, its division of labour, and its members' positions in the concrete settings where they work. But while virtually all occupations called professions (as well as others rarely so called) may be classified as such in labour force or census categories, rather few have the legal status of professions. In the selection of individual occupations for study, therefore, loose recognition as a profession by the general public, and even the occupation's own claim (so long as it is taken seriously by some consequential audience) may be employed to locate cases. Thus, not only traditionally accepted doctors, lawyers and professors, but also engineers, pharmacists, social workers, schoolteachers, librarians and many more to which the title is attached by some audiences but not others, can all be appropriate cases for analysis no matter how they might otherwise differ or fail to conform to various definitions.

The outcome of such a programme would be at the very least to add to our knowledge about a number of occupations, knowledge which would be all the richer for its emphasis on the special characteristics of each rather than on the comparatively little they share that corresponds to some simplistic model or ideal type. As important would be the consequence of forsaking the equally simplistic but less formally or self-consciously stated assumptions of recent emphases on 'professionalisation' - that occupational movements for professionalisation are necessarily oriented toward change and mobility, for example, rather than toward stability and security. By expanding the universe of occupations on which we have detailed and systematic data, and by analysing them as individual, historic cases, we could establish the ground for catholic comparisons that we lack at present. Such a foundation would go far toward portraying the variety of contexts and inconsistencies intrinsic to the notion of profession, as well as the varied role of the notion in the fortunes of a number of occupations and their members in English-speaking societies. Such a portrait is certain to be richer and more varied than that abstract essence toward which the traditional literature aimed, but in being so, it is likely to be more faithful to reality.

THE OBLIGATION OF DEFINITION

In conclusion, it is incumbent on me to address the problem of definition with which this paper began. It should be clear by now that I do not think the problem can be solved by struggling to formulate a single definition which is hoped to win the day. The concrete, historical character of the concept and the many perspectives from which it can legitimately be viewed and from which sense can be made of it, preclude the hope of any widely-accepted definition of general analytic value.

It is precisely because of the lack of any solution to the problem that I feel that serious writers on the topic should be obliged to display to readers what they have in mind when the word is used - that is, to indicate the definition upon which their exposition is predicated and, for even greater clarity, examples of the occupations they mean to include and those they mean to exclude. Provided with such guidance, readers will then be in a position to judge whether X is really talking about the same thing as Y. If X means to refer only to those few occupations recognised by almost everyone as professions, possessing very high prestige and a genuine monopoly over a set of widely demanded tasks, while Y means to refer as well to occupations which try to ameliorate their low prestige and weak economic position by referring to themselves as professions, then each is talking about incomparable categories and both the writers and their readers should be aware of the fact.

The same obligation should be recognised by those who write about 'professionalisation', though clarity is more difficult because of the processual character of the concept. Even if one defines the traits constituting the end-point toward which the process is assumed to be headed, how many of those traits, and in what degree, must an occupation display before it makes sense to talk of it as involved in a process of professionalisation rather than in a process of merely improving its economic or status position? If it does not make sense to talk of the professionalisation of labour in general as the terms and conditions of its work improve over time, what characteristics must exist before it *does* make sense to do so? Must one use the term only retrospectively to label the process by which present-day professions have attained their position? Is there a distinctive difference between professionalisation in particular and the collective efforts of occupations in general to improve their job security, working conditions, income and prestige? No doubt on these issues, as on those connected with defining profession, writers will differ, but they are unlikely to be able to debate the relative virtues of those differences if they are not self-conscious about what they are. It is precisely because differences are inevitable that their specification should be an obligation for the writer and a requirement of the writer by the reader. Such an obligation may not increase consensus, but it would certainly increase the clarity and precision of a body of literature whose status has been vague and chaotic for too long.

ACKNOWLEDGEMENTS

The basic substance of this paper was written while I was Fulbright-Hays Senior Research Scholar at the Laboratoire d'Economie et de Sociologie du Travail (CNRS), Aix-en-Provence. I wish to express my deepest thanks for the hospitality and intellectual stimulation of M. Guy Roustang, then Directeur, and M. Marc Maurice, Maître de Recherche. An earlier version was read at the annual meeting of the American Sociological Association at Boston in August 1979. So many colleagues have commented helpfully on earlier versions of this paper that it is impossible for me to thank them all here by name.

NOTES

1. The evidence is overwhelming that *within* any given profession,
    differential life-chances are strongly influenced by the prestige of the
    educational institution from which one receives one's credentials. Thus,
    I do *not* mean to imply that in Anglo-American countries élite
    institutions of higher education play no part in occupational careers. I
    am arguing only that in English-speaking countries, occupational
    identity and commitment are considerably more developed than identity
    as an élite educated class or trans-occupational technical-managerial
    stratum. Thus, the institutional concept of profession is more relevant to
    them than to European nations.

2. In the United States there are considerable advantages attached to being
    in an occupation that has been officially recognised as a profession.
    Needless to say, when it is employed as a legal and administrative
    category, 'profession' must be defined in such a way as to allow practical
    discrimination among occupations and occupational roles by those
    administering the law. The legal status and definition of professions in
    tax, immigration, labour and other bodies of law (including the rules of
    evidence) simply beg for thorough investigation and analysis.

2 Professional Autonomy and the Social Control of Expertise

DIETRICH RUESCHEMEYER

I

The sociological analysis of the professions is in turmoil. Whether this condition will prove to be a productive ferment for significant developments or end in confused exhaustion is not easily decided at this point, although - not surprisingly - I lean toward the former prognosis. The study of expert occupations transcends in importance the confines of occupational sociology; it is of interest not merely because it deals with complex work and prestigious occupational groups. How expert knowledge is deployed in different institutional forms, how it is controlled, how it is used as a resource of power and a basis of privilege, and how in turn different institutional forms of deployment, social control as well as individual and collective advantage, are affected by other and wider social structures and processes - inquiries into these questions tell us much about the structure and the dynamics of society as a whole. That, furthermore, the subject is closely related to a - and perhaps the - central theme of classical sociology, the emergence of modern society and culture, becomes clear once we identify increased rationality in the pursuit of pragmatic goals as one of the major characteristics of that process.

In view of these interrelations it is not surprising that the development of this specific field of inquiry mirrors in many respects the history of sociology during the last generation or two.

After the Second World War research on the professions was marked by a retreat from broad historical and macro-sociological questions as we find them still in the work of Carr-Saunders (1928 and 1933), Marshall (1939), Parsons (1939) or Timasheff (1940). Symbolic interactionist studies produced a wealth of descriptive work combined with limited theoretical interpretations, while structural functionalists made self-conscious attempts at middle range theory-building with occasional forays into empirical investigation. Both kinds of work - the large bulk of it being done in the United States - took the institutional context of American society in the first half of this century largely for granted, and in both, basic assumptions and definitions of reality current among the actors studied entered into theoretical arguments, although functionalists were more receptive to dominant interpretations and symbolic interactionists included more of the perspectives of the 'underdog' - of marginal practitioners and clients less well served. This close and not fully examined concatenation between the theories and interpretations of the actors studied and those of their analysts seems partly a result of the virtual absence of intercultural and international comparison, and it probably derived further strength from the fact that the outlook and ethos of the scholars involved were in their fundamental premises similar to the outlook and ethos of the professions studied - both grounded in a middle-class culture that had developed its specific and by then seemingly stable form since the late nineteenth century.

In the 1960s, this pattern of limited heterogeneity broke apart into more sharply defined contradictions. More critical attitudes toward the established professions as well as toward the theoretical interpretation of their position in society went hand in hand with a revival of diverse political and ideological concerns among social scientists and with a critical questioning of the prevailing theoretical orientations in sociology. Even cursory reflection suggests several sources of this change that are specifically related to the subject of the professions, some of long standing, some perhaps only short-run phenomena. An unfavourable and often hostile attitude toward status privilege has a long and varied tradition in American society; it derives strength from changing conditions that reinforce egalitarian and democratic demands. Scepticism about the idea of progress based on expanding knowledge and applied technology grew with vastly increased possibilities for its destructive use and with new environmental concerns. The expansion of education and communication diminished the sense of awe toward occupations distinguished by their higher knowledge, while the related growth of advanced education fostered attempts of new occupational groups to acquire professional status, but at the same time built frustration into such attempts at collective status improvement because it vastly increased competition.

In conjunction with changes that put the general paradigm constellation in sociology into question, these developments gave a strong impetus to critical and often debunking studies of established professions and their work, studies which fused analytical with moral-political concerns and used a variety of critical yardsticks ranging from a model of uninhibited competition to substantively defined conceptions of the tasks of different professions and of the common good. A good deal of scholarly writing got drawn into social and political arguments about which groups deserved the coveted label 'profession' in the competitive process of collective status attainment. While some studies, following the leads of symbolic interactionism and ethnomethodology, sought to ground their understanding of professional work in the analysis of immediate interaction and the creation and maintenance of meanings mutually understood by teachers, practitioners and clients (Dingwall 1976), others insisted on the importance of the broader structural context. Value dissension, interest conflict and power resources received greater attention in theoretical models about professional work and its place in society and there is some evidence for a return to macro-sociological concerns and, based on genuine historical studies of expert occupations, comparative historical analysis.[1]

It is my contention that one can discern in these complex and apparently contradictory developments important continuities with earlier attempts at theory building, and that there is in fact cumulative progress in our understanding of expert occupations and in the identification of crucial open questions. In the following, I will sketch this theoretical development focussing on the issue of the social control of expertise.

II

Much of the early discussion of the professions got entangled in definitional problems, and this is even true of some current work.

Theoretically important issues were discussed in the form of different catalogues of defining characteristics (cf., most prominently, Greenwood 1957). It is the lasting merit of functionalist analyses that they began to conceive of these compilations of traits - as had been done with other ideal types, such as Weber's pure type of bureaucracy - as models that contained hypotheses about how different characteristics are related to each other, even though these theoretical ideas remained incomplete and largely implicit. The most fully developed of these functionalist models takes the social control of professional work as its central problem.[2]

Stated with utmost brevity and simplicity, the model begins with a knowledge-based competence held by experts, a competence accepted as pragmatically relevant for problems which are important for those directly beset by them as well as for others not immediately involved. This importance derives first from the weighty interests that are at stake, but it is also grounded in values to which less directly involved parties also have a commitment: receiving no adequate redress when being cheated on a contract is not only of concern to the party wronged; it also arouses moral indignation as well as anticipatory self-interest among others. The issue of social control arises out of the fact that the recipients of expert services are not themselves adequately knowledgeable to solve the problem or to assess the service received. Who then controls the experts in matters of such importance that protection against incompetence, carelessness and exploitation is particularly urgent? The answer of the functionalist model is bafflingly simple: the experts themselves. Individually and, in association, collectively, the professions 'strike a bargain with society' in which they exchange competence and integrity against the trust of client and community, relative freedom from lay supervision and interference, protection against unqualified competition as well as substantial remuneration and higher social status. As guarantees of this self-control they point to careful recruitment and training, formal organisation and informal relations among colleagues, codes of ethics, and professional courts or committees enforcing these codes.

Such models explain reality to the extent that it approaches their assumptions. Thus this particular theoretical construct is not to hold for all 'professions', however defined, but only for those expert groups that meet - in their relation to problems and clientele - the assumptions stipulated. The simplified version of the functionalist model given above can be - and has been - modified to include additional factors that sharpen or diminish the urgency and difficulty of the social control of expertise. A few of these must be mentioned even in a brief sketch.

A crucial question is whether the quality of an expert intervention can be judged by evaluating the result. To the extent that this is possible the control of expert services becomes easier; in turn, this consideration sets apart those cases as specially problematic, where the operation may well have been successful, though the patient is worse off, or where a case in court is lost in spite of excellent legal counsel. Another important variation recognised early is the extent of the competence gap between expert and client. Compare, for instance, the corporation equipped with a legal staff retaining a barrister for pleading its case in court with the severely ill patient admitted to the emergency unit of a hospital or, more generally, an illiterate clientele with a highly educated one. Finally, we find in some expert services - but not, or much less so, in others - a special need for trust between expert and client which gives additional support to non-coercive and unstandardised expert-client relations; examples are the conflict-related service of legal counsel requiring the sharing of confidences or person-bound therapeutic work where the relation to the patient itself is a therapeutic tool.

At first glance, the functionalist model appears to give an elegant if stylised explanation of the phenomenon of 'the professions'. If the fact that it coincided to a large extent with the interpretations advanced by these privileged occupations themselves stirred doubts, these doubts did not as such constitute stringent evidence against the explanation. Closer examination, however, both of the explanatory logic and of the evidence, which was fostered by the developments inside and outside of sociology indicated above, revealed severe flaws in this model.[3] As a functional explanation it violates virtually every rule in the functionalists' own book, and historical as well as intercultural comparative work showed that the flaws could not be repaired by a mere reordering of the logic of argument. Many have concluded that this finishes the discussion and that a completely new approach has to be taken. Yet these fundamental critiques can alternatively be viewed as a form of antagonistic cooperation leading to a broadened framework of theoretical problem formulations related to core elements of the original model. Such an alternate view, which retains the issue of social control of expert services as its organising focus, I will outline in the following.

III

Critical self-reflection among functional theorists themselves had identified early a number of pitfalls functional explanation has to avoid, though naive users of functional reasoning are especially prone to commit these errors (Merton 1949/1957; Stinchcombe 1968, pp.80-101). It is possible to order a good deal of the critical arguments against the model of professional self-control just sketched by discussing them under the headings of these general issues of functional analysis. Merton (1957, p.25) lists three interrelated postulates which, though common, should not be taken for granted:

> first, that standardized social activities or cultural items are functional for the *entire* social or cultural system; second, that *all* such social and cultural items fulfil sociological functions; and third, that these items are consequently *indispensable* [italics in the original].

In spite of his warnings, all of these postulates were often assumed rather than investigated in functionalist analysis of the professions. Least explicit was perhaps the second postulate of a 'universal functionalism': it simply formed the background of many of these interpretations of the role and social position of the professions. Making it problematic would have led to an inquiry into the conditions under which purported solutions to the control problems of expert services come about and are reinforced - or break down - when obstacles are encountered, an issue to which I will return immediately.

The first postulate Merton debates, that of the 'functional unity of society' was pervasive indeed. Already in the very definition of the control problem, emphasis was put on *societal* values that are at stake or, in the formulation of Parsons (1968, p.536), on the requirement that the experts' competence 'be put to socially responsible uses'.[4] This overlooks the possibility - and indeed the very common reality - that the reference values of a profession's work are not shared across all strata and classes of society;

certainly justice and order - but on closer inspection even health and illness - are typically understood in different ways by different sections and interests in a society.[5] Similarly, the professions are said to strike a bargain 'with society'; yet even if there is a clear metaphorical element in this formulation, it obscures that special institutions and groups and, underlying them, particular structured interests are the parties in this bargaining process and in the subsequent arrangements of social control.

Crucial for any functional analysis that aims at causal explanation is the question of what happens if the state of affairs to which certain patterns are said to contribute is not maintained[6] or, in the case of the model of professional self-control, what happens if the expert groups do not fulfil their part of the 'bargain'? The genetic-historical correlate of this question is: how was the position of professional autonomy and privilege attained in the first place? and, in particular: was this process - ephemeral variation and complication aside - indeed grounded in the issues of control that arise through the use of expert knowledge in the solution of socially as well as individually crucial problems?

Theoretical arguments and empirical investigation have made it clear that there are many other bases of professional privilege and especially of professional autonomy than the bargaining chips identified by the functionalist model - commitment to a service ethos and the claim of effective individual and collective self-control. The privileges of the professions are closely akin to those held by any group that ranks high in the stratification system. This suggests that they are similarly grounded, namely in the power resources different groups derive from their position in the division of labour. Furthermore, once attained they are more easily defended, so that we should expect 'survivals' of uncertain duration, which have their original basis in past patterns of culture, politics and the division of labour, though part of their power resources may be used to acquire new functions in a changed political economy as well as to shape public acceptance of their claims to useful expertise and a service ethos. In the short run, it is certainly clear that many professions have the resources to withstand a good deal of public criticism without seeing their privileges diminished.

The functionalist model implies that tensions between the 'goal state' of effective self-control and the actual state of affairs lead to corrective changes; but this remained an implied assumption, rarely made explicit and never fully specified and investigated. The considerations just reviewed suggest that such 'feed-back' mechanisms are present, if at all, only to a very limited extent and that other factors, not included in the model, buttress professional privilege and autonomy - even in the face of a considerable gap between reality and claims to effective self-control. This gives credence to a view of the professions common in earlier economic analyses (Friedman and Kuznets 1945; Kessel 1958) and more recently powerfully advanced by Eliot Freidson (1970a & b) in sociology, which sees the machinery of professional organisation as a tool for acquiring and maintaining a privileged and autonomous position and only secondarily, if at all, as an instrument of professional self-control. A 'profession' is then conceived as 'distinct from other occupations in that it has been given the right to control its own work' (Freidson 1970a, p. 71).

Finally, there is the third of the postulates Merton discussed critically, that of 'functional indispensability'. His stipulation that alternative solutions to a given problem - here the social control of expert services - must be explored in order to arrive at a full analysis is consistently violated by the functionalist model of professional self-control. In view of the historical and comparative evidence, the assumption that self-control is the only possible solution to the problem is perhaps the most glaring shortcoming of the model - a consequence of the parochial concentration in much of recent sociology on contemporary conditions in the United States.

Expert services can be - and they are and have been - controlled in many ways other than through the occupational groups and organisations of the experts themselves. Johnson (1972; 1977) and Rueschemeyer (1973a; 1973b, especially chapter 1) arrived independently at very similar typologies of different institutional forms and suggest hypotheses about their empirical conditions. Control of expert services by consumers is the one major alternative to professional self-control and control by third parties, especially the modern state, the other. In both, the power balance between expert practitioners and the major groups with which they deal is tilted to the disadvantage of the experts so that consumers or third parties can define their needs for service relatively independently and - often with the advice of loyal experts - can control the quality of performance of the practitioners. Among the major factors influencing the balance of power resources are the relative size and the elasticity of demand for and supply of expert services, which in part are shaped politically, the degree of differentiation of expert-client relations from diffuse status-orientated stratification patterns, the political power resources of different groups and also - influencing several of the other conditions - changes in the extent and character of knowledge that is widely accepted as pragmatically relevant. Underlying these more immediate causes are changes in the division of labour and the shifts in social organisation they give rise to.

Historically, expert-client relations embedded in diffuse status relations were common and in most pre-modern societies even the norm. In one typical pattern, experts were retained by powerful patrons and - with limited chances to change employment and to form associations with other experts - worked in a position of dependence on the high status consumers of their services. Architects, early accountants, but also lawyers, priests and physicians often found themselves in such dependent conditions. The reversal of this pattern of the consumer as patron is also, though less commonly, found in pre-modern societies. Especially in the law we encounter powerful patrons helping dependent 'clients' with learned advice as well as other resources in exchange for labour and political support. This latter configuration clearly has shaped a good deal of the cultural legacy from which modern professional ideologies - with their claims to noble service and authority - were tailored.

It appears that the pattern of professional self-control emerged from both of these forms through skilful exploitation of the opportunities offered by expanding potential demand in the course of urbanisation, increasing market exchange and capitalist industrialisation (Larson 1977). Seen in historical perspective, it combines in a remarkable way elements of older, though modified, corporate status privileges (reflected explicitly in the German usage of Akademiker*stand*, Anwalts*stand* or Ärzte*stand*) with an increasing standardisation of service through more systematic education and less diffuse and personalised relations to the clientele.

On the European continent, the early modern state provided with its increasingly rationalised organisation a different context for the growing utilisation of expert services. Public bureaucracies were here far more important for the early developments of 'professionalisation', both as consumers of expert services and as supervising and controlling agencies. This established forms of recruitment and training in public universities as well as institutional controls and cultural orientations which remained of lasting importance even after capitalist forms of exchange and production came into their own on the Continent. It is against this background that we can understand why, for instance, in Prussia/Germany it is the ethos of the civil servant that has informed the outlook and orientation of professionals *(Akademiker)* and other white collar occupations even when commercialisation and industrialisation advanced conditions more favourable to somewhat greater professional independence (Rueschemeyer 1973b; also Kocka 1977, pp.174ff., for white collar employees; Kaelble 1978, for executives of large corporations).

In the further development of the capitalist political economy - in England and the United States as well as on the Continent - the large modern corporations became major private consumers of expert services and attained a degree of concentration of resources so that they, too, could establish bureaucratic controls similar to those created by absolutist rulers and to the later forms of expert employment by the modern state, although under modern conditions alternative employment opportunities - varying with changes in supply and demand - tend to be more easily available than in the earlier period and thus favour somewhat greater independence and professional identification across different places of employment. This spread of bureaucratic employment of expert practitioners is seen as not easily compatible with professional work and even as a twentieth-century crisis of the professions in much of the Anglo-American literature, while similar alternatives to professional self-control were long taken for granted in continental social science, as, for instance, Max Weber's analyses of bureaucracy show. In a long-term historical and comparative perspective, then, the pattern of professional self-control is only one of several different forms of the social control of expert services and it is by no means the pattern toward which others converge in a long-run process. To conceive of it as the only, or even the predominant, institutional form of expert services is an act of cultural and historical parochialism.

The different types of social control of expert services distinguished above are generally found in mixed form. Even the greatest degree of autonomous self-control is typically secured by legal intervention and government guarantees in the form of licensing, inhibition of unauthorised competition and publicly stipulated minimum standards of professional training. Major client groups exercise varying degrees of 'lay control' through their choice of practitioners in the market and through the terms of employment of professionals in their organisation even where the professions have secured a large measure of autonomy for themselves. In turn, even in bureaucratic employment or under third-party supervision, expert practitioners derive from the special character of their services a core of autonomy which, though different from profession to profession, is greater than the irreducible autonomy found in other occupations. While it is crucial to distinguish here with Freidson (1970a) between autonomy in the immediate execution of work and autonomy in the institutionalised regulation of the relations between experts and clients, the irreducible core of autonomy in the actual delivery of expert services remains a resource of power and influence that can become the springboard for more extended institutional independence and other privileges.[7]

Before concluding this review of alternative modes of the social control of expert services, one last alternative must be mentioned - the case of a lack of effective control. Especially if the recipients of expert services are economically, socially and politically weak, we find both in history and in contemporary modern societies many instances where clients are protected neither by their own control resources - a strong market position or organisational means of control - nor by professional self-restraint nor by effective third-party interventions. It is the structured incidence of such 'anomic' relations between marginal consumers and - often also marginal - practitioners that constitutes the strongest empirical argument against the functionalist assumption that the 'need' for 'socially responsible uses' of expertise will in fact secure adequate safeguards. In the words of William Goode (1969, p.300), who explicitly rejects such naive functionalism:

Societies, like people, need a great many things they will not get. At best, if a social structure needs something, that will mean no more than that opportunities will be seized if they appear, not that opportunities will in fact appear.

IV

Perhaps the theoretically most interesting critique of the model of professional self-control transcends the criteria of a causally adequate functional argument. Renewing problem formulations from the sociology of knowledge, it inquires into the nature and the determinants of the major independent variables of that model - the experts' knowledge and the norms and values surrounding the problems to which it is applied. To the extent that the knowledge accepted as pragmatically relevant, the values and the material and immaterial interests involved in the problems which are the object of expert services cannot be taken as given, but must be seen as shaped in large measure by enterprising groups of self-proclaimed experts who succeed to a varying degree in anchoring their claims in culture, political and socioeconomic institutions; to that extent, the dilemma of the social control of expertise itself - that is, the generating core of the functionalist model - has to be viewed as the product of the expert groups themselves. While I consider this formulation an overstatement which must be severely qualified, this line of questioning raises fascinating problems of far-reaching consequence.

To begin with the *pièce de résistance*, with scientifically established knowledge, it is clear that when scholars themselves, or philosophers of science, reflect on its nature they take a much more complex - and a far more sceptical - view than sycophantic formulations extolling 'the best available knowledge of our time' let on. Without entering these complexities, we know that scientific knowledge ineluctably derives from the questions asked, and these are in large part socially and culturally determined rather than by the objects of study themselves. In fact, the demands and interests crystallising in professional practice constitute one of the mechanisms through which such determination takes place, and they are by no means a selective force but also on occasion - especially before a more differentiated institutionalisation of scientific investigation is established - a hindering one (Ben-David 1971, pp.24-7, for a discussion of examples from antiquity). Scientific knowledge is, furthermore, always preliminary and it is contingent on what Kuhn (1970) has called the 'paradigms' of fundamental concepts, assumptions, problem formulations, accepted modes of investigation and standards of empirical adequacy. It is also clear, and perhaps especially so to social scientists, that the rigour of standards of empirical testing and thus the reliability and validity of specific explanations and predictions as well as the extent to which different propositions are theoretically integrated and thus mutually reinforce each other's credibility, vary drastically from one field of investigation to another.

In the last hundred or hundred and fifty years, it is knowledge of this character that has increasingly become, as Freidson (1970a, p. 343) formulates in his evaluative discussion of medical knowledge, 'the special knowledge of the profession which justifies its autonomy'. It therefore does not surprise us when we see enterprising occupational groups claim 'scientific knowledge' and succeed in gaining acceptance for such assertions even though this claim to scientific status for their expertise should be viewed as marginal or even wholly unacceptable by those in a position to judge. Examples are the recognition as *Wissenschaft* of the humanities in the reorganised German universities of the nineteenth century (Ben-David 1971, p.112f.) and the proclamation of legal studies as a 'science' that accompanied the establishment of law teaching as a professional pursuit in the United States (Auerbach 1971); the claims of modern economics should be a rewarding object of study in this respect, too.

Even where the claim to scientific knowledge is beyond doubt for a competent observer, however, the issue of public as well as pervasive professional acceptance remains as a critical factor as far as the consequences for professional organisation and public recognition are concerned. Early developments in modern medicine are instructive:

Challenged by homeopathy on scientific grounds, orthodox medicine (in mid-nineteenth-century America) could not muster, in response, a demonstration of therapeutic superiority. ... before the rise of bacteriology in the 1890s, orthodox medicine could not offer any substitute for 'heroic' therapies. The bulk of the profession, its self-confidence undermined from within, rejected the discredit cast upon its technical tools. The emergent orientation toward scientific medicine was therefore an additional factor of disunity, which compounded the conflict of interests between élite and average practitioners and condemned inclusive professional associations to ineffectiveness. (Larson 1977, p. 132)

Scientific investigation itself acquired full cultural recognition and social-political support in a similar, though much more drawn out process of enthusiastic promotion and recurrent breakdowns of institutional support. From the seventeenth to the early nineteenth century, it 'moved in the wake of more embracing theological-philosophical movements', themselves 'a-scientific or even anti-scientific in content' (Ben-David 1964, p. 468) and was embedded in organisational forms resembling those of religious sects:

> They burst into life with great *élan* amidst considerable enthusiasm on the part of groups of individuals rallying around a few charismatic leaders. They settled down into routine soon thereafter, once the force of the intellectual revolutions which inspired them had subsided (p. 469; also Ben-David 1971).

Only in the latter part of the nineteenth century did science become institutionalised in a more differentiated and stable fashion and only then did it acquire the cultural acceptance and power of legitimation we now take for granted.

If scientific knowledge were the only or even the main factor behind the special position of knowledge-based occupations, independent of particular historical socio-cultural constellations, we could not account for the peculiar character of the old professions of law, medicine and religion before the rise of modern Europe nor for the apparent fact that knowledge seems to be universally associated with high and privileged social status. In fact, it seems that even the early forms of modern professional autonomy developed prior to the establishment of science as a culturally dominant and pragmatically useful pursuit. In an analysis of changes in the doctor-patient relationship in nineteenth-century England, Waddington (1977) accounts for the fact that by the middle of the nineteenth century doctors had largely emancipated themselves from the control of patients and attained considerable professional autonomy in terms of the consequences of economic growth and urbanisation - the growing number of middle class patients, the decline of patronage dependency, the more impersonal character of life in the larger cities, the differentiation of personal relations from professional ones and the swift development of professional associations whose norms of professional behaviour fostered solidarity among physicians and a trustful dependency on the part of patients. It is possible that ultimately we have to conclude from such findings that knowledge, of any kind, plays a much more limited role in shaping the social forms of expert service than so far assumed. At present, I deem it more plausible to consider the grounding of occupational expertise in scientific knowledge as a special case and to focus on similarities and differences in the consequences of various types of knowledge competencies. A few indications must suffice here.

Being learned in major cultural traditions, consensually accepted as valid and pragmatically relevant - at least in basic outline and on the part of dominant social groups - confers quasi-charismatic prestige and constitutes a powerful source of expert authority and legitimation of privilege. Expertise in scientific knowledge can then be seen as one variant of this more general phenomenon, one in which it is easier than in others to separate cognitive from evaluative components of the 'knowledge' of experts and through such decomposition to increase the opportunities of social control.[8] In history *and* in contemporary society, many learned occupations do not have the basis of their competence in science.

Another distinction between different kinds of competence used by expert practitioners, often noted as crucial in its social consequences (Jamous and Peloille 1970; Johnson 1977; and, focussing on the special character of 'person professions', Goode 1969), cuts across the distinction between science-based and other kinds of knowledge. Partly determined by the knowledge used and partly contingent on the problem situation dealt with, the expert intervention may be relatively standardised and in the extreme subject to a judgement of its quality by an assessment of the outcome, or it may demand complex adaptations of general knowledge to the particular situation and thus require learned 'judgement', intuition and even informed methods of trial and error. It is the latter form that is the most powerful basis of autonomy in the immediate work situation and it is the latter, too, that is the most resistant to a decomposition of the practitioners' competence into increasingly specialised and more easily controlled subtasks.

The knowledge base of a given form of expertise is made up of different components and their composition varies from one set of experts to another. We need to know much more than we do now about the consequences different forms of knowledge have for the control dilemma of expert services and for its various possible solutions. Similarly, our knowledge is very limited when we consider the forces that shape the different patterns of knowledge, their transmission in education and training as well as their presentation to various publics as pragmatically useful and effective.

Professional interests do affect the knowledge base itself as well as its public acceptance. Exaggerated claims of validity and effectiveness, selective development of knowledge, protective maintenance of mystique and complexity, over-education with the aim of professional respectability and limitation of access to the profession are more or less common. Furthermore, the professions do have, in varying degree, a special voice in determining normatively what constitutes a problem fit for, and in need of, expert intervention; thus, doctors influence our conceptions of illness which separates that special state from a condition of normal social responsibilities, and lawyers shape our views of justice and order, fostering, for instance, a more formal and procedural than substantive conception of these values. However, it would be a fundamental mistake to draw from these preliminary and incomplete insights the conclusion that the reference points of the previous analyses of expert services - pragmatically relevant knowledge as well as the values and norms surrounding the problems to which it is applied - are simply or primarily a function of the interests of the expert groups themselves.

That the knowledge base and the conceptions about purpose, goals and propriety of expert intervention are subject to change and have important indeterminacies, does not mean that expert groups can shape these changes and indeterminacies at will to their advantage. This view vastly underestimates the stability of major components of culture, in part due to their institutionalisation in differentiated institutional spheres, as well as the power of the major interests grounded in the basic structure of the division of labour and, finally, the difficulty of intentional intervention in long-term socio-cultural change. On closer inspection, such a conception represents a facile functionalism, different in content and reference points, but similar in its flaws to the functional model just reviewed.

V

What is to be done? Where does the study of expert occupations stand and where should it go?

Eliot Freidson, who was a major force in developing the critique of functionalist notions about the professions, has advanced a counterview which has attracted a large following. Focussing on structural aspects rather than on orientations and ideology and discarding functionalist considerations, he made the grant of autonomous self-control the defining characteristic of 'profession' and emphasised the political power required for attaining such autonomy (Freidson 1970a). While recognised knowledge was seen as one of the bases of this power, its role was played down in the initial central arguments though later it moved to front stage again (Freidson 1973). Recognising that 'professionalism', as a particular historical formation, is highly specific to England and America - an 'Anglo-American disease' - and at the same time the fulcrum of intense group struggles, he now proposes (in this volume) to move away from an exclusive concern with 'the professions' as inevitably tied to folk sociology and political entanglement and toward a broader analysis of occupations and occupational groups grounded in our understanding of class and stratification, of work organisations and of group formation. A variety of models of different professions and quasi-professions can then be situated in an inclusive typology of occupations.

I propose a different, though not necessarily incompatible strategy of investigation, one more in continuity with previous theoretical work on the professions, which I view, as Freidson does, 'as virtually the only sustained effort at systematic theorising about occupations in institutional terms', but also as a theoretical effort with implications far beyond occupational sociology. What has emerged as the central theoretical issue of this field of study, that of the social control of expert services, its different institutional forms and their structural conditions, remains a powerful generator of problem formulations and hypotheses which do have implications for the study of other occupations but perhaps more importantly concern the role of knowledge in history, contemporary societies and the future and, beyond that, have close links to the major issues in the analysis of societal structure and change.

The fact that the reference points of the control dilemma - the character of expert knowledge, its recognition as pragmatically useful and its differential distribution, as well as the interests and normative considerations involved in the problems to which expertise is applied - are all historically variable and to an extent subject to the impact of 'professional projects' (Larson 1977)[9] complicates the analytic task and may limit the generalisability of specific findings, but does not create insuperable obstacles for this line of investigation. Comparative historical and intercultural studies hold the greatest promise because the problems identified concern to a large extent broad aspects of societal structure and culture as well as their long-term historical change. This is not only the surest way to transcend the particularities of Anglo-American conditions, but also the most fruitful way to explore hypotheses about how different forms of the social control of expert services and the resultant position of knowledge experts in society are related to different types of knowledge and education, value patterns and their change, professional organisations and privileged access to political decisions, the changing structure of markets as well as the institutionalised power relations in different parts of the system of the division of labour.

In searching for the causes of different institutional forms for the social use of expert knowledge, the factors identified by Freidson (in this volume) are of crucial immediate importance; yet particularly an approach that stresses the role of the political power of different expert groups must inquire further into the conditions of that power. These seem ultimately grounded, first, in the fundamental structure of the division of labour and its change.[10] Related to that - but to an unexplored extent independently variable - are, second, the changing structures of state organisation and, third, cultural developments and continuities.

Such a macro-sociological approach, which complements more limited inquiries, can also throw more light on the broader social and cultural consequences of increasing uses of knowledge in social life and its varied forms of institutionalisation. Among these consequences are the emergence of modern conceptions of individualism, which did not simply grow out of entrepreneurial ideologies; the role of education in modern societies, which was strongly affected by the different patterns of professionalisation; the legitimation of equality of opportunity *and* of inequality of results based on educational qualification and occupational performance; and the impact a generally increased standing of expert knowledge has for democratic opinion and decision formation.[11] If for these consequences there exists already a substantial historical record open to investigation, their understanding could also inform our visions of the future, in which the growing use of knowledge and its institutional forms play such a central role - whether we think of Weber's process of continued rationalisation and his image of an 'iron cage', of varied predictions of a technocratic post-industrial society or of Gouldner's (1978) conception of the intelligentsia as a 'universal class' which, albeit flawed, carries the eschatological hopes that concept held for Hegel and Marx.

NOTES

1.   For the latter see M. S. Larson (1977) or B. J. Bledstein (1976); cf. my introduction to a special issue of *Geschichte und Gesellschaft* (Rueschemeyer 1980). It is also noteworthy that during the last two years the Davis Center for Historical Studies at Princeton University has carried out a special project on professions under the direction of Lawrence Stone. This new interest leaves behind older, fundamentally ahistorical constructions of a 'natural history' of professionalisation; see, for instance, Caplow (1954), pp.139-40 and Wilensky (1964).

2.   I think here especially of the work of W. J. Goode, R. K. Merton and the later work of T. Parsons; see Goode, Merton and Huntingdon (1956), Goode (1957), Goode (1960), Merton (1960), Parsons (1968); Goode's last contribution (1969) meets some but not all of the criticisms developed below.

3.   For the development of this critique see, among others, Rueschemeyer (1964), Freidson (1970a and 1970b), Johnson (1972), Rueschemeyer (1973a), Johnson (1977), Freidson (1977).

4.   Parsons (1968) makes this a part of the definition of 'a full-fledged profession'; yet, as in other instances of the functionalist literature, I believe to extrapolate only slightly if I interpret the remnants of definitional arguments as assertions of functional and causal relations between variables. Thus, although Goode (1969, p. 277) speaks of a basic body of abstract knowledge and the ideal of service as 'the two generating qualities' of professionalism, his argument makes clear that he sees the latter as a response to the problem of controlling expert services, which are potentially harmful.

5.   The interrelations between legal developments, socio-economic interests and the legal profession - its allegiances and its organisation - are particularly instructive for this problem, though the insights gained here should provide important leads for the study of other professional fields, too. For instance the same author, Roscoe Pound (1953), speaks of the period from the American Revolution to the Civil War as an 'era of

decadence' in regard to the professional organisation of lawyers and as the 'golden age' of American law, because in two or three generations the heritage of the English Common Law was transformed to fit the emerging American political economy. Morton Horwitz (1977) documents the ways in which this development favoured entrepreneurial and mercantile interests over those of farmers, workers and consumers. The very strong impact of business interests on constitutional law after the Civil War is analysed by Benjamin Twiss (1942). For a comparison with developments in nineteenth-century Germany see Rueschemeyer (1973b, pp. 160-83).

6. Cf. the excellent discussion of Stinchcombe (1968, pp. 80-101); the necessity to identify 'feed-back mechanisms' in order to move from the mere statement of positively functional consequences of different phenomena to an understanding of their causal conditions follows also from Merton's (1949/1957) critique of the three common but problematic postulates of many functionalist analyses.

7. Macro-social consequences of these power resources of experts in the overall context of changing balances of power and systems of stratification in industrial societies are discussed by Lenski (1966, pp. 313f. and 316). That even lawyers in the Soviet Union acquired a peculiar work organisation as well as associational representation (cf. Friedman and Zile 1964; Barry and Berman 1968) is indicative both of these general bases of autonomy in expert work and of the particular foundations of a certain independence of experts involved in dispute settlement.

8. This is the tack taken by Freidson (1970a) in his differential assessment of the different components of medical knowledge. It is ironic that in their own writing, which presumably claims also the authority of 'knowledge', many of his followers insist on the legitimacy of fusing evaluative and cognitive arguments.

9. 'According to Webster, "project" means "a planned undertaking". As the term is currently used in sociological analysis, it does not mean that the goals and strategies of a group are entirely clear and deliberate for all members, nor even for the most determined and articulate among them. Applied to the historical results of a given course of action, the term "project" emphasises the coherence and consistence that can be discovered *ex post facto* in a variety of apparently unconnected acts.' (Larson 1977, p. 6, footnote). As the term is currently used, then, it clearly involves unresolved - if not in principle unresolvable - analytic problems akin to those of functional causal arguments.

10. A few theoretical forays into this problem area may be noted. Freidson's (1970b) work on 'professional dominance' refers not only to static relations between occupations but also to the consequences for the course, and the outcomes, of inter-occupational division of labour. Professional dominance can then be contrasted and compared with the implications of 'managerial dominance' and of an absence of organisational relations of domination in a given field of work (Freidson 1977). Rueschemeyer (1977) introduces more generally considerations of power in an argument for a more process-orientated study of

structural differentiation and de-differentiation, which applies also to occupational division of labour. Though partly autonomous, the power of different groups has to be explained ultimately in the context of such factors as population change, developments of technology, changes in economic production, exchange and distribution, class formation as well as developments in the basic cultural orientations and especially the cognitive premises of socio-cultural life. Johnson (1977) makes an interesting, but highly speculative attempt to explain different forms of professional knowledge and expert control by the relation different expert groups have to the capitalist class structure.

11.   These issues of the broader consequences of varied forms of professionalisation have recently received more attention; see Daheim (1973), Bledstein (1976) and Larson (1977).

3 The Rivals: an Essay on the Sociological Trades

P. M. STRONG

One of the many problems that sociology faces is the sheer number of its rivals - unlike, say, physics, which may be reserved mostly for physicists, anyone can play. Not only are there competing social sciences, but everyone has to be something of a social scientist just to get by in this world. Everyone, that is, is obliged to gather data and test hypotheses. Although there may be more or less rigorous ways of doing this it cannot be denied that the central activity is the same.[1] Thus, as well as an ethno-methodology, there is an ethno-sociology, an ethno-psychology and so on.

There is also a third form of competition, one which comes neither from the academy, nor from the laity, one by which we are all influenced but which rarely receives the attention it deserves: novelists, journalists, film-makers and dramatists are, at least in part, also professional students of the social world. Their primary audiences may differ, as may some of their aims and, in consequence, their modes of analysis and communication, but quite a few of their findings and methods are the same, a fact which is all too often ignored, at least by ourselves - the consumers of our wares often make far less of a distinction. Here, as elsewhere (Bittner 1965), we seem to have been misled by an essentialist definitional procedure which concentrates on the differences between phenomena and neglects those other matters which they have in common.

There may, of course, be other motives in all this. We

sociologists have had good reason to be stand-offish. To breach the university's walls and claim a serious place therein, sociology, like the other social sciences, has been obliged to draw a fairly rigid line. Its demarcation from those other professional analysts who cater to the mass market, has had to be made as severe as possible.[2] We have felt obliged to play up those special things which we alone do and to keep quiet about those which we hold in common. However, now that we have gained some sort of place within the academy, another possibility suggests itself. Might we not learn something from a closer look at our rivals' activities?

This is not, of course, a new suggestion and, to a rather limited extent, it is one which has already been followed. What I wish to argue here is that far more could be gained from a serious study of others' methods and findings. At the same time, such a study might throw an interesting light on the way we currently analyse our popular rivals. There is some evidence that sociology's analysis of professions such as medicine is biased by its own ambitions (Strong 1979b). How much more may we be biased against direct competition? How far, for example, are scathing exposés of media bias simply knocking copy (Anderson and Sharrock 1979).

What relevance has this to law and to medicine? Two answers may be given: first, just as they illuminate many other areas of social life, the methods and findings of our rivals may help us understand the work of the professions (to illustrate this, some of my examples will be drawn from medical novels; no doubt legal novels will be equally instructive); second, it is not clear how far we can go in understanding other occupations' behaviour unless we grasp that of our own.

SOME SIMILARITIES

We may begin by considering some of those traits which, perhaps unexpectedly, the sociological trades share in common. Here, the first point to note is their mutual influence. On the one hand, large parts of sociology have grown directly out of the literary and journalistic traditions. The most obvious example is that of Park, a central figure in the Chicago School, who had been a journalist as well as having studied at Heidelberg (Dingwall, *et al.* 1980). But there are many other, rather more neglected influences. Steiner

(1978) has argued that the study of both internal and external speech derives from the novel, and before that from the letter and the diary, and, before that even, from meditational religious exercises. Moreover, not only techniques but whole analyses have been borrowed. Trilling (1972) argues that Diderot was a crucial influence on Hegel. Likewise, Kumar (1978) sees Dickens and other nineteenth-century novelists as centrally informing the sociological vision of the industrial revolution.

Similarly, although the ethnography of British rather than colonial life is only a recent development within academic sociology, the discipline having been associated with the statistical method from its earliest beginnings (Abrams 1968), there has been, for over a century, a major tradition of such work by novelists, journalists and social reformers (Keating 1976); a tradition which culminated in the work of Orwell, perhaps the most influential British social analyst of this century.

At the same time, one may, tentatively, argue that social science, in its turn, has begun to affect its competitors' production, at least in the United States. Two distinct trends may be discerned, though the same writer may work in both conventions. On the one hand, the growing cult of the fact may well account for the modern American cultivation of its opposite, the surreal fiction of Heller, Pynchon and Doctorow; if realism is captured by sociology, some novelists may take refuge in surrealism. On the other hand, there is the development of increasingly ethnographic forms and methods within both the novel and journalism.[3] Discussions of this hybrid, called 'faction' or 'the new journalism' by some (Kakutani 1980; Wolfe 1975), focus principally on the overlap and rivalry between the novel and journalism. One may also surmise a sociological influence. This emerges most clearly in 'Radical Chic' (Wolfe 1975) where Wolfe's ethnography is prefaced by a review of the sociological literature, but the genre as a whole, though typically lacking such overt ambitions, has some of the flavour of social science research. It emphasises lengthy and direct involvement with one's subjects, sometimes over a period of years; it places great stress on the recording of actual speech; and it stresses the need to consider the apparently trivial, the story behind the story, the background that is normally omitted from conventional journalism.

This mutuality of influence is matched by a mutual ambition. Even if social analysis is something which everyone does, those who engage in it professionally are still tempted by delusions of grandeur. Indeed, perhaps the principal occupational deformation in the written arts, the social sciences and in journalism is the belief that one's particular profession holds the key to the meaning of social life. Though some apparently think otherwise (Runciman 1970), there seems little doubt that most sociologists have a very high opinion of their calling (Collins 1975). Indeed, there is a touching tendency for each social science to assume that it, quite plainly, is the Queen of the Sciences.

This egocentric, if understandable, belief can be found elsewhere too. Poets seem no less ambitious on occasion. There is Shelley's famous claim, in 'A Defence of Poetry', that 'poets are the unacknowledged legislators of mankind', the equally grandiose claim of the French poet René Char, 'A chaque effrondrement des preuves, le poète répond par une salve d'avenir', which very roughly translates as, 'Wherever man's knowledge is found wanting, the poet sallies forth with a vision of the future' (cited in Steiner (1971)), and the German cult of the Poet or *Dichte* (Gay 1970). Journalists, likewise, scarcely seem reticent in their claims. Of course, just as sociologists and poets worry a lot about their actual influence, journalists may often see themselves as hacks and hackettes. Nevertheless, to call oneself the Fourth Estate is hardly unambitious, while the very names and nicknames of newspapers tell us much about their occupational pretensions — *The Times* (the Thunderer), the *Guardian*, the *Globe*, the *Tribune*, the *Observer*, the *Examiner*, the *Mirror* and *Le Monde*.

As this list also reminds us, journalists seem to worry as much as sociologists about their proper analytical role. Should one simply observe, examine, or, if a mirror, reflect the times, or, should one be a guardian or a tribune of the people? Similarly, just as sociologists or some of them, develop revolutionary tendencies from time to time, so too do poets from Wordsworth to Blok. More common, perhaps, is a desire to reform. Recent medical novels, for example, such as those by Shem (1980) and by Douglas (1977, 1980a, 1980b) share a suspicion of high-technology medicine and a desire to treat patients in a more humane fashion which is very close to their counterparts in medical sociology.

At the same time one may suspect that, despite these occasional ambitions, whether revolutionary or reformist, journalists, novelists and sociologists are typically analysts rather than practitioners. Advocacy is of course a central component in each, without which they would be weaker, but so, at the same time, is a certain scepticism and distance. Each is marked by an engagement with and a retreat from the world, a constant movement backwards and forwards which ends, if one stays in the profession, largely, though not wholly, in a withdrawal, for these are the picturing not the tinkering trades. Commentators who are too committed to particular types of action limit their appeal.

We also share, at least in part, a common location in the academy. Sociology has come very late to the university, compared with the other social sciences, and although it has found a base there in a way which the arts or journalism have not, even they have increasingly strong academic connections. Not only are there now departments of journalism and creative writing but the academy is now a central source of employment for many writers (as witness that modern phenomenon the university novel); its members and ex-members increasingly comprise the major audience for many arts; and, 'English' has become a theoretical subject like any other.

Since they are analysts not practitioners, sociologists, writers and journalists all have relatively weak professional organisations in bourgeois democracies though, given their different working conditions, the NUJ is much stronger than the BSA or PEN. They also share a common interest in free speech or, more accurately, freer writing. All three trades are vulnerable to censorship and where that is not practised overtly each, in their different ways, can be bought. Jobs, commissions, grants, pensions, patronage of one kind or another, all pose common dilemmas.

National traits are also important. Just as there are distinctive national sociologies, even if the differences are somewhat less marked than formerly (Shils 1980), so these are mirrored in the arts (and, to a somewhat lesser extent, in journalism). Shem's technique for describing the life of the junior hospital doctor, derives from that modern American surrealism described earlier, while Douglas's more restrained, more documentary style stems from the British tradition of Powell, Isherwood and Amis.

To this list of common origins and influences, of shared ambitions and institutions, one must also add a common interest in research, a keen theoretical ambition - on some occasions at least - and a fascination with speech and what it may reveal. Research is paraded as strongly by many journalists and novelists as it is by sociologists. Journalists conduct interviews, research documents, undertake joint projects with Insight teams and hire quantitative researchers to undertake polls. And so it is with novelists. Le Carré flies to Hong Kong; Arthur Hailey studies Ford and airport management; historical novelists like Farrell produce meticulous reconstructions of the Indian Mutiny and the Irish troubles; traditional crime writers check on poisons, and novelists of manners keep diaries to record events and people in much the same fashion as ethnographers.

Theoretical ambition is perhaps less obvious amongst journalists and writers but, in a way, this is no less true of sociology, where a lengthy tradition and major career constraints keep most research and theory well apart. For all this, some practitioners of each trade still manage to combine the two. One can, however, be misled here. Sociologists and journalists with theoretical ambitions typically announce these in a somewhat ponderous fashion. In the novel, by contrast, such aims may well be concealed. An example may, in consequence, be worth considering at some length.

Take, for instance, the series of twelve novels by Anthony Powell, *A Dance to the Music of Time*.[5] Many reviewers have seen this as a study of the author's times, as an amusing documentary record of literary and bohemian life in London from the 1920s to the 1960s, and so it is. However, more specifically theoretical concerns may also be discerned, though extensive theoretical passages are rare [6] (Spurling 1977). On my reading, the series is also a study of character, or characters.[7] What sorts of people are there in this world? How far do they change? To what extent is character immutable? These are the questions to which the series is addressed.

This theoretical concern is more readily seen if we consider the series, not as a piece of psychiatry or social psychology, the only social sciences to have considered character thus far, but instead as something more akin to interpretative sociology. Thus, while Freud receives some attention, as in Powell's respectful treatment of General Conyers, a late convert to Freudianism, his most favoured analysts are the English Renaissance writers on character, Aubrey[8] and Burton, who prefer a more naturalistic description of the range and variety of adult character. In line with this, his observations are drawn, not from the consulting room, but from the mundanities of everyday intercourse, while very great pains are taken to record only what the narrator directly observed, or had reported to him on good authority. He certainly engages in speculation as to what might have happened but treats it as such, continually emphasising that multiple interpretations of the data are possible, that there are many important matters to which he has not had access and that only limited and tentative conclusions may be drawn.

His method is to record what happens, over the course of sixty years of the narrator's life, to the large group of people that he meets and meets again during this period; what they made of themselves and what he made of them. This explicit treatment of his own life as data is further exemplified by his treatment of dialogue. Like several other British novelists in the realist tradition, he presents dialogue directly, and unadorned by any authorial comment. As in qualitative sociology, dialogue is seen as evidence and, therefore, to be presented and digested on its own. Interpretation and comment come either before or after the evidence, not during, and are explicitly defined as such. Dialogue is treated as an actual record of what happened, to be carefully distinguished from the observers' reactions and speculations.

Finally, he makes considerable use of 'natural experiments', the sociological, or in this case literary, device, of studying those natural contrasts which crop up from time to time. Two comparisons are central here, the first being those incongruous occasions, of which the book is full, when characters that he has previously encountered in quite disparate walks of life, happen to meet. A further, equally powerful device, is that of the Second World War. Prior to this, he has introduced a series of characters from a great range of settings. War-time mobilisation acts as a single institution which grades them all according to its distinct purposes, thus serving as an external check upon their nature quite separate from the whims of the observer and the contingencies of their previous situation in life.

It is therefore possible to see Powell as making a serious empirical and theoretical contribution towards the development of a sociology of character. Indeed, for those interested in observational methods, it is hard to see how a longitudinal study of any magnitude could be carried out in any other way.

One might, however, still argue that this work, and novels like it, merely ape social science conventions: that, whereas sociologists actually have research designs, cite data and distinguish between warranted and more tentative conclusions, novels are simply works of fiction, mere simulacra of the real thing.[9] There is, of course, something to this argument and some crucial differences between literature and social science will be considered later. For the moment it is worth concentrating on the shared concern for speech which is typical of both the written arts and, increasingly, of sociology.

For Powell, as for many modern sociologists, speech is the central data source, indeed the most characteristic human product. In consequence, both share a central belief in displaying speech as evidence. Of course, novelists have a license to invent their speech, and thus to heighten its qualities for dramatic impact,[10] which is not granted to the journalist or sociologist. Whereas in sociology dialogue is a found object, produced ideally by forces external to the writer, it is the creation of literary authors. However, in several respects this divide is not as great as might appear. Not only is the method of demonstration the same but, given the research that novelists do, it cannot be claimed that their dialogue is wholly invented. Even the surreal speech that is so distinctive a feature of Orton's comedies was based in part on the systematic collection of real-life instances (Lahr 1980).

Moreover, the methods followed by interpretative sociologists in the selection and analysis of speech bear certain other important resemblances to those used by literary artists. If the sociologist is present at the moment of speech-production, whether as observer or interviewer, then he or she plays some part in the creation of the dialogue. Unless mechanical recording is used, sociologists necessarily invent at least some of what they report. Besides, though sociologists may not legitimately seek to heighten or improve the speech they collect, for purposes of quotation they certainly seek out the most concentrated, the most dramatic instances they can find. Finally, in informally analysing their material with colleagues, they commonly exaggerate for dramatic effect, using a whole range of literary devices. Often, it is only after the story or the joke that they realise that this was no joke, that this contained important elements of the truth. In the preliminary stages of analysis, dramatic methods can therefore play a central part in hypothesis-generation. If the quotation used by the qualitative sociologist is not too far from the heightened dialogue of the literary artist, it follows that, with only a little licence, one may use the work of at least some novelists much as one might use that of fellow ethnographers.

A personal example can be drawn from my own observational study of doctor-patient consultations (Strong 1979a). One of the central interpretative difficulties that I faced was the lack of comparable material from other studies. In particular, whereas I had fairly strong evidence that one particular set of rules, the bureaucratic format as I called it, was standard in NHS consultations and common in the American consultations on which I had data, what I took to be a further distinct mode, the 'charity' format, was used by only one of the American doctors in the study. Was this simply an idiosyncracy of this particular doctor, or not? Consultations with other doctors in Britain suggested that something like this format may well have been fairly common in the past with the very poorest patients, while modern studies of casualty departments revealed that something approximating to it was still used with the most stigmatised of patients. I therefore included it as a separate mode although my analysis remained highly tentative. The following dialogue, however, which in certain respects closely resembles the charity format, suggests a wider incidence of the form, and in turn, a broader analysis of its origins:

Dr	How long has she been ill?
Mother (M)	Five days now.
Dr	*(Whispers to Feldsher)* Diphtheria. *(To Mother)* Why have you left it so long?
Grandmother (GM.)	Five days, sir! Five days!
Dr	Quiet, woman, you're only in the way! *(to M)* Why have you left it so long? Five days? Hmm?
M.	*(Sinking to knees and banging head on floor)* Give her medicine. I'll kill myself if she dies.
Dr	Get up at once or I won't talk to you. *(M. gets up. GM. starts praying).*
Feldsher	That's what they're all like. These people!
M.	*(Furiously)* Does that mean she's going to die.
Dr	*(Quietly)* Yes, she'll die.
M.	Give her something! Help her! Give her some medicine!
Dr	What medicine can I give her? Go on, you tell me. The little girl is suffocating, her throat is already blocked up. For five days you kept her ten miles away from me. Now what do you

	want me to do?
GM.	You're the one who's supposed to know.
Dr	Shut up!

This dialogue is from a story by Bulgakov (1976). I have left the dialogue unchanged but removed some of the author's comments and set it out in sociological rather than novelistic conventions. The story was first published in Russia ten years after the revolution. Bulgakov had trained as a doctor and had spent 1917-18 working in a remote peasant community, an experience which formed the basis for a collection of short stories. Whereas I had seen the doctor who used the charity format as something of a villain, Bulgakov portrays himself as a hero in these stories and plainly expects his Soviet readership to do the same. I had explained the open abuse of patients in the charity format as largely the product of the doctor's belief in the idleness, immorality and stupidity of her patients; she was white, her patients black and poor. For Bulgakov, by contrast, though he certainly views his patients as culturally primitive, the point of such a style is to force the benefits of modern medicine on an ignorant, superstitious peasantry. Only by being so aggressive will his patients learn to consult immediately, to take proper precautions and so on.

Thus, this particular story ends happily. The doctor performs a tracheotomy, much against the women's will; the little girl recovers, and as the Feldsher remarks later, from then on his practice flourishes. The peasants believe he has performed a miracle and, thereafter, flock to him. He in turn comforts them as best he can with modern medicine. And here again there is a link. For, of all the doctors I observed, the doctor who used the charity format was the most concerned to emphasise the scientific basis of western medicine, not just to me but to her patients also. She, above all, was concerned to root out ignorance and dispel superstition.

SOME DIFFERENCES

Having argued that sociology is rather closer to journalism and the literary arts than some might imagine, I now turn to consider those differences that do, after all, divide them: in particular what makes social science scientific?

Perhaps the most central differences between the conventional literary artist and the journalist or social scientist is the very different nature of the truth which they claim to serve. The journalist and social scientist seek to establish that their claims are firmly based on actual incidents and specific individuals. Thus, even though they may for professional purposes, guarantee their subjects' anonymity in return for access, they nevertheless stress that behind the 'sources in Whitehall' or 'the people of Hicktown' there are indeed real people; thus establishing both their veracity and their morality. By contrast, artists normally strive, at least supposedly, for a general but not a specific truth, for a truth to life - however defined - but not a truth to particular individuals. Thus the morality of artists is often established in quite the reverse fashion to that of sociologists. Instead of guarantees that the story really happened, we get promises that it has all been made up. Here is an example, picked at random, of this somewhat implausible claim:

> The persons and incidents described in this book are fictional: any similarity to specific individuals and events is unintended by the author. The places too - with the exception of certain points of interest in New York - are imaginary and not intended to represent specific places.

Thus one exalts facts, the other the imagination; both conceal the extent to which they necessarily make use of the other's procedures. At the same time, such rhetoric does point to a very real difference. Gellner (1974, p.28) puts it this way:

> In any system of ideas or convictions, truth is the first and pre-eminent consideration, and its absence cancels any other possible virtues. This point may now seem obvious or even trite. Yet its sustained and ruthless application is anything but innocuous. It is radical, revolutionary and deeply disturbing. It requires that we look not to things, not to the world, but instead to the validity of what we *know* about things or the world. ... So real intellectual sovereignty lies in the norms of cognition...

A sustained concern for truth therefore entails the public display of one's methods, for only in this way does one reveal not what one knows but how one knows it. And it is this public display which is the essence of science. For what is displayed can be checked by others, and, if possible, reproduced by them. Whereas writers and even journalists aim to construct individual works, works that stand on their own, the only novelty allowed the scientist is to be first. After that, ideally, everyone should be able to do the same. All they have to do is follow the methods. Scientists' methods are public, available to everyone after publication; those of artists are trade secrets, part of their mystery, and are typically concealed.

Here, then, is a vital difference. At the same time, one cannot go too far with this. Not only may some modern novelists display at least some of their methods, but it would appear that even the hardest of natural scientists fail to spell out all of the procedures which they follow in their research, indeed that they are sometimes unable to do so (Mulkay 1979). A central part of methods it would seem is tacit knowledge, developed and shared by those who work together but resting unformulated and thus unavailable to those without personal contact.

Finally, at least in the social sciences, there would seem to be strong social influences on which methods do get displayed and which are ignored. In sociology, for example, we are most explicit about those procedures which we ourselves have invented or developed, that is quantitative procedures. Most qualitative methods, however, since they pre-date the discipline, are largely ignored in qualitative reports. There has been little methodological writing about them until very recently; there are major researchers, such as Goffman, with many volumes to their credit, who have not published a single line on their techniques; and, while quantitative data are conventionally available to other researchers for re-analysis, no such traditions exists in qualitative research; field-notes, indeed are often jealously guarded.[11]

Science is therefore public, or at least normally strives to be. However, in another, crucial sense it is closed off from the world. Indeed, it is this central ambiguity in its relation to the world, and the specific form that this ambiguity takes, which is one of its most distinctive features. Its isolation from the world stems from the revolutionary nature of the search for truth. All radical movements, as Bittner (1963) notes, seek a unified and internally consistent interpretation of the meaning of the world. As such, they require for their survival and growth a fairly strict demarcation from the fuzzy, ad hoc and heterogeneous meanings of everyday life. An active segregation from the world is the standard radical policy.

However, the very procedures by which the radicalism so necessary to science is maintained, may also serve to limit and curtail scientific investigation. This problem is but one instance of the general paradox which confronts any kind of radical movement or occupation which is more than purely self-regarding. Radicalism can only be maintained by separation from the world and yet, where this outer world is still of interest to the inner group, whether as object of study or object of practice, it must also be constantly admitted, a process which continually threatens either the faith of the practitioner or the rigour of the analyst.

Since science's primary role is that of commentator rather than practitioner, the set of transformation rules[12] and practices by which the radical's dilemma is resolved have taken a special form. Whereas radical movements of a more practical nature often proclaim that they have found the truth and try to establish a world-order based upon this,[13] doubt is firmly institutionalised within the scientific realm. Science travels hopefully but rarely claims that it has arrived. It allows the world the chance of proving it wrong, though 'the world' can only do this on the scientists' terms.

To put this more concretely: scientists try to enforce a set of rules which place strict limits on the entry of the outside world into their realm. Every scientific paper, be it ever so short and its subject ever so tiny, is nevertheless supposed, at least in principle, to make claims about and build upon, in a logical and verifiable fashion, our knowledge of the rest of the entire natural and social world; an ambitious aim. Thus, supposedly, nothing can be admitted to our writings unless it is capable of being checked by the reader, either via the presentation of original data and a methods section or through reference to other work which upholds similar standards. Everything else must either be explicitly held in abeyance or overtly assumed for present purposes (the *ceteris paribus* or *etcetera* clause in science). In this fashion the outer world is admitted to the corpus of scientific knowledge only after it has, at least in theory, undergone the most rigorous scrutiny; a scrutiny which is practically embodied in the use of external references by scientific journals. Moreover, every member of every discipline has a right, even a duty, to challenge, disprove or modify what has earlier been agreed or just taken for granted. Nothing is sacred, even after it has undergone positive vetting.

These sceptical, cautious and cloistered arrangements constitute the distinctive institutions of science which separate it from other more worldly activities. Within it, ideally, one's audience and judges are solely one's colleagues who, again ideally, have, like oneself, a purely disinterested commitment to truth. By contrast, sociology's more popular rivals are necessarily constrained by the requirements of their own, rather different, audience, the mass audience, whose interests are more practical, more ideological or more aesthetic.

At the same time, of course, one must remember that these are only idealisations. The peculiarly disinterested institution of science develops only in special circumstances and remains constantly vulnerable. According to Collins, the collegial pursuit of independent truth arises under the following three conditions: the development of an educational system large enough for teachers to become inward-looking; a relative autonomy from outside control; and some degree of internal differentiation within the school system - the key group in the development of science are those most insulated from the outside world, the teachers of teachers (Collins 1975).

But, even given these conditions, and the firm creation and institutionalisation of science, the outer world constantly presses upon it. Scientists face a constant struggle to segregate themselves from the inducements offered by governments, pressure groups and publishers, all of which may provide alternative sources of funding and prestige to those of their colleagues. There is a never-ending struggle to ensure academic control of, or representation upon, grant-giving bodies; to ensure freedom of publication - and to make sure that the line between academic and non-academic publishing is distinct.[14] A struggle that is made all the harder by the fact that, at least within the social sciences, the majority of academic practitioners have many other aims besides the scientific. The pursuit of ideological, practical and aesthetic aims dominates large areas of social science and constantly threaten the distinction between the different types of picturing trades. Just as journalists and novelists may have theoretical ambitions so, in their turn, academics often write with others in mind besides their colleagues. In actual practice, audiences, interests and markets overlap quite considerably. Nevertheless, despite such blurring, the constant academic struggle does achieve something. The peculiar cognitive emphasis of science is made socially manifest in that isolated collegial structure which renders science distinct.

The other features which are often claimed as defining characteristics are at once both subordinate to this and, on closer examination, clearly visible in many non-scientific enterprises. Certainly within science they are to be found in a highly concentrated form and used in a far more rigorous and systematic fashion. But the system and rigour is the product of the peculiar institutional and ideological form that science takes.

Cumulativeness, for example, the way in which scientists explicitly build, via references and reviews, on the work of their predecessors and competitors, although clearly a central feature of science, can nonetheless be found in somewhat different form in literary traditions. Not only do writers develop the innovations of their predecessors but they may also make more or less explicit references to their works, sometimes in highly elaborate forms. Thus the central theme in both the works of Steiner referred to earlier is the nature, and very recent decline, of classical literary culture which, for the classically educated reader, formed a complex web of allusions and developments.

Likewise, though Collins (1975) stresses as fundamental the scientific aim of explaining everything and of doing so via the method of controlled comparison, such aims and methods can, as we have seen, be found elsewhere. All radical groups have such an aim and the method of variation can be found in all who reflect upon the world; it is certainly central to Powell's method. What makes science distinct is not the unique possession of these features but the unique rigour with which they are pursued, even though not all scientists are as rigorous as they might be.

So it is also with quantification. Quantification, of a kind, can be found in every type of writing about the world, while qualitative work is still central even in the most mathematised of sciences. Certainly, sophisticated quantification is characteristic of science in an advanced stage of development, and even so-called qualitative sociology is increasingly far more quantified than its literary counterparts. Such developments occur, so Kuhn (1961) suggests, because of their advantages in settling disputes. By contrast, as Collins (1975) points out, more literary styles trade off an essential ambiguity. It is their very complexity and ambiguity of meaning which renders literary classics re-readable and thus classics. This same complexity and ambiguity creates the possibility of literary criticism as an organised enterprise. It is not merely that classics are ambiguous; it is also that ambiguous texts are more available for the debate which elevates literature to classic status. The clarity of science and the fuzziness of art both serve collegial purpose.

So finally, it is with literary style or dramatic mode. On the one hand, the best scientific writing is practical, precise and orderly, it is both usable and disposable. It serves, not as a monument to itself but as an aid to collegial communication. Once this has been achieved it can be dispensed with. Likewise, though there is some truth in Walpole's observation that 'the world is a comedy to those that think, a tragedy to those that feel', such genres are typically barred from science. At the same time, the distinction is not wholly clear. Sociology has both tragedians and comedians; scientific style also has its rhetorical side (Gusfield 1976).

CONCLUSION

Science is a particular tune played on a set of instruments which all of us share in common.[15] Some instruments receive far more prominence than they do in more everyday tunes, others get merely the lightest, occasional touch. Care, precision, consequence, reliability, parsimony, focus and contrast are turned up, emotion and prescription are turned down, though they never completely disappear. Within the austere collegial melody of science even the slightest emotional shading can have a suitably dramatic effect.

What renders science distinctive, then, is not so much the instruments that are played, for crude variants of these can be found wherever we look; nor even the particular tune, for everyone plays brief snatches of this from time to time; it is rather the sustained and collaborative elaboration of this particular melody in preference to all the others one might play.

For all its fragmentary ubiquity, getting to play this tune in any serious manner can be a most difficult task and in some areas, of which sociology is one, the band as yet plays in a rather halting and ill-coordinated fashion, while there is some confusion over the choice of instrument. However, the need for more practice should not prevent us, as it so often does, from listening to that same melody when it is played by our more popular rivals. They may play in a different key and with a somewhat different emphasis but the tune can often be heard all the same.

The very fact that some topics and methods are conventionally the preserve of artists has meant that many have shied away from them in their eagerness to establish their own practice as scientific. But dependence on a mass market is not always a bad thing. Scientists must proceed cautiously, moving ahead only with the assent of a fair number of their colleagues. Artists and journalists are not so dependent upon their colleagues' approval but can appeal directly to the laity. Sales are the only criterion. In consequence, they are freer to experiment with new forms and new techniques such as film, audiotape and video-methods that only now are inching their way into sociological approval.[16] The purity of science is brought at the cost of a certain conservatism.

What can we then learn from literature and journalism? Clearly the popular genres are normally restricted to the more descriptive or ethnographic side of social comment though, bearing Powell in mind, we should pay attention to their more elaborate theoretical constructions. As far as methods go, we may learn as much from their old techniques as from their new ones. Keeping a diary is still a profound method of studying daily life and one far too little utilised in sociology. And as for topics there is much to be learned. Such commentators can often gain access to many of the places which sociology itself is unable to describe by any except the most remote methods. Leys' (1978) recent account of China; Crouse's (1974) account of American presidential campaigns and the role of the mass media; and Wolfe's brilliant essays on such topics as navy fighter pilots in Vietnam; all these represent areas to which sociologists would find access rather difficult. For in such work it is often the writer's special job, whether as journalist or as art historian/diplomat (Leys), or else their very fame as popular writers, that gives them their entry.

Sociology is also a lengthy business. Its characterisation as 'slow journalism', or the view of the latter as instant sociology, are both apt. We often take a long time to hear of what is going on in the outside world and when we do find out, it can take even longer to get into the field. Finding money, time, contacts and doing some reading: all this is a slow business. For a discipline which has made a speciality of the modern world we are somewhat at a disadvantage compared to journalists. The pressure for daily or weekly production may often trivialise their comments but it does keep them in touch with what is going on.

Artistic ethnographers also write about many subjects which sociologists find it practically difficult to investigate. The obvious example here must be that of the family, not one of sociology's high points but the setting for much of the greatest work in the novel, film and drama. Families, being private places, are rather difficult for the self-styled observer to cope with, but seem quite manageable for the more discreet artistic observer who, of course, only writes 'fiction'. Finally, there are many important topics in micro-sociology which till now have been far better explored by artists than by sociologists. Character, consciousness, emotion: all these have received a far more subtle empirical portrayal by our rivals and we have much to learn from them.

A moral: Our literature reviews should not ignore literature.

ACKNOWLEDGEMENTS

I would like to thank Sheila Adam, Janet Askham, Mick Bloor, Gordon Horobin, Klim McPherson, David Oldman, Bernard Smith, Clare Wright and the editors for all their comments and conversation.

NOTES

1. Anyone who has reported their research findings to a group of those whom they have studied knows the problem. Living a life, for all its biasses, is a formidable method of data-gathering.
2. History and anthropology have not faced this dilemma quite so sharply. Since their wider audience is unfamiliar with their subject matter, they have been able to lean heavily on the qualitative methods also used by the laity and by more popular commentators. Sociologists, however, since they have dealt neither with natives nor the dead, but primarily with living members of their own society have been obliged to use more quantitative methods to gain an edge over their competitors.
3. See for example the work of Mailer, Capote and the anthology by Wolfe (1975).
4. There are of course important differences as well - particularly the aggressive stylistic flourishes developed principally by Wolfe.
5. Published in London by Heinemann between 1951 and 1975.
6. The most extended theoretical passage occurs perhaps in *Books Do Furnish a Room* (London: Heinemann, 1971) pp.153-4 and 157.

7. A useful guide to the characters is Hilary Spurling's *Handbook to Anthony Powell's Music of Time* (1977).
8. See also Powell's study, *John Aubrey and his Friends* (1980).
9. Clearly Powell's manner of handling dialogue cannot be a simple imitation of academic interpretative sociology, since no such thing existed at the time that he and various other British writers developed this mode. It seems more plausible to argue that both this style and sociology are joint products of a heightened consciousness of social science which affected British culture generally in the interwar period. See M. Lane, *Brave New Weltanschauungen: the intellectual context of sociology in Britain*, paper given at BSA annual conference, Lancaster (1980).
10. e.g. two junior doctors talking in Casualty,
    'Nothing in trolleys?'
    'No. So it's back to the suffering millions in triviatrics I suppose. I'm sure they just come in there out of the rain' (Douglas 1980b).
11. There is, for example, no qualitative equivalent to the SSRC's quantitative databank. (Conversation analysts must be excepted from these strictures. Their special openness to other's analysis of their data stems, perhaps, from their use of group methods of training and analysis; from their reliance upon mechanical recording and from the novel character of their work - this is an original sociological method.)
12. This term is taken from Goffman (1961) and refers to the procedures by which the outer world is transformed so that it may enter the world of conversational, or in this case scientific, discourse, in an appropriately dressed manner.
13. Contrast Baumann's (1976) account of conventional socialism.
14. See, for example, the sustained attack upon OUP by Marshall Sahlins (1979), which concludes: 'Like the marketing of automobiles or toothpaste, academic research is submitted to the one characteristic sense of criticism left to American society: Caveat Emptor. So the publishing decisions of academic presses, and ultimately the nature of scholarly research, are drawn irresistibly into the orbit of the average common opinions of the consuming public. It's a scandal.'
15. Indeed for G.H. Mead, research methodology was 'only the evolutionary process grown self-conscious' for it is an essentially problem-solving activity. 'The animal is doing the same thing as the scientist is doing.' See Reck (1964), ch.3.
16. Collins (1975) argues that, in fact, many of the most important contributions to the social sciences have been made by 'role-hybrids', that is by academically oriented non-academics, who bring to the academy empirical material and analyses which have, hitherto, conventionally been excluded.

Part II

Professional Work

In the second part of this volume we move to a group of papers dealing with specific institutional settings for professional work. Gordon Horobin and Maureen Cain both address aspects of general practice. Horobin begins with a discussion of the shades of meaning around the notion of professionalism and its opposition to the concept of the amateur, one who performs services for satisfaction rather than gain. In bourgeois society, the professions hover on the margin between tradesmen and gentlemen. Their appeals to the morality and mystery of their work in an attempt to establish a charismatic authority may be seen as a defence of their status since, as Paterson's discussion of judges reminds us, there are social strata above the professions. Hospital medicine has become routinised, but general practice still has substantial elements of charisma. This poses problems for clients, arising out of the issue which Rueschemeyer identified, of the social control of expertise: the impersonality of bureaucratised hospital doctoring and the creeping paternalism of general practice are equally unacceptable. These are, however, necessary consequences of the division of labour and the consequent role of trust in social relationships. The general practitioner can only act as a, necessary, mediator between layman and specialist by cultivating that trust to a degree which makes paternalism unavoidable. The concept of mediation or translation between presenting problems and available remedies is also central to Cain's paper. Again starting from the problem of expert knowledge in the division of labour, Cain addresses the radical critique of law as an instrument of social control, that lawyers' work is founded on the suppression of clients in the interests of a ruling class. She points out, however, that the principal clients of lawyers are the bourgeoisie, whether as individuals or as corporate bodies. While policing may involve social control, lawyers' work is that of translators, taking everyday problems defined by clients and resolving them by reference to the body of legal discourse, a reference which may, of course, involve considerable creative elaboration. The failing of the more usual critique lies in its insufficient attention to empirical practice. The analysis of practice is the necessary preliminary to attempts to classify occupations on the basis of identifiable rather than supposed similarities and differences.

The next two papers, by Phil Thomas and Geoff Mungham, and Marc Galanter, consider the changing market for legal services and its effects on practice. Thomas and Mungham present a detailed analysis of the legal community in a British provincial city. Their paper returns to a theme raised, as we have seen, by Parsons, namely the similarity between professions and businesses as economic enterprises and the place of altruistic and self-interested motives. They show how the market for solicitors' work has altered with the development of criminal legal aid and the threat to established sources of income from divorce, conveyancing and personal injury claims. Where the returns from criminal work had been too limited to support more than a small number of firms, they had now increased while other firms felt under economic threat. The original specialists had, however, established an effective cartel. Thomas and Mungham show how the duty solicitor scheme was created and evolved, ostensibly as an act of public service but chiefly as a significant part of the struggle by outsiders to break into the cartel. Galanter charts the rise of mega-law in the United States. He notes the parallel development of large corporations and large law firms, with increasing internal specialisation and stratification, wider geographical coverage and exhaustive tactical and strategic involvement with clients. The source of the demand for legal services lies in the proliferation of laws and regulations promulgated from a variety of sources, and the simultaneous waning of belief in the determinacy of legal doctrine. Corporate bodies are in continuing tension with legality, seeking to arrive at some accommodation with attempts to regulate their own affairs and to exploit its possibilities for defending or advancing their own interests against rivals. The demands of such actions for lawyers' services are such that only a large and complex firm can meet them, with corresponding implications for costs, restricting, in turn, the availability of such services to all but the wealthiest. At the same time, Galanter observes, the scale of finance both makes the highest quality lawyering possible and frustrates those involved by the organisational implications.

The work settings of professionals are the subject of contributions from Celia Davies and Topsy Murray, Robert Dingwall and John Eekelaar. Both papers reject the supposed necessity of conflict between professionals and bureaucracies. Davies uses data from a comparative study of the development of nursing in the UK and the USA to consider the historical experience of the different societies and its implications for hospital and community practice. She demonstrates the limitations of approaching this analysis from too narrow a concern with professions and bureaucracies, a concern which tends to muddle and obscure the immanent logic of these developments. In particular, we need to set occupational development into a societal context, against evolving class and gender relations, the prevailing political culture and the economic basis of practice. Murray, Dingwall and Eekelaar take a somewhat different tack. They present comparative material on solicitors in private practice and in the employment of local government authorities to show the continuities in the rhetoric adopted to describe their work. Professional work has a Janus character, a public face of resolving problems of social or natural order and a private face of personalised service. The 'natural' mode of fee-for-service private practice by a strongly organised occupation is a structural realisation of this ambivalence. How is this reconciled with the hierarchical bureaucracy of a local authority? The authors point to the lawyers' success in reproducing for themselves the conditions of private practice and its implications for other departments and for the workings of local democracy.

4 Professional Mystery: the Maintenance of Charisma in General Medical Practice

GORDON HOROBIN

Provost Sirrah, here's a fellow will help you tomorrow in your execution. If you think it meet, compound with him by the year, and let him abide here with you; if not, use him for the present, and dismiss him; he cannot plead his estimation with you; he hath been a bawd.

Hangman A bawd, sir? Fie upon him! he will discredit our mystery.

Provost Go to, sir; you weigh equally; a feather will turn the scale.

Bawd Pray, sir, by your good favour, - for surely, sir, a good favour you have, but that you have a hanging look, - do you call, sir, your occupation a mystery?

Hangman Ay, sir; a mystery.

Bawd Painting, sir, I have heard say, is a mystery; and your whores, sir, being members of my occupation, using painting, do prove my occupation a mystery: but what mystery there should be in hanging, if I should be hanged, I cannot imagine.

Hangman Sir, it is a mystery.

Measure for Measure, IV.ii. 23-44.

INTRODUCTION

This paper is for the most part about medical practice, particularly

84

general medical practice of the British variety, within the context
of a more theoretical discussion of some aspects of professional
work. I do not fully share the concern of those sociologists (and
others), who wish to address the question of what differentiates
professions from non-professional occupations. Freidson (1970a)
has already written probably the best account of the essential
features of professional work in his 'Profession of Medicine' and
Roth's (1974) sardonic look at the 'attribute school' makes me
very wary of following that path. Nevertheless it is necessary to
start somewhere and it might be useful to take off from those
analyses. I shall begin therefore with a consideration of some of the
characteristics of 'profession' as both an analyst's and an actor's
concept. This will lead me to take seriously some of those
attributes of professional work which have perhaps been dismissed
too lightly in recent work as mere political rhetoric. In attempting
to apply this reasoning to British general practice I shall use some
of the field-data collected by Jim McIntosh and myself (Horobin
and McIntosh 1977) but I shall also be trying to apply a
sociological perspective to the mundane background knowledge
which we all possess as societal members.

THE MEANING OF PROFESSION

Whilst it is perfectly true, as Roth points out, that any of the
attributes of profession listed by such writers as Greenwood, Gross
and Goode can also be found in occupations not usually assigned
to the category 'profession', we all (Roth included), use the terms
'profession' and 'professional' both descriptively and analytically.
Thus Roth (1974, p.21) quotes Friedman (1965) approvingly:
'"This essay avoids, in general, the uses of the term profession as
an expression of a discrete category of occupations." Perhaps
sociologists would benefit from avoiding the term also'. He then,
one paragraph later, says: 'Because of the centrality of
professional services in a complex society, professional control
over professional affairs affects the general welfare' (p.22).
  I do not want to get bogged down in a semantic quibble but it
does rather look as though sociologists have just as much difficulty
as anyone else in doing without the word 'profession'. This is not
surprising since we have to think and write with a vocabulary
which we share with lay persons. (I should add that my dictionary

defines 'lay' as 'non-clerical' or 'non-professional'.) More than that, the occasioned uses of everyday concepts constitute part of the data on which we then perform sociological analyses, which we, in turn, reflexively validate by our own background members' knowledge of the world and our own everyday social reasoning.

'Professional' sociological usages and everyday theorising ('lay sociology') interpenetrate. In particular, the spokesmen of professional and professionalising occupations formulate and reflexively construct their work, just as members of those occupations accomplish profession in their day-to-day work and contact with other occupations. One example of the former is contained in a recent book by a general practitioner about general practice. The first chapter on 'the role of the doctor' begins with a section headed 'medicine as a profession'.

> Professions are distinguished from trades by the length of training, the depth of special knowledge and by codes of behaviour. Medicine is different from most other professions not by virtue of the length of training (which is extremely long), or the depth of knowledge but by its code of behaviour and by its concern with people, rather than buildings, structure or accounts. This involvement with people is shared with priests, nurses, teachers, social workers and to some extent with lawyers. It is not characteristic of architects, actuaries, accountants and engineers. (McCormick 1979, p.13)

Such an interpenetration of analysts' and actors' theorising does not, of course, imply that spokesmen read and use sociological works; some may do, but most probably do not. This extract from McCormick's book could easily be mistaken for the work of almost any of the 'attribute school' writers.

Freidson's discussion of professionalisation begins with an important aspect of profession often ignored by the 'attribute school'. This is the broad distinction between 'professional' and 'amateur', a distinction which Freidson sees as that between work and non-work. 'What makes the activity, "work" is its exchange value. What makes a performer a "worker" or a "professional" is his relationship to the market' (p.17). From this point of view, professional is not distinguished from amateur by any intrinsic features of the activity, nor by differences in skill, but solely by relationship to the market.

I am not sure about this. In everyday language, 'professional' is often used adjectivally of any performance to denote features of that performance which have nothing to do *directly* with exchange value. An amateur, do-it-yourself home decorator can 'do a professional job', just as an amateur footballer can bring off 'a professional foul'. This usage of 'professional' does indeed have connotations of skill or excellence or efficiency and, perhaps, of commitment to an end to which the activity constitutes the means. Freidson (1977, p.15) warns us that '...confusion lies in the fact that the word profession is used to refer both to concrete historical occupations and to an intellectual construct or ideal type, without consistent attention to the relationship between the two'. We may say that, whilst *typically* professional work is undertaken in the context of the market, any given concrete activity may have professional and amateur features attributed to it.

The notion of market value is not wholly unambiguous. The 'amateur' athlete who has travel expenses to meetings paid by sponsors and is compensated for loss of earnings, has market value to promoters and is an integral part of a market economy. Housewives and volunteer workers, to whom Freidson denies strict market value and hence the status of performing professional work, do sometimes have exchange value granted them: in courts of law household tasks have been assigned wage values and the voluntary sessions 'given' by consultant physicians and surgeons in the pre-1948 'voluntary hospitals' had their work costed when they joined the NHS. It is also true, of course, that these doctors' free services were given partly for research and clinical experience, partly from strictly charitable motives and partly to establish marketable reputations in the private sector of pre-NHS British medicine. We would be purists indeed if we called their hospital work 'amateur'.

'Professional' as against 'amateur' may also have connotations of discipline, of the instrumental rather than the expressive. This meaning is obviously allied to, but not identical with, those mentioned above. For example, in a recent book review Robert Towers (1979) writes:

> There is a hint of amateurishness in *Birdy*, sometimes inspired, sometimes not. The obsessive vision that propels and sustains Birdy on his long flight has a once-in-a-lifetime quality about it, a quirkiness that does not augur well for a successor...

The *Cement Garden*, by contrast, seems entirely professional in its execution, the work of a young man whose private demons, however unruly, have been successfully harnessed to a career.

To call an activity, or aspects of an activity, or even a person 'professional' is not necessarily to apply a seal of approval. In sport, for example, the professional player is often held to be socially inferior, if at the same time technically superior, to the amateur. In English cricket until recently, 'gentlemen' (i.e. amateur) and 'players' (i.e. professional) had separate pavilion facilities, and professionals seldom achieved the captaincy of their clubs. In more individual sports, such as tennis and golf, professionals hold respected but wholly separate, socially inferior positions. This is even more the case in the aristocratic sports of hunting, shooting and fishing where the 'professionals' are literally servants - hunt-servants, stalkers, gillies.

Of course, this class of non-productive labourers are not, and were not, regarded as members of 'the professions', but they performed professional services for their amateur and socially superior employers or clients. Such relationships took their shape and meaning from the distribution of power, wealth and status in aristocratic society. Professional work in bourgeois society had different origins and different meanings, but the two 'professionalisms' have co-existed since the alliance and interpenetration of bourgeoisie and aristocracy began. 'There is no real contradiction between privilege bestowed by blood and privilege bestowed by gold in constitutional balance. Blood, for instance, decides in the case of certain army posts, whose incumbents hold them by virtue of family connections, nepotism or favouritism; but gold gets its due through the circumstance that all army commissions can be bought and sold for coin of the realm' (Marx 1953). Even in our more 'meritocratic' society, the notion that members of a certain class are good at 'leadership', for example, is widely held, and is scorned only by 'professional' sceptics such as sociologists and trade unionists.

My contention is, then, that 'profession' in the bourgeois sense of a special kind of occupation also carries ambiguous connotations of 'professional' as non-amateur, as describing services performed for gain rather than satisfaction or obligation, of skills acquired rather than naturally endowed and of lowly, client-dependent status as against the honorific independence of the gentleman.

PROFESSION AS MORALITY AND MYSTERY

Turning now to the issue of occupational differentiation we can see that those occupations which are generally accorded the title of professions base their claims to special status on a number of grounds which together or separately might be used by any other occupational group. This is why the attribute game has provided endless fun, if not profit, to sociologists. As Roth (1974) points out, the notion that only professions have subcultures is negated by the 'distinct and pervasive patterns of occupational life' found amongst dockers, seamen, miners, etc.; prostitutes also claim that their service is a social good and a community service; a lack of demarcation of work and leisure is equally true of policemen as of dockers; and so on. These claims rest less on profession as an objective category of activities and more on moral evaluation of work (Becker 1970). 'Proper conduct' is crucial in this. Dingwall (1976, 1977b), writes of 'accomplishing profession', drawing on his analysis of the uses of the term by health visitors. Their uses included those familiar attributes of autonomy, special skill and knowledge, but also 'commitment' and 'comportment'. For the health visitors, being professional meant having a particular orientation to the job and displaying oneself as a particular kind of person.

These aspects of 'mystery' are nicely illustrated in the exchange between the pimp and the hangman in *Measure for Measure*, quoted at the beginning of this paper. The use in this of 'mystery' as articled trade and as 'enigma' precisely makes my point that our own usage of 'profession' carries both meanings (as well as others). This is most apparent when the label 'professional' is used, stripped of any connotation of high moral purpose or high social standing, for the killing trades - hangman, professional hit-man or soldier ('Join the Professionals', as the Army recruiting slogan has it). From this point of view, then, the professional-amateur distinction becomes again a dominant theme.

In the course of fulfilling our social contracts we make moral judgements of work. These judgements use a variety of cross-cutting (and often contradictory) criteria, including productiveness, social importance, scarcity value, degree and type of mystery. We also judge work performance by the quality of the product (in so far as we can assess this) and by the work style of the performer. The amount of trust we feel justified in placing on the work done for us is a measure of both the moral status of the occupation and of the work performance we can expect.

The point that the so-called professions themselves appeal to the moral status of their work is well argued in a recent paper on the creation of a professional ideology in the nineteenth century.

> Central to this process was the formulation and diffusion of a unique ideology based on the concept of service as a moral imperative. This provided doctors, lawyers, clergymen and the members of an evergrowing number of other occupations with an article of faith with which to justify their claim to superior status and special privileges, such as self-discipline. The ideal of service allowed the professions to reconcile the concept of the gentleman with the necessity of work for a living and to formulate a definition of their relationship with clients and with society. (Duman 1979, p.114)

PROFESSIONAL AUTONOMY

The notion of self-discipline or autonomy has been a central one in recent work on professionalisation. There is little doubt that doctors have been very successful in establishing high status, protection from lay criticism and favourable terms on which to define and monopolise work tasks. Medical work is what medical workers say it is. Medicine is, by common assent, the archetypal profession.

Yet it is also important to recognise the limitations on this collective monopoly of power and to assess the degree to which differentiation within the collectivity may affect the locus of that power. We must also examine critically the notion that individual practitioners enjoy an autonomy which is somehow derived from that of the collectivity.

In Britain the divisions between the public health, general practice and hospital sectors have a long history of often quite bitter dispute. The National Health Service Act of 1948 only acknowledged and institutionalised those divisions, it did not cause them, just as the 1974 reorganisation has done nothing to diminish them. The different degrees and sources of political power of the hospital consultants on the one hand and the general practitioners on the other were skilfully exploited by Bevan in setting up the NHS. The GPs were as divided as they were independent, and being geographically isolated from each other were rather like the French peasants described by Marx (1953) as 'potatoes in a sack'.

> In so far as millions of families live under economic conditions of existence that separate their mode of life, their interests and their culture from those of other classes ... they form a class. In so far as there is merely a local inter-connection among these smallholding peasants, and the identity of their interests begets no community, no national bond and no political organisation among them, they do not form a class.

To continue the metaphor, the hospital consultants, already heavily unionised through the Royal Colleges, bargained more cohesively and thus successfully with the Minister. They formed already 'a class for itself'.

This *is* only a metaphor, but the point is perhaps worth making that the insistence on 'independent contractor' status on the part of the GPs and local competition for patients (which necessitates collective regulation through 'professional ethics and etiquette'), weakened their bargaining position with both their hospital colleagues and with Government. While they remained relatively free to organise their own practices, they had little power to influence recruitment, selection, training and licensing. In comparison, doctors in the hospital sector had a much greater measure of influence over these issues, but because of the combination of bureaucratic and collegial control, relatively less freedom over their own work practices.

It would seem, therefore, that in a health service financed from taxation, and under the ultimate financial control of government, there are some quite powerful constraints on the ability of the dominant occupational groups to determine the conditions under which they work. In Britain, the doctors collectively have by and large retained the right to determine what conditions shall be deemed 'medical', and, as individual practitioners, what treatment any given patient will receive. But they have increasingly had to cede ground to government and to 'administrators' over issues of policy and resource allocation. Health Board administrators with a predominantly managerial ideology can and do take decisions which profoundly affect patients and staff, including medical staff. Finally, in the past few years, so-called 'ancillary staff' have begun to use their collective power in such issues as private beds in NHS hospitals and, in pursuit of their own economic interests, have defined 'medical emergencies' (Manson 1976).

The degree of professional autonomy would appear to have been higher in the United States than in Britain, and the imbalance in favour of specialist medicine over general practice or family medicine greater still. Specialists organised themselves earlier - the American College of Surgeons and the College of Physicians were formed in 1913 and 1915 respectively, while the Academy of General Practice did not appear until 1947 - and, despite the recommendations of the Mills Commission and the Willard Committee in 1963 and 1964 for more broadly trained physicians, there was little response from the medical schools (Stephen 1979, p.266). It was left to the Federal Government through the 1976 Health Manpower Bill, to try to force compliance on the schools by making federal capitation grants conditional on the schools increasing the proportion of primary care graduates to 50 per cent by 1980. Even an American government can limit professional autonomy in this way, though whether it has the political will to back up its threat remains to be seen.

PROFESSIONAL CHARISMA

A related theme to that of mystery is that identified by Kosa (1970) as the 'professional charisma' of medicine. For him 'medicine has two ancient links with the original, undifferentiated and unprofessional charismatic authority. One is represented by the Biblical "power to heal sickness and cast out devils" (Mark 3:15) ... the other is represented by the Hippocratic oath ... which refers to that ability of healing and that mastery over death which no profession save medicine can claim. It does not matter whether or not that ability and mastery are real; at times of distress the public perceives and invokes them' (p.31).

Kosa sees this charismatic character as peculiar to medicine and clergy, although he notes that some Protestant denominations have weakened or eliminated the charismatic authority of the clergyman. He compares medicine with law and accountancy, and finds that neither of these has, in the 'public mind', the same aura. The accountant 'deals with the business, but not the personality, of the client' and 'a wilful activity necessitates legal services which are initiated, and can be terminated, at the will of the client; but the necessity of contacting a doctor emerges out of circumstances which are beyond human control' (p.27). To extend Kosa's argument, I see the moral quality of medicine as residing in the alliance of public and profession against the common enemy, 'disease'. There is no conflict over ends - by definition, disease is an evil - although there may well be conflict over means as evidenced by disputes about 'unnecessary' medical procedures or operations.

By contrast there is no common objective in law, unless it be some relatively abstract, though powerful, conception of 'justice', or of the 'Rule of Law'. In practice, there are lawyers for the 'good guys' against those for the 'bad guys', so that the moral position of the advocate is uncertain. Lawyers tend to play in a zero-sum game; doctors do not. This difference has, of course, been noted by Parsons (1954) and Rueschemeyer (1964), and I believe it to be a very important one. Not all lawyers, of course, actually engage in advocacy but their work is predicated on the possibility that competing interpretations of fact and of law arising from competing interests will have to be represented and argued in court or tribunal. There is always an antagonist, actual or potential, and whilst the law may be impartial, lawyers are not. Reverting to the earlier argument, the morality of their work is suspect, and with it their charisma. Judges may still be accorded charismatic qualities, however, partly because of their high social and economic standing, partly because of the mystique of the legal ritual and partly because they embody the law's impartiality. They are not automatically exempt from criticism and occasional ridicule, however. If, as Paterson suggests in this volume, the judges are in certain respects 'above the professions', their status derives from these charismatic qualities and is reinforced by their more aristocratic origins (at least in Britain) and style of life.

Rueschemeyer's other main distinction between the law and medicine is less convincing. His argument is that medicine rests on the discovery of natural laws while legal norms derive from decisions, influenced by the actions of lawyers themselves. Further, he claims, much of a lawyer's competence comes from general rather than specifically legal knowledge, and from his interpersonal skills. I think this difference is overstated. Medical knowledge is also in large measure constructed, whilst Rueschemeyer's characterisation of legal competence as '... generalised intellectual skills, various areas of knowledge outside his speciality, and skills in handling interpersonal relations ... ' could almost as well describe the work of the British general medical practitioner (p.22).

If, however, Rueschemeyer were making not a positive statement about substantive differences between law and medicine in this respect but a statement about general beliefs in such differences he would be on surer ground. There is certainly a generalised public belief in the scientific basis of medicine precisely because disease and illness are perceived as natural, malignant phenomena.[1] The knowledge gap between doctor and patient is not greater than that between lawyer and client - indeed there is probably much more do-it-yourself medicine than law - but the gap is less resented in medicine. Lawyers are seen to create the circumstances under which their knowledge and skill are needed whereas doctors are seen to use their knowledge and skill against the natural enemy.

Special knowledge is important, though, as a characteristic of many trades, but in some it goes beyond mere 'know-how' or the tricks of that trade. Apprentices in the middle ages were instructed in the art and 'mystery' of their craft. In our more sceptical age, mystery surrounds especially those crafts which seem to shape our world and deal with matters which seem beyond our control and comprehension. Medicine and Science with a capital 'S' are perhaps the most obvious examples of such esoteric worlds.

MEDICAL PRACTICE AND PUBLIC ESTEEM

My argument thus far is that medicine bases its claim to be a profession on several grounds and that its claim is honoured by the public on similar grounds. Whilst I do not want to argue with Freidson and others that autonomy is an important ground, claimed by and often fought over, by the collectivity itself, I believe that in state financed health services there are similarly important limitations on that autonomy. 'Profession' and 'professional' as actors' categories draw less on that aspect than on those which critics of the attribute school have tended to throw out. Amongst these characteristics are what I called 'morality' and 'mystery' which contain, I think, the charismatic elements to which Kosa drew our attention. None of this is to deny that we may often regard doctors' claims to special privilege with some cynicism and distrust. The growth of self-help groups in society at large may also be cited as evidence that a sizeable minority find medical services inadequate for some purposes. But I do not believe that these trends fundamentally affect my case, for the most radical criticisms of medicine come, not from such illness groups, but from 'minorities' who have seen medical dominance as reproducing the class relations which have brought about their oppressed status, e.g. radical women's movements and black urban Americans. Here too the most common solutions appear to be women doctors and black doctors, albeit organised in collectives rather than on entrepreneurial, bureaucratic or capitalist lines.

Such radical criticism appears to have gained less support in Britain than in the US and I would suggest that the NHS is largely responsible for this. After all, paying for something that does not work is presumably more likely to produce frustration than receiving the same ineffective care 'free'. A great deal of care in both societies, however, can be seen to be effective, and a good deal more cannot be evaluated at all. Thus, perhaps not surprisingly, medicine and medical practitioners still enjoy considerable public esteem.

GENERAL PRACTICE

With the continuing growth of specialisation in medicine, the survival of general practice may appear as a paradox to be explained. There are good grounds for suggesting that general practice in Britain has done more than merely survive. It has staged a remarkable recovery from the apparently moribund state of the late fifties and early sixties. This is not to say that general practice has solved all its problems, for an old contradiction remains unresolved. This is the contradiction between the GP as 'Primary Care Specialist', and the GP as 'family counsellor'. Both conceptions are contained in the political rhetoric of the Royal College of General Practitioners and attempts at being both produce practical dilemmas for the doctors.

It is perhaps not strictly correct to call it an 'old' contradiction for, in the pre-NHS days when solo practice was the norm and many GPs also did hospital work, the tension between medical care as technical work and as supportive counselling was relatively unimportant. Of course, as Jewson (1976) and Armstrong (1979) have argued, the rise to dominance of hospital medicine in the nineteenth century placed the general practitioner in a position of clientship to the hospital while remaining in an entrepreneurial, patronage relationship with his own clientele. The two systems of medical work, say these writers, produced and sustained two cosmologies of medicine. They differ, however, in that while Jewson claims that hospital medicine superseded 'bedside medicine', Armstrong sees the latter, 'biographical medicine', as he names it, as remaining in exchange relationships between hospital doctors and general practitioners to re-emerge in recent years as a separate, but not necessarily subservient specialism.

Armstrong sees the 'emancipation of biographical medicine' as having occurred through the break with hospital medicine. Blocked mobility into consultant grades forced the GPs to organise themselves through the Royal College of General Practitioners. Perhaps, in this way, 'the potatoes in the sack', the 'class in itself', did become something of a 'class for itself'. In its 'strong' form, this emergent cosmology of biographical medicine places the patient and his biography at the centre of 'the medical gaze' and relegates hospital medicine to a purely technical role; in its weaker form, the two cosmologies are different, but equal.

To what extent, though, do ordinary GPs conceptualise their tasks in this way? And what about the public? Or, to turn these questions around, what relevance do these intra-collegial debates over the 'proper place of general practice' have for everyday medical work and the participants' views of it?

Data from general practitioners suggest that the dilemma or contradiction mentioned earlier is very much a feature of GPs' theorising (McIntosh and Horobin 1977). On the one hand medicine is seen as a body of scientific knowledge and as a set of techniques, for which the GP feels himself to be relatively poorly equipped. On the other hand the tasks of counselling are also regarded as specialised activities which potentially bring him into competition with social workers, nurses, marriage guidance counsellors, psychologists and psychiatrists. Here are some examples.

Dr 'Patterson' ... patients here are very much consultant oriented, and no matter how much you may feel you're on the right lines for treatment, they do expect to go along and see a consultant. ... I think that this being very much a teaching hospital area ... the GP becomes a second or third rate citizen. This is never by a direct assault, but more by implication ... .

Dr 'Smith' You see, to me, a doctor is a scientist. He should try his best to be a scientist all through and only then can he do justice to his profession. However sympathetic or kind one wants to be towards a family, he can't be a social worker. If I am a social worker, I am doing an injustice to my profession.

Dr 'Bothwell' Because we're so over-burdened by relative trivia and social problems, we cannot utilise the skills for which we're trained ... we're trained to treat medical problems ... I would think that 30 to 40 per cent of my time is spent on what I've been trained for. The bulk of the rest of the work could be done by health visitors, social workers, district nurses - who are much cheaper and who are even trained for the job.

Drs Smith and Bothwell appeared to represent a minority view amongst our sample; most of the respondents appealed to a different set of work orientations which emphasised personal involvement with patients' problems, 'family doctoring' and continuity.

Dr 'Richards' There's much more than medicine in it ... we're not general practitioners, we're family doctors, which means you're a family friend.

Dr 'Jackson' [These problems] are not non-medical; they're part of life and really that's what we're dealing with.

Dr 'McKenzie' People come here for a reason and I am prepared to deal with anything.

These respondents for the most part endorsed those parts of the official rhetoric (see e.g. Royal College of General Practitioners 1977) which incorporate the roles of family doctor or counsellor and specialist in ordinary disease. While there were differences between urban and rural, and between solo practitioners and members of group practices, they were differences of degree only. What most of the practitioners seemed to be saying was that the satisfactions of practice lay in 'helping people', whatever the problem, whereas the frustrations lay in their inability to exercise their technical skills more fully because of the pressure of time.[2]

Dr *'Macmillan'* The satisfaction is derived from the whole purpose of the job which is to make people better in all senses ... there's still some sort of fascination in trying to work out people's problems and deal with them.

Dr *'Lawrence'* The reward I think is knowing that perhaps you've done your best for your patients and if the patient at the end of the day says 'thank you' ... [but] you could do a lot more given the opportunity and time is the great factor here. It would be nice, for example, to do all your own minor operations ... remove cysts, do stitching and all these sorts of, eh well, do a complete work-out for somebody with say cardiovascular problems - but this needs half an hour at least ... .

These doctors have given up the notion of being specialists and of being involved in hospital medicine but the idea of coping with the medical problem is still a potent force in their ideologies. They accept that their work is less technical than they would perhaps like, but 'craftsmanship' is still possible in accurate diagnosis and illness management (Freidson 1975). And the gratitude of 'deserving' patients counterbalances the irritation of dealing with 'trivial' presentations.

There is, however, another element in the GP's ideology and with this I want to draw out one of the most powerful of the myths of medical work and relate it back to my earlier theme of profession as mystery. This is the myth of 'heroic intervention'.

THE DOCTOR AS HERO

In Marcia Millman's (1976) fascinating account of 'the backrooms of medicine' there is a chapter called the 'Great Save'.

Standing around, waiting for the police to arrive, the resident and the intern made bets on whether the case would be a real emergency or just a teenager who had swallowed too much aspirin. But at least, they assured one another, this time they knew it wouldn't be some old alcoholic who would 'waste' all of their time in the Coronary Care Unit. (p.49)

Most GPs have little or no opportunity for heroic intervention for, generally speaking, life-threatening illness is referred immediately to hospital. Even those doctors who practise in areas remote from hospitals do relatively little life-saving. But the realities have not destroyed the myth. One of the respondents expressed this theme very clearly.

Dr 'Scott' You come to a house where something awful has happened and there's the mother and a couple of daughters and the neighbour from next door and they're in a terrible state. Now I suppose this is just appealing to my sense of power or something, being able to walk in and take charge and in a minute or two they've settled down and they're not panicking because you've arrived and all their burdens are on your shoulders and they don't have to worry any more because the doctor's there ... this I find profoundly satisfying as long as I can, in fact, cope with what's happening. By this I don't mean that I can cure the patient, but that I can cope with the situation. If he's dying of a coronary, well I can't stop him dying, but I can maybe help ... the number of people whose lives you save in the course of your career, you can probably count on the fingers of one hand - it's scientists and public health people that save lives. Most doctors merely alleviate suffering, whether physical or mental, and it's being able to do that ... we alleviate by technical skill (or) by presence or personality ... . When I went in for medicine I had the feeling that maybe I would take out an appendix on the kitchen table ... now this has been a big disappointment of my life as a GP that whatever I can do, there's someone else who can do much, much better. I can diagnose tonsillitis, there's an ENT surgeon who is far better than me at that; I can diagnose appendicitis, hearts, whatever you can think of, there's someone who is much better than me at it and these people are all now available to the population. It's not as much fun being a GP nowadays as it used to be. The only thing is that if it's fun anywhere, it's fun out here. At least, out here, I have - I admit this with shame - I have delivered an extended breech with the nurse giving chloroform at one end and praying and me delivering at the other end and swearing, and the baby lived, the mother lived, and everything was all right. Now when you've done that, it's almost like winning the pools. I shouldn't ever have got myself into that position but it's a wonderful feeling when you get yourself out of it. Now this, I think, GPs had in the old days, they had much more exciting lives ... .

I am not trying to say that Dr Scott is typical of general practitioners - in some ways his willingness to bare his soul makes him unique. But there is no doubt that many of his generation did and do still appeal to the heroic myth. Whatever tasks a doctor performs, whether routine or unusual, he seems to measure it against this standard of 'the great save'. Nor, probably, is this confined to doctors. Nurses, ambulance drivers, policemen, even boy scouts no doubt cherish the hope that somewhere, sometime the chance will come to bring off such a coup. But what is peculiar to the doctor is that the successful action, the save, is seen to be brought about through the use of the esoteric skills for which he trained and which, by and large, remain untested and unused.[3] In practice, the policeman, the nurse and the ambulance driver probably perform more life-saving actions, but they perform them through skills anyone can learn. They lack mystery.

On the less dramatic level, we can see in Dr Scott's account the more usual performance of mystery - the acceptance of responsibility by mere presence. However sceptical we may be of the claims of medicine and its practitioners, we do, as Kosa said, place our faith in them when we cannot cope by ourselves. It is true, of course, that we invest hospital medicine with technical powers additional to those more home-spun ones of the GP, but we attribute those powers to the institution rather than the person. Hospital staff may possess charisma, but for the most part it is routinised; it is the charisma of office, not of person. There are exceptions, of course; anyone can quote the names of a few specialists who have attained local or even national eminence. But they remain 'doctors' or more anonymously still, 'the hospital'. '*The* doctor' remains, for most people, their 'own' general practitioner.

I take the reasons for this to lie in the heroic myth shared by doctors and public. For both, the archetype is the solo practitioner, disparaged by the label 'horse and buggy doctor', who, in the myth, brought us into the world, smoothed our fevered brows, and eased by magic potions the anguish of illness. By contrast, in this folk memory, the hospital was the hospice, the infirmary, the place to which the dying were sent. I always suspect that the proverbial gratitude which patients express to hospital staff is really gratitude for having got out alive!

The strength of the GP's charisma is also derived, paradoxically, from his familiarity (the friend of the family function) and from his 'moral superiority'. By this I mean that, like the priest, he deals in sacred matters, converting mundane problems to moral issues. He has the power to induce guilt by opening up our private lives for inspection, but by transforming pain and fear into illness, he can also absolve us. Like the policeman and the clergyman, he is 'never off duty', so that he must be seen to lead a life of probity. Thus we, as patients, are faintly surprised when 'the doctor' treats us as equals and demonstrates his own ordinariness.

This moral superiority, of course, is a potential weapon, available for use by the GP, on 'suitable occasions'. What occasions might be suitable, however, are not clearly apparent, and are certainly not part of what is conventionally regarded as diagnosis and/or medical decision-making. The point that moral judgements are made in medical practice and that patients are engaged in doing moral work in their encounters with doctors is probably a commonplace of contemporary medical sociology. I suggested some years ago that

> despite the claims of many both within and outwith the profession that the role of the doctor is ethically neutral, it is extremely difficult to see how such (moral) judgements could be eschewed ... . If patients wish to be treated 'as human beings' and not simply as bodies to be mended or diseases to be cured, then they cannot object to the social nature of their humanity being scrutinised and its relevance to therapy assessed. (Horobin 1973, p.367)

Of course we do, as patients and as critics of medical hegemony, complain about both the impersonality, the 'objectification' of the person in hospital medicine, *and* the pressure to uncover the private, undiseased parts of our lives which is inherent in biographical medicine of the Balint variety. This is to say no more than that the patient's agenda, derived from his own theories of illness and his own biographical relevances, may conflict with the doctor's agenda. We know they are different - if they were identical we would not need to consult the doctor for purposes other than access to resources - but we cannot understand why they differ in these particular ways. Our response to expertise is therefore ambivalent. The division of labour is the division of expertise which depends on the shared assumption that almost all work needs special skills, that we do better to concentrate on our own skills, leaving others to their own, and that this arrangement is functional for the community. As Simmel (1950, p.313) argues:

> Our modern life is based to a larger extent than is usually realised upon faith in the honesty of the other. Examples are our economy, which becomes more and more a credit economy, or our science, in which most scholars must use innumerable results of other scientists which they cannot examine. We base our gravest decisions on a complex system of conceptions, most of which presuppose the confidence that we will not be betrayed.

We all have to trust members of other trades to ply their trades on our behalf, and this applies to bus drivers, food packers, and car mechanics as much as to doctors, dentists and lawyers. We license each other, albeit with misgivings and with institutional or legislative safeguards, to tell us what we need and to produce it for us. Of course expertise places the non-expert in an exploitable situation, hence our ambivalence towards it. All experts claim legitimacy for their contribution to public welfare, but this is not, or at least not primarily, a confidence trick played by the professions in pursuit of autonomy and monopoly power. It is rather an inherent feature of the division of labour. If we have to agree to others performing tasks in exchange for the tasks we perform, we at the same time grant licences to them to become expert and to use their expertise on our behalf. We also expect the expert to inform us what is in our best interests, for how can we know this when the technical grounds for such judgements are, by definition, outside our competence. Even when experts leave us with choices, we are more often than not reluctant to exercise such choice; 'what do you recommend?', we ask. Of course, 'experts' pursue their own self-interests at the same time and we can seldom know when interests coincide and when they conflict. Nor can we rely, if we ever could, on the free play of market forces to effect a coincidence of public and private good. We can only maintain a healthy scepticism of any claims to place public welfare above private interest.

Duman (1979) points out that the ideal of service served in the nineteenth century as a counterweight to the ascendant *laissez-faire* business ideology. In so far as the members of the professions themselves believed in such an ideal and oriented their behaviour in accordance with it (and therefore against pure self-interest), they created the conditions under which trust could be offered and accepted. It is part of my argument that this notion of service is still a fundamental part of the actor's conception of professionalism, constrains professional behaviour and is built in to the 'contract' between profession and public. Other occupations have adopted the professional rhetoric and even if they have done so in order to enhance their status and monopoly or guild power, they have had to accept the concomitant constraints on self-interested behaviour. If we, the public, see 'profession' as more trustworthy than 'trade', we help to institutionalise trust-worthiness as part of the licence we accord to those who set up as experts. The rhetoric becomes an integral part of the reality. This is not to deny the reality of such self-interested behaviour as that discussed by Thomas and Mungham in this volume. We need always to ask the question, *cui bono?* or, as I said earlier, to maintain a healthy scepticism. But the fact that the medical profession has, for example, tended to restrict entry to the profession so as to preserve status, jobs and income, does not imply that I should withhold my trust in the ability and intention of my doctor to act in my best interests. Scepticism and trust are not necessarily incompatible.

In the case of general medical practice, then, the logic of expertise forces the expert to adopt a paternalistic stance and the non-expert patient to accept it. The position of the GP, however, is not straight-forwardly that of expert in relation to the non-expert patient, for beyond the GP are the specialists. In some respects one could regard patients, GPs and specialists as, in Schutz's (1964) terms, man-in-the-street, well-informed citizen and expert respectively. But clearly some patients are well-informed citizens or even experts in their own illnesses (Macintyre and Oldman 1977). Further, it is probably only when the GP has performed the initial expert task of transforming signs and symptoms into an organised illness, that the patient can formulate the help he requires as possibly beyond the competence of his GP. After all, even GPs and hospital specialists consult their 'own' GPs about their illnesses. I would further argue that it is precisely in these circumstances where further specialisation and sub-specialisation has occurred that the 'intermediate expert' is constrained to adopt a paternalistic stance.

However, the 'trade unionisation' of general practice ideology which turns the GP into a primary care specialist, operating in group practice with a so-called 'team of ancillary workers' threatens to undermine the basis of biographical medicine by fragmenting care still further. This creates a dilemma for health service policy of choosing between fragmentation plus a possible increment in consumer choice and a more thorough-going version of family doctoring with its concomitant problems of paternalism.

Meanwhile the GP's charisma is maintained through the paradox that increasing knowledge and control through science creates new uncertainties (the more we know, the more we realise how much more there is to know). Such an argument runs rather against the more usual one that science, in the long run, reduces uncertainty. As one writer has it,

> Magic and experimental science advance hand in hand, often indistinguishable, setting up their flimsy ring-wall against chaos. As human control widens and is consolidated, the resultant shrinkage of the unknown will curtail divine prerogatives. All weather-gods are diminished by meteorology. (Green 1979)

We place the GP in the position of the well-informed citizen who can mediate between the world of science and our own mundane concerns. But we also attribute to him the power to mediate between those same concerns and the hostile forces of disease. He is the weather-god that is not diminished by meteorology!

ACKNOWLEDGEMENTS

Many of the ideas in this paper were formulated and reformulated during discussions with Philip Strong and indeed the title was suggested by him. He also drew my attention to the piece of Shakespearean sociology which prefaces the paper.

NOTES

1. We should beware of throwing out the baby with the bathwater in rejecting any scientific claims of medicine or of refusing to regard diseases as natural phenomena. Whilst we certainly need to treat the medical enterprise as the construction and application of knowledge (Freidson 1970a), we need also to recognise the massive reality of disease. Cancer, coronary thromboses, peptic ulcers, typhoid fevers and even humble arthritic pains are certainly social constructs, but they are also biological facts.

2. This preoccupation with 'time' is quite crucial to an understanding of general practice work, a point I elaborate in a forthcoming paper. Crudely summarised, time is both a real constraint and an account. It is real in that the GP must schedule his consultations to average six minutes throughout the working day and week. It follows from this that his task is not just to determine what this or that patient needs, but which patient needs can be coped with in six minutes. When, however, the GP talks about the constraints of time he is also talking about his own conceptions of what is 'proper' general practice work: trivial illness and inappropriate consultations take time which should be devoted, in his view, to more deserving patients.

3. Bittner (1975) makes a related point about the 'essential nature' of police work.

> While everybody might respond to the call of an emergency the policeman's vocational ear is *permantely and specifically attuned* to such calls, and his work attitude throughout is permeated by preparedness to respond to it, whatever he might happen to be doing... . I do not intend to imply that everything policemen attend to can be thus characterised. That is, the special and unique police competence comes into play about as often as practising medicine, doing engineering, or teaching - in the narrow meaning of these terms - come into play in what physicians, engineers and teachers do.

5 The General Practice Lawyer and the Client: Towards a Radical Conception

MAUREEN CAIN

'Tis a wonderful thing, Sir, that Men of Professions do not study to talk the Substance of what they have to say, in the Language of the rest of the World

Sir Richard Steele, *The Conscious Lovers*

INTRODUCTION

In this paper I use some of the results of a very small scale piece of research to address one theoretical and one more practical problem relevant to the sociology of lawyering.

I shall argue that the concept of profession, even in its most radical formulations, obscures more than it reveals about the work people do, and that *alternative concepts based on the specific practices of various occupational groups* should be substituted. A completely different classification of occupations would of course result. I argue that the alternative formulation situates jobs in a general theory of social structure, whereas the sociology of the professions has *either* been confined to 'middle range' theorising and ignored this problem *or* sought to bridge the gap between jobs and the social order by empirical statements based on implicit and (therefore) ill-formulated theories. Radical formulations have asked about professions in the class structure, but have presumed the usefulness of the notion of profession itself. I claim to be able to theorise the relationship between some 'professional' jobs and social structure in a way that opens up new avenues for empirical research.

The practical question which this paper also addresses is 'how can one tell when and whether a lawyer has done a good job?'. The legal profession[1] offers only a limited range of negative criteria, although there exist many eulogies of good practice from which rules of conduct could be extrapolated by a neophyte practitioner (e.g. Malcolm 1966; Megarry 1962). But the main concern of these works is to inhibit legal deviance rather than to encourage legal competence - whatever that may be.

Another approach to the competence question has been to ask clients, retrospectively, how satisfied they have been with the service they have had (Rosenthal 1974). Such measures are often not independent, for many lawyers advise clients what it is 'reasonable' to want, and thus supply the criterion by which they are to be judged (although Rosenthal did construct an independent measure). More important, no survey of clients (or lawyers) could yield a *sociologically relevant* analytic category. Such research can only discover whether lawyers are doing a good or a bad job in terms of common sense criteria, themselves embedded in, if not derived from, the ideology of lawyers themselves. Only if the sociologist constructs her own categories, and constitutes her data in terms of them, can the terms of debate as defined by lawyers be avoided, and a genuinely independent measure be created.

PROBLEMS WITH THE CONCEPT 'PROFESSION'

Given the limited scope of a paper, I will for reasons of economy develop a critique of the concept 'profession' in relation to the work of Terence Johnson (1972). Criticisms made of it are here being required to stand for a more general critique. Johnson's work merits this special position both because it has been influential in this country - Bankowski and Mungham (1976) use it, for example, and it routinely appears on 'English Legal System' booklists - and also because he explicitly takes issue with ideologically determined empiricist and common sense definitions of professionals in terms of the 'traits' which they possess.

For Johnson the basis for differentiation between occupations is *control* over the producer-consumer relationship. Thus he defines professional jobs as those of producers who *define both the needs of the consumer and how those needs should be met*. Typically, he says, this position of control results from the fact that the clientele (consumer group) is large and heterogeneous. Conversely, producers in this situation tend to be a relatively homogeneous group, collegially organised. Control is exercised in terms of the rhetoric of a diagnostic relationship.

Johnson's approach represents an advance on classic statements such as, for example, that of Carr-Saunders and Wilson (1964); first, because it is *relational*; second, it questions the taken for granted *desirability of professionalism* and third, it departs from *empiricist nominalism*. The last point is demonstrated by the fact that according to Johnson's definition neither a lawyer working for a company nor a lawyer working for a neighbourhood centre would be a professional. The fourth merit of Johnson's approach is that it allows for *mobility of jobs between categories*, although he does not attach as much significance as Hughes (1958) to the efforts of the 'professionals' themselves in this regard.

There are, however, crucial difficulties with Johnson's argument. First, he assumes a *theoretical need* for a concept of profession, yet does not indicate the body of theory which requires and situates this concept. Secondly, and as a result, his formulation is *reactive*. Certain occupational groups style themselves as professions and the concept is defined in terms of a set of purported characteristics. In the standard works the need to protect the client from the consequences of his own ignorance have been emphasised. High standards of technical skill and of ethics, for example, are argued to be necessary because the client cannot judge the service he receives. Professions are treated as necessary deviations from the free market model of supplier-consumer relations. Johnson says no, it is not like that. Rather, the characteristic of professionals is their control over the client. He substitutes an alternative, indeed a radical alternative, but he does not transcend the debate. Thirdly, Johnson posits certain kinds of relationship as a permanent, i.e. non-historic, logical possibility. The *ideal definition* remains, while in historical time various occupational groups move in and out of the category. The concept of profession itself is timelessly correct. Plainly this error too derives from the first one, for if the concept 'profession' has no theoretical existence, and yet is recognised as a concept, it lacks all material grounding.

In sum, Johnson falls victim to the same snare which he saw to have trapped his predecessors. People doing certain jobs have characterised themselves - and been characterised - as professions: this concept with all its ideological trappings has been incorporated into sociological analysis so that even its harshest critics are incapable of transcending it, and conduct their discourse in its terms. Thus Johnson replicates these occupations' concern with their own organisation and their rhetoric of the ignorance (vulnerability) of the client. His analysis reinforces the notion that there really 'are' professions, and by claiming the mantle of radicalism for a perspective which emphasises professional control over the client inhibits the development of an adequately theorised alternative to the conventional view.

More recent work (Bankowski and Mungham 1976; Illich 1977; Medcalf 1978; Scheingold 1974) emphasises that lawyers control not merely, or even at all, by over-the-desk domination of clients, but more subtly. Lawyers peddle the language of the law, legal symbols. Lawyers coerce the experiences and life situations of their clients to fit these definitions. Lawyers are responsible for individualising and de-politicising issues. This is inevitable if an issue is to be constituted in terms of legal discourse. Law is hegemonic, and subjects all who come within its scope to a reconstitution of their problems in terms of a fundamentally bourgeois set of ideological categories.

The struggles of radical lawyers to get off this hook are well documented, most classically perhaps by Lefcourt (1971). Two points are more interesting for the current argument. First, there is the recognition that to trade in categories and interpretations must necessarily be to trade a way not just of perceiving but also of constructing situations. This point of view recognises that language is never value free, that discourses are creative. These points are accepted in the current argument.

Secondly, there is in these works the assumption, not demonstrated, that *therefore* lawyers are to be thought of as social controllers. This view, indeed, is shared with scholars of many political and sociological persuasions. As O'Gorman (1963, p.5) has put it 'sociologists from Ross to Parsons have described the legal profession as a major mechanism of social control'. It is with this view that this paper take issue. So far radicalism both in defining lawyers as controllers of individual clients and in defining them as controllers because of the ideological discourse which they sell has reached a position from which only negative statements can be made: lawyers don't help, they control; professionalism does not protect clients, it defeats them. Radicalism can and should offer an alternative formulation which is positive, which makes it possible not just to see that one's previous knowledge was incorrect but also to understand more about the world. Without such positive formulations and theorisations the world cannot be changed.

Such an alternative formulation cannot be achieved without an examination of the various concrete practices of people doing jobs. Ideologies cannot be transcended in the realms of thought and reason. Identifying the specific concrete practice of an occupational group is, of course, a theoretical as well as an empirical task. When the specific concrete practices of several such groups have been identified, then a new and theoretically grounded basis for their classification may be achieved. The research on lawyers, presented below, could have provided a basis for continuing to classify together lawyers, doctors and vicars. But it did not. An approach to the material world - research - can yield both a theoretical alternative *and* a concrete rebuttal.

THE SPECIFIC PRACTICE OF LAWYERING

Sociological wisdom, then, whether conventional or radical, has emphasised the importance of lawyers as agents of social control. Some, like Parsons (1962) saw this as a positive function of the law and its practitioners. The social control function of lawyers then takes on moral overtones. 'Attorneys mediate between the established normative order guaranteed by the state and divers interests and developments in society' (Rueschemeyer 1937b, p.173), it has been argued, following this basically Durkheimian line of reasoning. By contrast, the radical position has interpreted control as suppression, and has focussed attention on the ways in which lawyers appropriate the right to know what their clients need. Thus the corollary of the expansion of access to lawyers is a limitation on people's confidence and ability to assert their own needs in their own way. Thus not only Johnson (1972), but Rosenthal (1974), Bankowski and Mungham (1976), Foucault

(1977) and Illich (1977) emphasise the controlling function of lawyers. This controlling and canalising of experience, it is argued, is carried out for the benefit of, if not directly on behalf of, the ruling property-owning class.

By contrast, the research reported here suggests that controlling is not what British solicitors - even those at the bottom end of the market - spend most of their time doing. Indeed, to anticipate a little, in sixty-seven of the eighty-two cases which I observed and recorded the client announced his need and set the objective for the solicitor. There was a significant minority of exceptions (ten), and some doubtful cases (five). These are described and analysed in the final section of this paper. But certainly the predominant evidence was not of clients being subordinated.

The specific practice of lawyers which *was* identified was that of *translating*. Clients bring many issues to the solicitor, expressed and constituted in terms of a variety of everyday discourses. The lawyer translates these, and reconstitutes the issues in terms of a legal discourse which has trans-situational applicability. In this sense law is a meta-language. Its material significance, however, derives from the fact that it is also the workaday language for certain state authorised adjudicators.

So far this argument has not departed far from the 'radical social control' position outlined above. The thrust of that position, however, is that clients' needs are taken from them (the transitive verb to need becomes a noun) and adjudicated by alien authorities, often to the disadvantage of the client. *But clients are typically the institutions (legal persons) of capitalist society, and middle class people*: the model professional in the occupation's own terms deals even more disproportionately with clients such as these (Smigel 1969; Carlin 1962; Handler 1967). A small part of law work, and that of a very low status, is concerned with the working class. Does not this call into question a view of lawyers as controllers of the masses? Does not this necessitate a definition which is based on neither lawyers' rhetoric nor a reaction to it but on what they actually do?

The view which I share with such disparate theorists as Antonio Gramsci and Max Weber is that the model of lawyers as both agents of the bourgeoisie and translators is correct theoretically as well as empirically. Lawyers are translators - that is their day-to-day chore. They are also *creators* of the language into which they translate. The radical position is not to argue against the evidence that lawyers are (a) primarily controllers of (b) the masses, and that this effect is achieved by the appropriation of clients' needs. The radical position argues rather that lawyers are *conceptive ideologists* (Marx 1976, p.60) *who think, and therefore constitute the form of, the emergent relations of capitalist society.* The remarkable correlation between the increase in the number of lawyers and the increase in the volume of capital (Smigel 1969; Auerbach 1976) is thereby explained. To think, for the first time, a debenture share, say, is a creative act which the antecedent development of capitalist relations had made possible, and, in some form or other, necessary. It is in this sense that lawyers are conceptive ideologists. Their primary client is the bourgeoisie, in its various forms of organisation. Weber too (1954, p.291) pointed out how finely attuned to the typical problems of the middle classes are those areas of law which lawyers have refined, polished, and expanded on behalf of their typical clients. It is in this sense that lawyers can also justly be characterised as the organic intellectuals of the bourgeoisie (Gramsci 1971, pp. 5-23), thinking the class's advance through a close institutional relationship with its day-to-day practical concerns.

These points are elaborated elsewhere. Here the position may be summed up by saying that the control task may recently have been added to the conceptive ideological and translating practices, but it is these latter which constitute the lawyer's work, and in terms of which his job should be sociologically defined.

This paper uses research to demonstrate the meaning and possibility of translation and its typicality within legal practice - a crucial point if it is to be identified as the specific practice and thus theoretically the defining characteristic of lawyers. Situations in which translation did not occur are accounted for.

Creative translation - conceptive ideological work - is not discussed in any further detail here. Such work is undertaken primarily for large institutional clients and is discussed more fully elsewhere.

Thus this paper supplies only a part of the substantiation which the foregoing analysis requires. What it does is demonstrate that even for 'one off' individual clients the most common practice of lawyers is translation rather than control. Control, in the form of either transformation or refusal to translate, is a minority practice even at this 'bottom' end of the occupation. It is therefore argued that translation is the specific practice of lawyers in terms of which their place in the social structure should be theorised. Indications of how this latter task might be done are offered but not developed in this article.

THE RESEARCH

The research was begun in January 1974, and was designed as a pilot study for a larger project which was not, in the event, carried out. Cases started during the research period were followed up to their conclusions, in one case four years later. Observation was carried out for a total of nine weeks in the offices of four solicitors. The two metropolitan solicitors were found by personal contact. The two provincial solicitors were the only two who agreed to the research following a random mailing of solicitors in the town. Given this data base the research perforce aims at *conceptual* rather than *theoretical* generalisation. This in any case is a correct objective for a pilot study.

A total of 82 cases was collected for analysis. In most cases I was allowed to read the case file as well as to observe solicitor-client encounters and to attend court. The first lawyer with whom I worked, however, (Lawyer A) did not allow me to examine files. Details of the cases are set out in Table 5.1.

Firm A was a one-man practice in the metropolitan centre. As Table 5.1 shows, he dealt with a lot of litigation work. Firm B was a high street practice in a suburb, which had five partners. Here litigation was a separate, specialised job. However, the partner with whom I worked claimed to be a general practitioner, and the distribution of his cases supports this. He also — and this is important — attended the local county court on behalf of his firm.[2] Firm C was a provincial branch practice in a north country town, carried largely by a managing clerk. The firm had several offices in small towns in the rural hinterland, and a partner from one of these would attend 'my' branch office on two days per week.[3] This firm depended heavily on conveyancing. Indeed, all but one (the compulsory purchase) of the non-conveyancing cases came to the firm because of associated conveyancing work.

In the larger provincial firm (D) the research was done with the probate partner. His debt gathering work was handed over to a colleague once the legal aspects of it had been sorted out. One of these involved the sale of the lease of a sea front catering

TABLE 5.1   Types of cases studied, by firm

Nature of task	Firm				Total
	A	B	C	D	
Conveyance*	—	1	23	3	27
Family and divorce	5	8	—	—	13
Debt collection	1	3	1	2	7
Planning and compulsory purchase	1	2	1	—	4
Will making	—	1	1	4	6
Unsatisfactory contracts	—	3	—	—	3
Deed polls/affidavits etc.	—	4	—	—	4
Personal injury etc. damages claims	2	1	—	—	3
Landlord/tenant	3	1	1	—	5
Crime	2	1	—	—	3
Probate	1	—	—	1	2
Other	1	1	3	—	5
Total cases	16	26	30	10	82

* Cases involving both sale and purchase for one client are counted as one.

concession, which was eventually repossessed by the vendor. The other was part of dealing with the affairs of a builder who had emigrated. The researched partner also conveyed his house and negotiated with the Inland Revenue Department on his behalf.

Thus both the provincial lawyers dealt primarily with undisputed matters, while disputes represented the bulk of the work of the two metropolitan firms. This was emphasised by the distribution of cases in which there was no second party or 'other side'.

The characteristics of clients are also important in any account which seeks to refute 'domination of the masses' as the most useful

TABLE 5.2   Unopposed cases, by firm

	Solicitor				Total
	A	B	C	D	
No second party	2	6	24	7	39
Total cases	16	26	30	10	82

way of theorising lawyers' practice. Unfortunately, the social class of the private citizens could not be determined. In the table below 'property owner' means someone making a living by buying and selling houses and flats.

Solicitors A and D each had a client in the category 'business/commercial' which had more than two directors. The rest of the clients in this category were working on their own or in partnership. In firm B this was because the senior partner had the larger company clients; in firm D it was because larger clients were more rarely involved in probate matters. In the two smaller firms the distribution of types of clients in the sample is likely to be a fairly accurate reflection of the clients of the firm.

This considerable dependence on private people as clients meant a large number of 'one off' or at best occasional clients. A problem of continuity of workload was posed for the lawyers (Carlin 1962; Galanter 1974). Lawyer A resolved this problem by building up a *reputation*. This was possible because his clients were part of loose knit but effective networks of relationships. Because he had a largely immigrant clientele he was in a position analogous to that of a lawyer in a small town where networks are complex and gossip channels effective. Eight of the 16 clients of lawyer A were West Indian, and two were Asian.

TABLE 5.3   Types of client, by firm

| Type of client | Solicitor | | | | |
	A	B	C	D	Total
Private citizen	12	19	25	7	63
Private landlord/property owner	2	2	1	—	5
Business/commercial	2	5	4	3	14
Total	16	26	30	10	82

Lawyer C was new to the town and aware of both this problem and that of breaking into an established market. The problem of getting work was tackled in three ways. First, a gap had been found at the bottom end of the market, conveying (or transferring) small terraced houses with local authority mortgages. Secondly, the firm prided itself on speed and efficiency, both as a profitable practice in itself, and as a means of building up a reputation with estate agents. Files of this firm would contain 30 letters on average for a conveyance, roughly half being despatched by the firm. (In firm D by contrast, a conveyance file could contain over 90 letters.) Finally, this firm (C) depended on the patronage of certain key land and estate agents who acted as brokers for clients and cases. Some of the consequences of this are discussed in the section on outcomes, below.

I have no evidence as to how lawyers B and D got their clients. They worked, however, in larger firms and in each the senior partner (with whom I did not work) had large commercial and industrial clients.

TRANSLATIONS

Discursive translation is a lawyer's defining skill. Even a simple conveyance of a newly built estate property - easy money for the lawyer, with a standard form of contract - involves some translation work. In drafting the contract a planning authority condition that the future occupants do not erect fences has to be translated into a restrictive covenant. Client purchasers require that this be translated back into everyday discourse. In the language of everyday it emerged that 'no one is going to say anything if you don't let it (the hedge) get too high'. The existence of the covenant, however, provides the possibility of its future invocation. Its breach would make possible a future legal solution even if the real grounds of complaint were quite other.

Translations undertaken on behalf of clients involved both translations of *objects* and of *concepts*. The skill of the lawyer existed in ensuring that the relationship between the statements in his legal discourse was such that it would lead to a legal outcome which would translate back *directly* into the outcome chosen by the client as formulated in his or her own, non-legal discourse. At the intermediate stages such direct retranslation is not necessary, and quite often not possible.

Three examples are taken from the research outlined in the previous section as illustrative materials showing what is here meant by translation. While these examples are not meant as proof it is still necessary to describe the data from which they are drawn. In the final section an analysis of the fifteen deviant cases is undertaken.

In will making the client's choice of outcome was given centrality more regularly than in any other branch of law work which I observed. This was true for all the lawyers. The case below illustrates well what is involved.

> A client told Lawyer D that she wished to bequeath her money to her children, including her share of a house owned jointly with her husband. She was particularly concerned to secure these monies for her children in the event of her husband remarrying after her death. Lawyer D told her that a jointly-owned house would become the sole property of her husband after her death, and she could not in any way guarantee her share of the money invested in it for her children. However, the woman was pressing. Lawyer D then suggested to her that changing the ownership of the house to a tenancy-in-common would enable her half to be secured for the children. He explained that this was unusual, and would require her husband's consent. It was arranged that the husband would telephone Lawyer D, after discussing the matter with his wife, so that Lawyer D could explain what was involved. Eventually the husband agreed. The form of ownership was changed and the will was appropriately drawn.

In this case the objects in the client's discourse were her money (which for her existed now as part of a house, now as cash again), her children, her husband, her husband's possible future wife and family. The principal objects in the lawyer's discourse were the jointly-owned house and the possible tenancy-in-common. The client's discourse was dominated by conceptions of kin-based relationships; the lawyer's discourse was dominated by conceptions of relations involving ownership potentialities and capacities. Thus the husband and wife became joint owners and possible tenants; the children became beneficiaries; the possible future spouse did not figure at all. The house which in everyday discourse the wife and husband regarded as 'theirs' turned out in legal discourse to be capable of being theirs in many different ways. In other words, if the legal discourse had exactly paralleled the everyday discourse it would not have been possible to achieve a solution in one but not in the other. The discrepancy between the discourses is necessary, not a redundant mystification. The only point at which *exact translation* is required is translation of the objective in legal discourse into the client's chosen outcome. Clients do know and are entitled to know what they want; a good lawyer will achieve an exact translation of this in another discursive realm.

[*Further examples of translations are presented here in the original paper (Eds.).*]

Ability to translate is the specific skill of lawyers, and, it is argued, their definitive practice. None the less, they are not always willing or able to deploy this skill. The next section of the paper deals with these exceptional situations.

OUTCOMES

CHOICE OF OBJECTIVE

If the defining practice of a lawyer is translation, how then is the second question addressed by this paper answered? What is a good lawyer? All the non-matrimonial cases of which the start was observed were concluded without litigation - although four years later one was settled within a week of a scheduled county court hearing. Law is not, in most cases, a zero-sum game. The question cannot be answered, therefore, by totting up the number of a lawyer's victories, for in most cases there are no clear winners and losers. Retrospective appraisal by clients has already been rejected as a lawyer-influenced criterion. Appraisal by panels of other lawyers is hardly independent of the occupation's own biases. Paradoxically, the most useful criterion is that suggested by inverting Johnson's definition, with which this paper started out. If 'professionals' are those who determine both the needs of their clients and how these shall be met, are lawyers professionals? Is this in fact what they do? Rosenthal (1974) has already considered a related question, that of client participation. In this paper the measure of *who sets the objective for the lawyer* is used.

The choice of this measure is not arbitrary, for the argument now is that *typically a bourgeois client brings an issue to a lawyer, which the latter translates into a meta-language in terms of which a binding solution can be found. The lawyer may have to extend the concepts and objects of that discourse in order to achieve such an effective translation.* Plainly such an argument would be nonsensical if the client were not the one who stated the *outcome* which he wished to achieve. A 'good' lawyer is therefore one who accepts his client's desired outcome as his own objective. An analysis was therefore undertaken of whose chosen outcome was adopted by the lawyers studied.

TABLE 5.4   Determination of objectives, by client

Type of client	Determination of objective			
	Client's objective retained	Client's objective rejected	Doubtful	Total
Private individuals	50	10	3	63
Business/commercial	12	—	2	14
Landlords/property owners	5	—	—	5
Total	67	10	5	82

Table 5.4 makes several points very clear. First, most clients tell the solicitor what they want and he sets about getting it for them. Secondly, none of the recurring clients, those who bring regular business, had his objective rejected. This happened only to private citizens bringing 'one off' cases, Galanter's 'one shotters' rather than 'repeat players' (Galanter 1974).

VARIATION BETWEEN FIRMS

This pattern was apparent for all four solicitors, but it was most marked for solicitor B (the suburban practitioner) and least marked for A (the central metropolitan solo practitioner) and D (the practitioner in the large provincial firm).

An additional variable is needed to account for the variation between the firms in the extent to which clients' chosen outcomes were retained or transformed. While the private person/other distinction accounts for most of the variance, it does not explain it all. This residual explanation is provided by an examination of the structural position of the practitioner and his firm. Two structural dimensions were of paramount importance. These were: first, the dependence or independence of the lawyer. This dimension examined whether or not the firm had a *patron* which disproportionately supplied it with work. The patron could be either a large client or a 'broker', in the case here a firm of land agents. The second structural dimension was occupational control, analysed as professional integration or professional marginality. This led to the typology set out in Figure 5.1 below.

	Professionally integrated	*Professionally marginal*
Patron	D	C
No patron	B	A

FIGURE 5.1   Typology of practitioners

DEVIANT CASES

The reasons for this allocation of lawyers to cells will become apparent as the deviant cases - those in which the client's chosen outcome was rejected - and the doubtful cases are examined.

Firm A has already been presented as a dependent for its flow of business on maintaining a reputation with its largely immigrant clients. No single client was identified as having the status of patron. The solicitor was strongly professionally oriented: he would regale one with legal anecdotes, the humour of which depended on a prior deferential attitude to barristers and judges; he was strict in his interpretation of professional ethics. Yet a one man business for immigrants in the commercial centre of the city was an anachronism. Moreover, although work was regularly provided for two sets of chambers there was no special tie with any other firm of solicitors. This lawyer was therefore classified as professionally marginal, in a structural rather than an attitudinal sense. He has no patron. Thus this lawyer accepted his clients' chosen outcomes as his objective both because *he needed to retain his reputation* amongst his relatively organised clientele, but also because there were no *countervailing pressures,* or no alternative rewards. His approach to clients was summed up in a remark I overheard him make to a colleague at the bar: 'You know me - I believe everybody'. He did. Even in private conversation he would explain how his client could not possibly have broken into the house in the way of which he was accused, because he was far too drunk at the time, and so on. Thus he fought his criminal cases, accepting the client's wish to 'get off' as his objective. Similarly, it was he who fought the photographs case [quoted in original paper] through to the Court of Appeal, and was successful. A pre-war immigrant himself, he believed to the full in the rhetorics of democracy, equal justice, and innocence until guilt is proven - and he practised accordingly. I suspect he believed that everyone else did too.

TABLE 5.5   Determination of outcome, by firm and client

Outcome	Determination of outcome by firm								
	A		B		C		D		
	Private person	Other	Private person	Other	Private person	Other	Private person	Other	Total
Client's objective retained	9	4	13	7	22	2	7	3	67
Client's objective rejected	1	—	6	—	3	—	—	—	10
Doubtful	2	—	—	—	1	2	—	—	5

Given all this, the deviant cases require explanation. In the one in which the client's objective was rejected the clients were a brother and sister whose father had died. There was no will. Lawyer A also worked for their late father's employer, a charity. There was a growing argument about £3000 which the charity had, according to lawyer A, loaned to the deceased. The children resisted this interpretation, claiming that it was an honorarium. Several times in the two meetings observed lawyer A pointed out to the children that they could seek alternative advice, and that they need not be embarrassed to do so. After the research period was over they did indeed change solicitor, and lawyer A withdrew from the case altogether. Here, then, the exceptional case proves the rule, since it resulted from the lawyer's attempt to achieve another client's chosen outcome.

One of the two clients of lawyer A classified as doubtful was a personal friend of long standing in the throes of a divorce. Lawyer A gave him a lot of advice about what was reasonable, but it was not invariably accepted. The case is classified as doubtful because the opinion of each party appeared to carry equal weight, and the advice was often about questions irrelevant to the legal issues of grounds, maintenance, and the house.

The second doubtful case was that of a man accused of driving while uninsured. He thought he was covered to drive another vehicle, and said he had been told as much on the telephone by his insurers. Lawyer A checked in his books, but said that it was as he had feared 'You are either insured or you are not. But the fact that you took the trouble to 'phone is a point strongly in your favour... I think we can save your licence'. The case is classified as doubtful because lawyer A demonstrably attempted to adopt the client's objective (not guilty). He discussed the matter with the client at length - I observed two three-quarter hour meetings - and examined the documents for a loophole with great care. However, he decided it was impossible to deny the charge. This client too eventually changed solicitor.

Lawyer A's failure to adopt the client's chosen outcomes involved in two cases (the children with the disputed inheritance and the uninsured driver) constituted a *refusal to translate*. The third case involved an *attempt to transform* the client's chosen outcome by persuading the client to accept a 'reasonable' objective.

Lawyer B emerges as the most prone to reject his clients' chosen outcomes. This lawyer was structurally integrated with the profession. The three high street law firms, and others in neighbouring suburbs, did a lot of business together, and were observed to help each other out with agency court appearances. Lawyer B also needed to maintain the good will of the local County Court if he were to remain a success. Thus lawyer B has been characterised as professionally integrated, although this turned out to be a rather mixed blessing for his clients. There was insufficient evidence to identify a patron.

Thus lawyer B was more dependent on the profession than on his clients. This meant that he was not willing to fight matters if there were a risk of this being regarded as 'unreasonable' by Court officers or fellow lawyers. He was not willing to take on cases with relatively unconventional chosen outcomes.

The six cases in which the client's chosen outcome was not adopted were:

(1) A plea in mitigation rather than a defence.
(2) A demand for 'reasonable' access, i.e. one evening, one week-end day and six week-ends per annum staying access. The

client had wanted either custody or to see his child every day. 'I don't want to feel I've twisted your arm,' said lawyer B to the visibly shattered client. He explained that he was tailoring his demands to what a court would regard as reasonable and be likely to allow.

(3) A divorce case. The client was dissatisfied with the amount of maintenance he would have to pay. He was told, 'You can always go back to the court if your circumstances change'. Again the attempt was to persuade him that courts are very reasonable.

(4) The fourth case also concerned a divorce. This woman was very determined that no provision for maintenance by her ex-husband should be made. Lawyer B insisted on a nominal maintenance being included, on the grounds that this could then be increased if, say, she became ill and unable to work. The woman did not return to complete the divorce, although she had been separated for three years.

(5) The fifth client whose outcome was not adopted was a man who was dissatisfied with the service he had received from a computer dating service. He was told that within the terms of the contract nothing could be done.

(6) Finally, a client complained about the noise caused by his neighbour. Lawyer B wrote to the neighbour, who called in to see him. Lawyer B then decided that the neighbour rather than his client was being 'reasonable', and wrote to the client suggesting various (expensive) building works which could reduce the noise.

Of these six cases in which lawyer B did not adopt the client's chosen outcome as his objective, numbers one to four involve an attempted *transformation* of the client's chosen outcome, and number five is a *refusal to translate*. Contracts are always capable of re-interpretation, and of having their implications elaborated.

The sixth case also involves a refusal to translate. Lawyer B, however, tried to resolve the issue in the terms of the presenting, everyday, discourse. Solutions in terms of this everyday discourse could have and may have been thought of by the client, who had come to the solicitor for a legal rather than an everyday solution. Such attempts to find solutions in the discourse of everyday were more typical of lawyer C.

Lawyer C was the legal executive/managing clerk who ran the small provincial practice. He has been characterised as having a patron and as being professionally marginal. The patron observed was an old established firm of land and estate agents. This firm did not pass all its legal work to lawyer C, but did pass two cases to the firm during the two-week sampling period. The practice is classed as having been professionally marginal because at the time of the research it was new to the town. Moreover, it was not popular because of its cut-price work. Lawyer C was not amenable to informal social control from the very strong local Law Society, because he was not eligible for membership.

Most of lawyer C's work, as indicated in Table 5.1, was conveyancing - a task which can often be carried out in everyday discourse. There were, however, three cases arising out of an original conveyance where a translation was necessary if the client's chosen outcome was to be achieved. In each case lawyer C refused to translate. In the first case he offered a solution in the terms of everyday discourse. But, of course, the client had only approached the lawyer because the solutions she could think of - those available in everyday discourse - were inappropriate or had been tried and had failed. The cases in which lawyer C rejected the client's chosen outcome are listed below.

(1) A woman had sold her home and handed over to her son the £4000 proceeds, on condition that she could live with him in the house he bought with the money. She was now unhappy living there, did not get on with the son's girlfriend, and wanted her money back so she could live elsewhere. She said it was a loan. The lawyer said there was no evidence that it was a loan and not a gift. He offered common sense advice such as that she should 'have a talk' with her son, but refused to accept that the money was a loan and take the necessary steps to recover it. 'She's been a silly woman and now she's regretting it,' he said. And on another occasion indicated that 'All she wants is a bit of hand-holding'.

(2) A woman had bought a terraced house with a local authority mortgage. She then found that one of the walls bulged, and wanted to get compensation from the surveyor. She was told she could not. This may have been correct, but no alternative was suggested. Her desired outcome was a bit of money to help with major structural repairs. It was lawyer C's job to translate the issue into a form which made this possible. Instead of this he left her to think of a solution and then rejected it as an inappropriate translation.

(3) The third client wanted confirmation that he rather than his neighbour owned a bit of land, and that his neighbour had no use rights. He was told he was wrong.

Thus lawyer C tended not to translate his clients' chosen outcomes, whereas lawyer B had transformed them so as to facilitate translation.

The three 'doubtful' cases of lawyer C are perhaps even more revealing. They also need careful attention because they are the only cases brought by business clients in which the client's objective was not unequivocally adopted by the lawyer. In two of them the outcome was in fact chosen by the patron - the broker land agents. The two clients, however, were apparently happy with the outcome.

(1) A man was buying a two-year sub-lease on some business premises. He wanted a guarantee that he could renew the lease on expiry. The freehold belonged to a local charity, of which the broker land-agent was secretary. The freeholder refused to put in writing any guarantee, such as that no comprehensive redevelopment of the site was planned. The client was advised of the situation, but, as lawyer C said, he wanted something cheap. He agreed to take his chance. The property had come to the attention of the lawyer through the broker. The client had been acted for on a previous aborted purchase.

(2) A man was offered an alternative plot of land with appropriate permissions, on to which he could transfer his small business, a 'kennels'. He would, of course, have the benefit of new drainage on the new site. The exchange was contingent upon planning permission for building being given on the vacated site. The client agreed, planning permission was given and the 'swap' went through. The client was content. However, the outcome had been chosen by the broker land-agent, who referred the client and explained what was needed to lawyer C.

(3) The third doubtfully determined outcome was from a builder who had been in financial difficulties. Lawyer C had conveyed his house in the teeth of a re-possession order from a loan company, and generally extricated him from the debts of his own dissolved partnership. Thus the case could properly be classified as one in which the client determined the outcome. Unfortunately, however, he did not pay lawyer C's firm. The

firm recovered their money by retaining monthly instalments paid to the client via them from the buyer of the client's house, to whom the client had lent £400 to secure the sale. As lawyer C explained to me, this was right in morality and common sense. I agreed. The surplus was of course paid to the client.

All of these doubtful cases of lawyer C were exceptional in that the client ran a one-man business, and was therefore likely to bring recurrent work to the firm. In all other cases the chosen outcome of business clients was adopted by the lawyer. This anomaly is now seen to be largely explained by the intervention of the *patron* - the broker land agent - who set the objective for both lawyer and client in two of the three cases. The third case resulted from the willingness and need of the firm to take work from any source while it was establishing itself in a new market. So lawyer C took on a notoriously troublesome client - and indeed, found a satisfactory way of handling the client himself, as well as his many debts and difficulties!

There is nothing to say about lawyer D, for he adopted his client's objective as his own in every single case. This absence of anything to say is perhaps the most significant fact of all.

REPRISE: THE TRANSLATOR

Lawyer D was professionally integrated, in that he was a member' of the local Law Society and worked routinely with other solicitors in the town. He is classified as having a patron/client because of the observed relationship with a large organisation which was one among a number of significant clients. The importance of the relationship cannot be demonstrated without an analysis of the accounts of the firm. There remains the possibility of a misclassification.

However, the concern of lawyer D to oblige this important client is shown by the case of the tenant farmer, summarised below. In this instance it seems that the client needed not so much advice on a course of action as *legitimation* from its lawyer. Once the client was in a position to show that it had received independent legal advice to the effect that the law was uncertain it went ahead alone to achieve its chosen objective. Such legitimation could not be provided by other than a high status firm. Thus this patron-client needed lawyer D's good standing in the local Law Society. They needed the scrupulous professional integrity which nearly proved such a stumbling block to them in this case. Their need for legitimation may have benefited lawyer D's other clients. Lawyer D's status was in part dependent on his willingness and ability to act as a translator for *all* his clients. Lawyers have long recognised themselves that their key task is translation, and it is the practice of translation which is accorded respect within the profession.

The case of the large organisation versus the tenant farmer is summarised below from a file of 63 letters, plus documents.

The tenant had been in partnership with his father, who had died. Lawyer D's client (the organisation) wanted to know whether it could release the tenancy on the land without the consent of the surviving partner (the son). They had an offer for compensation. D's reply was that this depended on whether the tenancy was an asset of the partnership: it was in the father's name, yet rent was paid by the partnership. On balance D thought it was a partnership asset and therefore the consent of the surviving partner was necessary for release.

Much later (there were many other aspects to the case) the client organisation wrote to say that they were seeking the son's consent but as there was a possibility that the offer of compensation would be withdrawn.

> 'We shall be pleased if you will give further consideration to the question of the release.... If you still feel the firm has no power to release the tenancy on the grounds stated we shall be pleased if you will advise us if there are any other grounds on which the firm could give the release without the surviving partner's consent.... If it transpires that there are grounds we shall appreciate your advice as to what redress Mr Blank would have, if any...'

Under pressure from an important client, D gave his client organisation the legal loophole it required.

> 'We still feel that our original opinion is correct.... However, we should point out that decided cases relative to the question all turn on the individual facts, and it could certainly be argued that the tenancy was not a partnership asset...'

The risk of litigation was pointed out, but the firm replied that they now intended to release the tenancy 'with or without the consent of the surviving partner', and did so. The son, apparently, claimed that the partnership had been formed expressly to prevent this happening.

OUTCOMES EXPLAINED

This section has argued that desired outcomes are typically chosen by clients, and that the exceptions to this are disproportionately private people bringing 'one off' cases. While this held true for three of the four firms, it was possible to account for the exceptions in firm C because of the business getting practices of that firm, and in particular its brokerage relationship with the land agent.

Explanations of the patterns for the other lawyers have been offered in terms of the degree of organisation of the clientele (lawyer A), dependence on the local civil court (lawyer B), and the need to maintain high status by performing highly regarded translation work, in order to be able to legitimate the practices of important clients.

This deviant case analysis, while yielding important insights, cannot be regarded as providing all the variables needed to explain firm by firm variations, as more research is necessary to construct a more refined typology, in particular one which could distinguish between the different types of professional integration here revealed, i.e. attitudinal, dependence on court, and dependence on the good opinion of high status practitioners.

But although more research is undoubtedly necessary, quite a lot has equally indubitably been achieved by this small enterprise. It is these advances which are noted below.

CONCLUSIONS

This paper has argued that a sociological definition of an occupation should be in terms of the specific practices of that occupation. Various materials, particularly those data constituted by research, should be used to identify these practices. A classification of occupations - if it is wanted - can then be constructed in terms of these various practices.

The correct theoretical location of the occupation can then be identified. This ápproach avoids the idealism lurking in other attempts to classify occupations, and in particular 'the professions', even when the attempt seeks to situate the professions in a radical theory of society.

In the case of lawyers the standard radical approach has been to assume the theoretical need for a concept 'profession', and then to redefine the content of this concept. The theoretical object 'profession' has been the same as for conservative theorists. In order to achieve this redefinition of the content of the concept 'profession', radical theorists have emphasised (i) the impotence of clients; (ii) the control of clients by professionals; (iii) the distortion involved in reconceiving issues in legal terms. The direction for research generated by this formulation of the issues would be a comparison of working class and middle class clients to demonstrate the greater vulnerability of the former.

However, if the specific practices of lawyers are examined it is readily apparent that most clients are *not* working class. To build a theory of 'lawyers as controllers' on an examination of their minority work with working class clients is therefore to miss the central point about what lawyers do, and it is this central point which should give them their place in a theory of the social formation. Also an empirical examination of relatively low level lawyers reported here shows that by and large lawyers do not tell clients what they want; clients tell lawyers the outcome they wish for. Moreover, the exceptions to this had to be explained in terms of the position of the lawyer in his local structure, including the structure of his relationship with clients; social class did not explain the deviant cases. It was therefore apparent that the specific practice of lawyers cannot be theorised as social control.

By contrast it has been argued that lawyers' characteristic and specific practice is *translation* into a discourse which they both use and create. Lawyers can thus be characterised as *conceptive ideologists*. It was shown that translation work is undertaken even for impecunious clients. However, since Llewellyn wrote in 1933 research has shown that lawyers do this work most and best for the haute bourgeoisie and the state which represents it. It is also appropriate therefore, to theorise lawyers as organic intellectuals of the bourgeois class.

The radical error arose for two reasons. One is the idealist scientific practice discussed above. The second source of error is the preoccupation with repression as the task of the agencies of the bourgeois class. True, there is a repressive task and there are repressive agencies; but for capitalism to be reproduced on an expanding scale there are also other necessary tasks. One of these is that of formulating and constituting new forms of relation appropriate to this expanding reproduction. This is the task of lawyers and of other conceptive ideologists with whom they should properly be classified.

That is the end of the argument, but given the theme of the conference for which this paper was prepared, it is necessary to add a footnote about classification. Soldiers, psychiatrists, and priests might on this basis be classified together as social controllers; doctors and perhaps teachers should be classified as sustainers: the proper theoretical place for them is as the maintenance engineers of labour power; playwrights, philosophers, accountants, sociologists, and lawyers must be classified together as conceptive ideologists.

ACKNOWLEDGEMENTS AND DISCLAIMER

Thanks are due to the Social Science Research Council, which financed this research, and also to the four lawyers and those clients who gave their time and help. Because of them I hope that this paper is of benefit to others, because that was their reason for agreeing to the research. I am grateful to the Law Society for giving me a letter acknowledging that the research did not involve a breach of professional trust and to Richard Abel, Philip Lewis and Terence Johnson for comments on this paper.

The paper was originally published in the *International Journal of the Sociology of Law*, vol.7, no.4. Copyright Academic Press Inc. (London) Ltd 1979.

NOTES

1.   It is legitimate to use the term here, for I refer to how an occupational group styles itself.
2.   County court work is, allegedly, uneconomic unless such a sub-specialism within a firm can be developed.
3.   Since the field work ended the practice has expanded and now employs two qualified solicitors in addition to the visiting partner and the managing clerk.

6 Solicitors and Clients: Altruism or Self-Interest?

GEOFF MUNGHAM AND PHILIP. A. THOMAS

INTRODUCTION

The collective voice of solicitors is expressed through the Law Society, which combines the functions of a governing body and a professional association for practitioners in England and Wales.[1] This London-based institution undertakes the major responsibility of projecting a public image of solicitors based upon client service overriding the baser desires of self-interest. The principle of altruism underpins the code of ethics and practice which provide regulatory guidance. Should a solicitor deviate from the rules of conduct then sanctions can be imposed by the profession. Throughout this paper evidence from a study of solicitors in Cardiff, a large provincial city, will be offered to show how the profession formally states that the client's interests should be, and are, put before its own. This places the solicitor in a less favourable position than the businessman who possesses greater opportunities to exploit a commercial relationship, possibly to the detriment of the other party. *Caveat emptor* may operate in the market place but not in the solicitor's office. In exchange for this public commitment the profession receives special treatment from the state, the community and the client. It is allowed by statute to undertake certain paid work to the exclusion of all others; it is a self-regulating body; its members are of high status and their financial rewards are considerable.

This paper deals with the relationship between the solicitor and the client. We consider the rationale and the manner of the legal profession's projection of an image of altruism and focus upon one legal service, the duty solicitor scheme, which was set up ostensibly to serve the community.[2] Our research into the origins and operation of this service highlights the rhetorical nature of the altruistic model and illustrates the internal politics, both local and national, of the profession.

A TROUBLED PROFESSION

Everett Hughes (1958, p.83) states that one of the manifestations of social unrest is in challenges to the prerogatives of the leading professions. The UK is currently experiencing considerable social unrest and the legal profession has been subjected to an unprecedented level of criticism and scrutiny. The profession is well used to the hositility, indifference or apathy of that majority of the people, who have traditionally been unable to avail themselves of its services because of insurmountable financial barriers. Since issues of property dominate legal work the propertyless have had little cause to encounter it unless they interfered with the interests of those with property. In the last thirty years, however, it has increasingly been the lawyers who have projected the legal solution to those who were previously estranged. With the introduction of the Legal Aid Act 1949, the Welfare State has created an enormous potential class of clients to whom the professional has turned. This discovery, of the reservoir of 'unmet legal need' (Morris *et al.* 1973), has also resulted in a closer relationship between the disenfranchised and the solicitors. The new clients have seen the profession at work and they are not pleased.

This groundswell of dissatisfaction was partially released during the 1960s and 1970s through inquiries into a number of key professional issues. For example, in 1967 the Monopolies Commission investigated the general effect on the public interest of certain restrictive practices so far as they prevailed in relation to the supply of professional services. In 1968 and 1969 the National Board for Prices and Incomes reported on the remuneration of solicitors. The reports, whilst vindicating certain activities, stated that solicitors were overpaid for conveyancing, which yielded over 50 per cent of their income. In 1967 the Monopolies and Mergers

Commission reported on the supply of solicitors' (and also barristers') services in relation to restrictions on advertising. The ultimate embarrassment came in 1976 when the Prime Minister announced the establishment of a Royal Commission to make a general inquiry into the law and practice relating to the provision of legal services in England, Wales and Northern Ireland. The Commission considered changes desirable in the public interest in the structure, organisation, training, regulation of and entry into the legal profession, although the final report has been seen largely as a vindication of the profession. Nevertheless, this wide-ranging set of inquiries does illustrate that the level of concern has risen to incorporate many of the lawyers' traditional users and allies.

THE PROFESSION'S RESPONSE

Such institutionalised criticism demanded a response. The profession, principally via its house journal, sought to account for the attacks in terms of a conspiracy theory. The pages of the *Law Society Gazette* in the late sixties and early seventies suggest that the conspirators included such august bodies as the British Broadcasting Corporation, Her Majesty's Government, the political left and right, the popular press, university academics and 'certain quarters' which remained unspecified.[3] The Council of the Law Society's unfavourable reaction to critical reports was predictable but it is more interesting to note the strong sense of resentment that the profession should be considered a proper subject for such investigations. This form of examination was seen as equating the professional relationship of solicitor and client with that of the market place. Such an equation totally misconceived the relationship and was ultimately detrimental to both parties.

> Law is not a business; nor merely is it a profession, which is defined in the Oxford Dictionary as a vocation or calling, especially one that involves some branch of learning or science, but is one of three learned professions. Is it really suggested that it is in the best interests of the community that the proper approach to remuneration is purely on a time basis, and supply related to the question whether there are sufficient people practising? Is the Church to continue for ever to be under-remunerated because just sufficient hear the call? Is the surgeon

to be remunerated purely on a time basis?... No profession worthy of the name has ever been impelled merely by the monetary reward. It expects, and has a moral right, to be paid properly for its skills and services. (*Conveyancer* 1972, pp.81-2)

As one solicitor (Williams 1973) wrote, 'did these eminent bodies have the slightest idea of the nature of the delicate area on which they were trampling with their feet?' The concern with 'greater productivity', he asserted, would kill the idealism of the legal profession. To practising solicitors law is not business.

Although the Law Society took the steps to establish a Professional and Public Relations Committee in 1971 and employed the public relations firm, Saatchi and Saatchi, to improve its tarnished image, it did not seek to present the profession on any sort of economic/productivity basis. How, in fact, does the legal profession project itself for public consideration?

DESCRIPTIONS OF THE LEGAL PROFESSION

The Law Society has characterised the profession in a number of official statements. The most common version is illustrated by its evidence to the Monopolies Commission of 1968 and repeated recently to the Royal Commission on Legal Services:

A body of men and women (a) identifiable by reference to some register or record; (b) recognised as having a special skill and learning in some field of activity in which the public needs protection against incompetence, the standards of skill and learning being prescribed by the profession itself; (c) holding themselves out as being willing to serve the public; (d) voluntarily submitting themselves to standards of ethical conduct beyond those required of the ordinary citizen by law and; (e) undertaking to accept personal responsibility to those whom they serve for their actions and to their profession for maintaining public confidence.

The language used throughout these public self-descriptions reflected general visions of altruism and service: 'public protection', 'willing to serve the public', 'public confidence', 'trust', 'special skill', 'the supply of professional services is very much more than a business transaction'. At the level of contentious and non-contentious business the Law Society has stated that

> The duty of a lawyer.. is clear and well understood. It is his undoubted duty to employ his skill, training and experience in order to ensure that his client's case is placed before the court to the client's best advantage and in the process thereof he must avail himself, on behalf of his client of every defence, be it technical or otherwise, which the law affords his client (1969, p.1). His (professional's) preoccupation must always be with the promotion of the interests of his client... (1968, p.5).

It is this special relationship, whereby the solicitor 'like all professional men always puts his client's interests before his own' (Monopolies and Mergers Commission Report 1976b) that is said to take the profession outside the market forces of the business world.

This position of service is also offered as the primary justification for the special privileges enjoyed by the profession.

> In order to protect the public from the charlatan or the quack, entry into the profession must be guarded, its standards policed, and its rules of practice defined in the first instance by the profession itself... The ground rules of completion are designed for the interests of the public and not for the interests of the profession alone. (Hailsham 1971)

The purpose of self-regulation and the code of ethics is to protect the public from the vagaries of *caveat emptor*. If the law is not a business then the controls of the market cannot be applied successfully and alternatives must be sought. Given the specialised nature of law, it is argued that only the professionals themselves are properly qualified for the task. The service nature of the profession means that self-control becomes the order of the day. The public statements and rules of practice provide protection if, indeed, the profession does operate in accordance with them, placing client before self in compliance with the altruistic model. Thus it becomes clearer why the Law Society is anxious to distinguish between professional services and business, to promote so vigorously an altruistic conception of the lawyer/client relationship. Without these fundamental distinctions the economic privileges of the profession are suspect.

This description bears marked similarities to those offered by a number of eminent sociologists who adopt the trait approach. Although comparatively little has been written about the professions in the UK there are those who see these occupations in the same altruistic light. The perceived breakdown of a traditional moral order during the industrial revolution and the expansion of the division of labour led to a search for new bases of moral integration. One such was the proposed establishment of communities based upon occupational membership. The professions seemed to offer a possible model. T. H. Marshall stated in 1939 that 'Professionalism is not concerned with self-interest, but with the welfare of the client'. Common good was paramount while individualism and self-interest were of lesser importance. Carr-Saunders and Wilson in their classic study of the professions endorsed the altruistic model:

> The attitude of the professional man to his client... is one of pride in service given rather than of interest in opportunity for personal profit. The professional man who gave a lower standard of service in necessitous cases, where his remuneration was little or nothing, would be regarded as an unworthy colleague by his professional brethren. (p.471)

Millerson in *The Qualifying Associations* took the work of twenty-two scholars on the professions, including Carr-Saunders, Marshall, Parsons, the Webbs, Tawney and Whitehead. He extracted the constant characteristics of their work to see which were considered essential to a profession. The common features were found to be: skill based upon theoretical knowledge; training and education; demonstration of competence by passing a test; integrity maintained by adherence to a code of conduct; a professional organisation and service for the public good. Underlying these definitions is the sentiment that the professional is a noble, independent individual who places public duty and honour before all else. In regard to the legal profession Millerson states, 'The lawyer emphasises the fiduciary nature of the professional/client relationship, the depth of learning, the cordial colleague relationship and sense of public service' (p.3).

However, people such as Johnson and Illich have rejected the trait/characteristic approach. Such an approach, they argue, simply restates the professionals' own self-presentation in seemingly neutral categories. To view them as members of a gentlemen's club, whose rules are predicated upon principles of service and public interest is to ignore the power structure of which they are a part. Instead Johnson (1972) looks outside the professions and attempts to understand them in terms of their sources and use of power and authority. He considers, for instance, the relationship between the state and the professions. Lawyers are adamant about the need to remain independent of the state so far as licensing for practice is concerned. Yet it is the state that ensures that only solicitors may be paid for transferring interests in land or that only doctors may issue death certificates. It is the state which provides the opportunity to practise in a monopolistic or restrictive fashion and it is the legal profession which reinforces the existing social order.

Illich is also sceptical of professionals' self-descriptions and has described them as definers of reality in their relationship with clients. They have the ability to determine a person's needs and thereafter hand over a solution to the problem in terms of their own definition. He suggests that professional authority has three elements:

> The sapiential authority to advise, instruct and direct; the moral authority that makes its acceptance not just useful but obligatory; and its *charismatic authority* that allows the professional to appeal to some supreme interest of his client that not only outranks conscience but sometimes even the *raison d'état* (1977, pp.17-18, emphasis added; see also 1975).

The altruistic model, where the solicitor acts only according to his instructions in the client's best interests, is the source of the profession's 'charismatic authority'. The protection of that model, and the benefits of legal charisma to individual clients, is the justification for the claims to power and privilege - power to determine the conditions of practice independently of the state and privilege in state protection for the monopolistic economic basis of that practice.

THE DUTY SOLICITOR SCHEME

All British criminal courts operate on the adversary system. Theoretically, parties should be represented by trained, qualified legal advocates who set out their client's case to the jury in the Crown Court, or to magistrates. Ninety-eight per cent of all criminal cases are heard in the latter courts. It was upon them that the legal profession focussed in the early 1970s in an attempt to improve its tarnished public image. The magistrates' courts provided an opportunity to do this while simultaneously bolstering flagging markets for solicitors, who were feeling the economic pinch of a depressed property and commercial market.

In 1971 'Justice', a group of liberal lawyers, published a booklet entitled *The Unrepresented Defendant in the Magistrates' Courts*. This publication, read in conjunction with several other contemporary research findings (Dell 1971; Zander 1969 and 1972), stated that only 4 per cent of defendants were represented by lawyers, usually solicitors. Despite the fact that practitioners must have been aware of the low level of legal representation in these courts the Law Society, in its evidence to the Royal Commission, explained the establishment of duty solicitor schemes in terms of the publication of these research findings.

There were both overt and covert reasons for the support of the Scheme by the Law Society, and the regional bodies, local Law Societies. The most important overt reason was this 'discovery' of a large group of people who were being effectively denied legal representation. 'Unmet legal need', an increasingly fashionable term, required action on the part of the profession. The duty solicitor scheme was projected as a public service by the Law Society: 'The prime object of a duty solicitor scheme is to provide unrepresented defendants with any legal assistance they may require and, in the context of the adversary system, to help ensure that justice is done and seen to be done.' Spokesmen for the Law Society and local schemes endorsed this view and suggested that it was a natural consequence of a socially aware profession which had over the years staffed and administered schemes for indigents at little or no cost.

The idea of a duty solicitor scheme to operate in a busy metropolitan magistrates' court may seem to many to be a natural consequence of all the other paraphernalia of a socially conscious profession. After all, we have had for years Poor Man's Lawyer sessions, political legal advice sessions, the legal aid scheme itself, and now, more recently, the neighbourhood law centres. It must seem natural that the profession should direct its attention to needs of prisoners appearing on overnight charges ... (Stevenson 1975)

The Lord Chancellor also supported the idea (Elwyn-Jones 1974):

A further possible development in this field (legal services) would be the greater use of duty solicitor schemes. These have the great merit of needing no further legislation ... So far as I know there is at present only one such scheme operating in London ... and I would hope that it would form a pattern of similar schemes in other parts of London. A number of local law societies have started such schemes outside London and I hope that many more will be initiated as soon as possible.

In Cardiff, which is the focus for the empirical data in this paper, the public statements followed a similar pattern of support. The Organising Secretary of the scheme stated: 'I suggest that solicitors who participate in the Cardiff Duty Solicitor Scheme are not motivated by money or profit.' The scheme was promoted as providing a more equitable and efficient distribution of legal services. Concern was expressed on behalf of those people in magistrates courts who were unaware of their legal rights and their entitlement to legal aid in certain criminal cases. The image of public service was strong although from time to time a recognition of the public relations benefits was made by the solicitors we interviewed:

The scheme might do solicitors a bit of good since we don't get a particularly good press at the moment. The general public seem to think we do nothing but skin them.

The scheme ought to be published more. We generally get a picture of a money-grabbing solicitor which is not really true. At least, it does not apply to me.

Nevertheless, the overriding impression left, after considering the public statements and documents of those involved in organising or endorsing the scheme, is the establishment of a service for that element of the community unable to help itself. The example of the bewildered, middle-aged lady accused of shoplifting was mentioned more than once in the interviews as the sort of person who needed help and made the scheme worthwhile. Such statements support the model of altruism, placing public/client service before self-interest. At a time when the credit of the legal profession was at a low ebb, the duty solicitor scheme could be advanced as practical evidence of its commitment to the theory of community service (Hillyard 1975, p.6).

Nevertheless, during the course of the interviews and our conversations with friends and contacts in the profession it became apparent that the local law society's publicly stated reason for the promotion of the scheme provided only a partial explanation of its inception. The *covert* reasons why the scheme drew widespread support from Cardiff solicitors was that it was part of an internal power struggle. This struggle was of an economic nature concerned with the competition for clients. Traditionally the criminal work in the busy city magistrates' courts had been dominated by three firms. There is evidence that similar cartels operate elsewhere in the UK.[4] It could be argued that just as some firms specialise in commercial work, other firms concentrate on criminal advocacy. However, some criminal lawyers were thought to acquire clientele by unethical methods. By flouting the rules of practice, which prohibit touting for business, certain solicitors were alleged to be able to place themselves in an unfairly advantaged position.[5]

Touting for criminal business was and is well recognised within the profession, and those in close contact with it.[6] The means to control such practices, given the implications of adverse publicity for a supposedly homogeneous profession, are, however, limited.

While the domination of the criminal market was well known within the profession nothing was done for two main reasons: first, solicitors were making a handsome living and were under no pressure to find or create alternative sources of income: and second, there appeared to be no way in which these cartels could be broken by ethical means:

During the mid-sixties the strongest pressures on the profession's practice were in the area of conveyancing. This was, and is, a particularly sensitive area for the average solicitor for their monopoly could be recognised by any member of the public and was a highly visible cost to anyone buying or selling a house. The profession was well aware of its tenuous position and the Council of the Law Society was under pressure from members to defend their favoured status and the scale fee, a form of price fixing, for assessing the charge to clients.

> The Council can only carry the profession with it so far. Many solicitors deeply resent the treatment they feel they have received over their remuneration. Despite continued inflation such small increases in remuneration have been conceded only after many years of negotiation. Now it would seem that they are not only to be denied an increase, but also to be faced with a reduction. No other section of the community has been treated in this way. (Law Society 1972, pp.386-7)

Private practitioners recognised that there might come a time when alternative sources of income would be required to replace or supplement the high-return, conveyancing market. 'If there is any sizeable reduction in conveyancing income, many practices could suffer to such an extent that they would be no longer financially viable' (Hart Jackson 1972, p.12). This awareness of impending disaster was exacerbated in the early seventies when a slump occurred in the property market. Mortgages became difficult to obtain, house prices stopped rising, commercial properties remained vacant and the economic squeeze began to hurt the profession. These factors, coupled with the abolition of scale charges for conveyancing, caused the lawyers to cast around for alternative sources of income. 'If conveyancing is to decline something will be required to fill the void and this cannot develop overnight (Bolton Law Society 1974; Blatch 1966). Further threats came from the withdrawal of legal aid for undefended divorces, with tacit official encouragement for do-it-yourself petitions, and the pressure for change to a no-fault system of personal injury compensation.

One of the areas to be examined was criminal work in magistrates' courts.[7] Increased expenditure on criminal legal aid made advocacy economically attractive to those firms which had traditionally ignored this down-market branch of legal practice. Criminal legal aid in the magistrates' courts cost £14 million in 1976, rising to £16¾ million the following year, an increase of 17 per cent. The Legal Aid Annual Report for 1976-7 shows that between 1973 and 1976 the number of cases granted legal aid increased by 54 per cent. Criminal legal aid has become big business for lawyers.[8]

Solicitors on the outside of the lucrative but tight criminal market wanted to get inside it. Not surprisingly, those who were already established had little sympathy for this proposed redirection of resources. One feature which did unite the profession was the need to retain the market for private practitioners and not allow lawyers from neighbourhod law centres to encroach:

> I for one, think this is a worthwhile service that private practitioners can give to the community and unless one wishes to see neighbourhood law centres and the like (who I hasten to add do admirable work in particular spheres) take over this type of work and who knows, all criminal work and after that ... (Stevenson 1975)
>
> The position is that the members of this association view with deep dismay the continuing spread in area and operations relating to criminal litigation of all London neighbourhood law centres ... If this trend is allowed to continue unchecked it may lead to more solicitors finding criminal defences unprofitable and yet another field of work will be lost to the solicitors' branch of the profession generally. (Lawrence 1975)

However, this was an insufficiently cohesive factor to allow an immediate and satisfactory settlement to emerge between the private practitioners. The outsiders either would not or could not resort to those tactics which were thought to have assisted the establishment of the three large criminal practices characterised by an 'outside' solicitor as 'The Barons' (Thomas and Mungham 1976; Smith and Thomas 1978). Yet without positive discriminatory assistance the would-be criminal advocates were unable to break the cartel. The answer which fell within an ethical framework was the duty solicitor scheme, as the Cardiff solicitors explained:

> There is strong feeling against the three firms who do most of the criminal work in the city. It is my view that the Duty Solicitor scheme was set up by certain parties to break this monopoly.
>
> I joined the scheme because I wanted to extend the criminal scope of my practice and this was one way of getting more contact with the courts and with prospective clients.
>
> The duty solicitor scheme gets our name known better: it is

valuable in that you get to know the clerks and some on the Bench. The scheme certainly helped me right at the beginning when I was starting up as a criminal lawyer.
One wants to break the power of the 'Barons'. The scheme offered the opportunity of doing extra magistrates work. I should like to say I joined the scheme out of humanitarian concerns but to be honest it was with a view to increasing business.

The scheme allowed the outsider, a solicitor with little or no criminal practice, to gain access to the criminal courts, receive a ready made clientele either through the cells or via the clerks and magistrates, represent these clients, get his face known, be talked about, be mentioned in the local newspaper and generally commence to build a reputation as a criminal lawyer. It was seen both in Cardiff and elsewhere as, in the words of one stipendiary, a form of 'legalised touting' (Morton 1977, p.293).

The dominance of economic terms of reference, to the possible detriment of clients, rather than matters of public service can also be seen over the issue of who was to be accepted as a member of the scheme. Clearly, if it was to be successful in redistributing work, those who controlled the market should be excluded completely or relatively. On the other hand the dominant firms, the 'Barons', were also those with the most experienced and often the most accomplished advocates, who could call upon a specialised back-up staff of articled and managing clerks. Thus, the issue arose between redistributing work to the inexperienced solicitor or maintaining the experienced trial advocate, the 'Baron', who was already in the dominant role.

Eligibility for selection as a duty solicitor has gone through three distinct and separate phases. Each one recognises sectional interests within the profession but has little or no regard to the public at large or the potential client. The rulings were created and administered by the local law society which represents all interested professional parties.

The respective eligibility rulings are: common eligibility; maximum of two solicitors per firm; and, finally the present criterion, 'substantial criminal experience' with no maximum number per firm. It became clear in the operation of the first category that, for example, strong social conscience or interest did not necessarily bring a concomitant skill in criminal advocacy. It also meant that the larger firms, particularly those with large criminal practices, could flood the rota with partners and assistant solicitors. Concern was expressed with the results of this free-for-all policy, both as far as the number of solicitors from large firms was concerned and in respect of the quality of advocacy:

> A free for all is dangerous. No disrespect to my conveyancing brethren but I wouldn't let them loose on a guilty plea of going the wrong way round a keep left sign.
> A free for all was a scandal. Too often their name was there but they either didn't appear, sending in someone else, or went only with someone else with them. This kind of operation is only for the benefit of the firm.

Such a rule would do little to assist the redistribution of work.

The failure of the common eligibility ruling led to its replacement by a limit of two solicitors per firm. This again failed to recognise that criminal advocacy is a particular skill and, on the economic level, militated against the large-practice firms which were able to field more criminally experienced lawyers than the maximum number:

> I do not think it fair that only two, or any *ad hoc* number, should be allowed to participate. For example, a firm with two partners would be getting 100 per cent attendance: a firm with eight only 20 per cent [sic].
> I think the idea of having numbers from each firm is really a dog in the manger attitude.
> The change occurred because of internal political reasons and for that reason alone and not out of the interests of clients. I think that clients, as it happens, have benefited but for the wrong reasons as it were.

This time it was the turn of the large-practice firms and 'Barons' to express successfully their concern.

Consensus was reached with the third and current criterion: that each solicitor must have 'substantial criminal experience.' The compromise between the professionally interested parties, the outsiders and the 'Barons', was arrived at by, on the one hand, removing the numerical ceiling which operated previously, to the detriment of the large firms, but also, by placing a limitation on these same firms, preventing them from flooding the rota with inexperienced staff. Again, in theory, this principle protects large practice firms from the 'inexperienced' practitioner anxious to obtain a slice of the client market. The reason for the accord rested in the way in which this eligibility test was administered. Each aspiring duty solicitor is obliged through a process of self-assessment to decide whether the requirement of 'substantial criminal experience' has been satisfied. Provided that all solicitors were competent and willing to make this judgement of themselves it would appear that the scheme had finally settled on a principle which would successfully serve the potential criminal client. However, once again the results of its application as observed by practising solicitors raise grave doubts about its effectiveness for anybody other than the practitioners themselves (Thomas and Mungham 1977).

All lawyers, like doctors, have their first client. Perhaps the secret is to keep that information from the client. Is it possible that the importance of 'substantial criminal experience' is being exaggerated? The position is different in so far as it affects the duty solicitor scheme. Most clients are first time offenders who are ignorant of their rights and the process through which they are being put (Thomas and Smith 1978). The level of dependence on professional assistance is highest with this client. It was stated frequently by solicitors that the effective choice of solicitor by the unrepresented defendant is either the duty solicitor or a named or identifiable solicitor. Given that these defendants are unlikely to know the names of solicitors the responsibility for acting quickly settles on the duty solicitor:

> There wasn't a single one (unrepresented defendant) who didn't say 'Yes, I'll have you.' They pounce on the man that appears whoever he is.

Under either of the first two criteria it was theoretically possible for a client to be represented by someone insufficiently experienced to handle the case. Currently, by virtue of being on the rota of solicitors, the advocate has undergone self-evaluation whereby he indicates publicly that he is competent to deal with criminal matters. Such a position, however, makes it more difficult thereafter for the solicitor to admit that the case presents too great a challenge and that it should be transferred to a solicitor with even more 'substantial criminal experience'. The duty solicitor has to take what turns up on the day and often act immediately, particularly as one of the administrative attractions of the scheme is to help the court clear the daily list. Although the client will usually be charged with a minor offence, cases can be complicated, whilst the out of town criminal may be involved in more serious crime. Perhaps the most important difference between the ordinary and duty solicitor is illustrated by the following statement of a Cardiff solicitor who discussed the purpose of vocational training through articles and experience:

> Solicitors are carefully nurtured taking the relatively simple cases and mitigation pleas. The duty solicitor takes what is presented on the day. Two murder cases have gone to the duty solicitor. Fortunately both firms are competent to handle this.

Comments from several solicitors, from both large and small practice firms, suggest that there remain on the rota solicitors who have over-valued or mis-stated their criminal experience:

> There are some people who really shouldn't be on the panel because they really don't know enough about the job.
> I think people who take on the job should know the job. Most do, lots don't ... Too many people taking it on who have hardly been in court before.
> Those allowed on should be those with some experience of this sort of work.
> In court once I noticed the duty solicitor going through a conveyancing abstract.
> Not every person who presents himself as the duty solicitor is competent to handle criminal matters.
> There are many people who appear in court who are basically conveyancers who are not competent to give other than initial advice.

Not only were disquieting statements made about certain rota solicitors but by rota members regarding themselves, which suggested that the present criterion for admission is a failure:

> I am not a criminal lawyer myself. I do conveyancing and probate. I used to do criminal work when I was in general practice but I haven't done criminal work now for about four or five

years. But I consider myself perfectly competent to be able to go to court, make applications for remand, make pleas of mitigation where there's a guilty plea and also conduct a case in such a way as to be able to pass it over to someone else in the practice. I won't do defended cases because I can't spare the time, not because I don't feel competent.

I'm a divorce man. When I get a case as the duty solicitor I pass it on to the criminal department.

Although the number of unrepresented defendants is reduced there is concern amongst practitioners that the quality of representation has suffered:

The quality has gone down.

I don't think they are doing a brilliant job as they don't have the experience. I hear some people in court and I say to myself 'I know why you are not here every day'.

The local law society holds out these solicitors to the general public as having substantial criminal experience but the rule seems to fulfil a symbolic role for the profession. As one solicitor told us, 'Substantial criminal experience? It is a formula without a meaning.'

CONCLUSION

The collegiate nature of the solicitors' occupational group encourages and maintains a feeling of identity, colleague loyalty and shared values. The group projects a version of the formal omnicompetence of all solicitors as a device for generating trust from the public which is used to making its own judgement of other occupations. The homogeneity[9] and close working relationship of the profession foster internal solidarity, understandings and deals (Baldwin and McConville 1977; Thomas 1978), whilst simultaneously informing the public of its protection via the code of ethics and the disciplinary powers of the collective organisation, the Law Society. However, as we have explained elsewhere (Mungham and Thomas 1979 and 1981) there are significant internal tensions which exist within the profession. At no time are these more apparent than when a possible downturn in the market for legal services is perceived. The scramble to redistribute existing resources and clients provides the conditions for the development of schemes such as the duty solicitor. The need for compromise is illustrated by the way in which the present criterion for appointment to the duty solicitor rota is operated. The Organising and Liaison Committees of the schemes are comprised of a small and identified number of solicitors. Peer judgement by the group of colleagues concerning substantial criminal experience is difficult given that criminal advocacy is only one part of their daily practice. The repercussions of alienating another solicitor in this matter might well be serious on other occasions in practice when a favour or understanding is required. Thus, a vetting process intended to secure the best quality of advocacy for the client is at odds with the need to encourage harmonious working relationships within the profession. The internal politics of the profession in a recession economy have not been resolved by this scheme (Smith and Thomas 1978) but it illustrates the irreconcilable tensions between individual economic advancement, collegiate unity and community/client interest, tensions which were recognised by our respondents.

But it's difficult, who should you look after - your solicitors who are trying to increase or break into criminal work or should you look after the client's interests by giving him only solicitors who are already tried and tested.
At least before the duty solicitor people were directed to lawyers who had qualifications in advocacy. They devoted their lives to it.
It depends on whether the duty solicitor scheme was set up to help the unrepresented defendant or to diversify criminal work.

The origins and development of the duty solicitor scheme cannot, then, be explained solely in terms of an altruistic model. While more people are represented and the court list is cleared faster, these are ancillary consequences of a scheme initially conceived to resolve economic struggles within the profession. Although the success of the scheme in its attempt to relieve these internal tensions is questionable, its public image remains heavily altruistic. The autonomy granted to the legal profession by the state and tolerated by the public is based upon its expertise and altruism. It is the idea of service which legitimates the exercise of professional discretion. The logic of this argument creates an unbreakable circle. The decisions of legal practice are made by solicitors because of their knowledge. The power thus created will be used exclusively for the client's best interest. The best interest will be judged by the professional.

> Professionals, in contrast to members of other occupations, claim and are often accorded complete autonomy in their work. Since they are presumed to be the only judges of how good their work is, no layman or other outsider can make any judgment of what they can do. If their activities are unsuccessful, only another professional can say whether this was due to incompetence or to the inevitable workings of nature or society by which even the most competent practitioner would have been stymied. This image of the professional justifies his demand for complete autonomy and his demand that the client give up his own judgment and responsibility, leaving everything in the hands of the professional. (Becker 1970, pp.96-7)

The Law Society's presentation of the duty solicitor scheme and its public reception is important as an illustration of the way in which solicitors wish to be seen, in order to legitimate the way in which they operate. This paper has provided an example of how the self-interest of solicitors is a more helpful way of viewing this group.

NOTES

1. Of the 34 090 practising solicitors in 1979, 27 257 (80 per cent) were members of the Law Society. (Royal Commission on Legal Services 1979, ch.29, para.25.)

2. Similar schemes operate in 107 magistrates courts in England and Wales. They are staffed by private practice solicitors on a part-time rota basis, under the administration of the local Law Society. The solicitor on call visits the cells to make his advice available to prisoners in custody and is generally on hand in the court building. His remuneration may come from the client but is most commonly drawn from legal aid funds. The first such scheme was established in Bristol in 1972 and followed shortly afterwards by a scheme in Cardiff, which served as a prototype for developments elsewhere (Thomas and Mungham 1973).

3. 'The fact that the programme (a BBC feature on conveyancing) was slanted against the profession to an unbelievable degree is something

one has come to expect. Yet another episode in the campaign of vilification against solicitors.' (Snowise 1972)

'The profession has been the ruthless subject of a publicity gimmick on the part of Her Majesty's Government ...' (Harris 1972). 'During recent years the consultant professions have grown resigned to the idea that they can expect little sympathy from those political views inclined to the left, and who naturally favour collective solutions to social problems. Events in the last few months have shown that no more sympathy for the professions and their rules of conduct is to be looked for on the right.' (Bennion 1971.)

'During 1963-4 the profession was subjected to a number of unwarranted and ill informed attacks by certain sections of the Press.' (Burrows, President of the Law Society, *Annual Report 1964-5*; Wegg-Prosser *op. cit.*)

'It would be helpful to ascertain to what extent the present breakdown in law and order *is* attributable to the repeated denigration of the legal system and lawyers by what some may believe is little more than popular journalism masquerading under the guise of representative, reliable and responsible research, conducted by persons of proven practical experience.' (Sir David Napley, *The Times,* 12 October 1977.)

4.   'The initiative for setting them up often comes from solicitors who are dissatisfied with the way that lucrative criminal cases tend to be channelled in the direction of a small group of criminal firms.' (Legal Action Group 1977.) 'At two courts it was suggested that the chief promoters of the duty solicitor scheme were local solicitors dissatisfied with the strangle hold exercised by a handful of firms on the criminal legal aid work.' (King 1976.) 'After we had published our report, *Complaints Against Lawyers*, in 1971, information began to reach our Secretary from a number of sources that in some areas and some courts unscrupulous firms of solicitors were resorting to undesirable methods of obtaining more than their fair share of legal work.' (Justice 1977, p.35) Legal aid generally is handled by relatively few firms. For example, in Birmingham over three-quarters of the firms have at least one solicitor on the legal aid panel. In practice, 10 firms, 6 per cent of the 173 firms in the city, account for half the legal aid work. Another 30 firms account for most of the remaining legal aid work. (Bridges, Sufrin, Whetton and White 1975.) On the national level 60 per cent of the legal aid money went to 14 per cent of all offices, i.e., 2350 offices in England and Wales shared £32 million while, 5800 offices shared £8 millions. 26 Legal Aid Annual Report [1975-6] Appendix 13.

5.   In London (1973) Morris and Zander showed how certain firms were more likely to be allocated legal aid work by the clerk of the court. 'It would seem from our interviews that the clerks themselves are concerned that the present system allows opportunities for improper conduct on the part of all those concerned: court staff, police and prison officers as well as solicitors.' The unethical procedures were not restricted to London as King (1973) points out. In his study of a scheme in Hendon, King reported solicitors speaking of the influence of the police in sending defendants to particular firms. One even suggested that a gaoler might

be receiving a 'back-hander' for his services.

6. As the Justices Clerks Society observed in their Evidence to the Royal Commission on Legal Services, 'Touting is done quietly and in such a manner as to leave the solicitor plenty of room for denial. This practice was carried on by a very small minority of solicitors specialising in criminal cases.'

7. Another area was welfare law. Hence the support of the Law Society for the extension of legal aid to tribunals. (Bankowski and Mungham 1974.)

8. 'The growth of legal aid provisions over the years has attracted considerable interest. From a pauper's beginning this aspect appears to have been turned into a lucrative field for lawyers.' (Police Superintendents' Association of England and Wales, Evidence to the Royal Commission on Legal Services, p.2.)

9. It is suggested that the recruitment of lawyers does not have the same social spread in the UK as in the USA. (Auerbach 1976; Carlin 1962; Smigel 1964; O'Gorman 1963) cf. Sir David Napley in his Presidential address to the Law Society (1977) when he talked of the middle classes being the backbone of the profession for recruitment purposes.)

7 Mega-Law and Mega-Lawyering in the Contemporary United States

MARC GALANTER

The characteristic features of the American legal profession are not new - large numbers, relatively easy entry, intense stratification, organisation into large firms, strong ties to clients, weak controls by the state or professional guild, a protean entrepreneurial quality, performance of varied functions in an extensive range of settings, and extraordinary prominence in public life.[1] The upper strata consist mostly of large firms whose members are recruited largely from élite schools and who serve corporate clients; the lower strata practice as individuals or small firms, are drawn from less prestigious schools, and serve individual clients. In their intensive and revealing study of the Chicago Bar, Heinz and Laumann confirm the picture drawn by historians like Auerbach (1976) and sociologists like Ladinsky (1963), Lortie (1959), and Carlin (1962). Law practice is a bifurcated structure, organised around different kinds of clients. They conclude that much of the variation within the profession is accounted for by 'one fundamental difference ... the difference between lawyers who represent large organisations (corporations, labor organisations, or governments) and those who represent individuals or individuals' small businesses'. (Heinz and Laumann 1978, p.1117). There is nothing to suggest that these features are being effaced in the American setting; indeed they seem to have become more general and more accentuated. But I think that to interpret recent trends purely in terms of American distinctiveness is to risk overlooking their wider portent. For implicated in them is what strikes me as the great innovation in lawyering in this century, the development of the large law firm and of a distinctive style of practice. It is an innovation pregnant with significance for the kinds of services lawyers provide, the sorts of clients they have, their relations with these clients, the way they relate to legal institutions and to the larger economic and political order. It marks a shift comparable to the movement from the individual general practitioner to hospital medicine.[2]

I would like to focus not on the large law firm *per se*, but on the closely related though distinguishable phenomena that I call, for want of better terms, mega-law and mega-lawyering. Mega-lawyering is associated with large law firms as their distinctive style, but it can be practised by smaller firms, by corporate law departments, by government agencies, by public interest law firms. And there may be large aggregations of lawyers who do not work in this style - e.g. some legal aid offices (Bellow 1977).

By mega-lawyering I refer to a cluster of features that characterise the corporate or organisational segment of modern American law practice. One or another feature may be less pronounced in a particular instance of mega-lawyering. Each of these features can be found apart from the cluster; indeed some may be found in very pronounced form separately from the others (e.g. the specialisation and intensive investigation exhibited by the plaintiff's malpractice or products liability specialist). It is the clustering of these features that constitutes a distinctive kind of lawyering.[3] To display the elements of this kind of lawyering, I shall indulge in a vast and (I hope) instructive oversimplification. Table 7.1 lists some of the principal contrasts between mega-lawyering and ordinary lawyering. Of course there are many intermediate cases. The listed terms do not reflect a discrete binary division. But neither are they points on continua along which there is some approximation of a normal distribution. The real world of American law practice is various and complex, but it displays significant traces of the bifurcated structure suggested by our model.

Compared to ordinary lawyering, mega-lawyering involves practice in much larger units. A survey of the twenty largest firms in 1968 provides a useful baseline by which to measure recent growth at this peak of the profession.[4] The largest firm in 1968 had

TABLE 7.1   Contrasting styles of lawyering

	Mega-lawyering	Ordinary lawyering
Organisation		
Size of units	Larger	Smaller
Specialisation	More	Less
Coordination	More	Less
Internal stratification	More	Less
Supervision and review	More	Less
Training inside firm	More	Less
Span of operation		
Range of settings (in which services are provided)	Many	Few
Scope of operations	(Inter)national	Local
Site of operations	Multiple	Single
Relation to clients		
Identity of client	(Larger) organisations	Individuals (and smaller organisations)
Client control	More	Less
Frequency	More continuous	Episodic
Duration	Longer	Shorter
Range of services	Wider	Narrower
Entry into problem	Earlier	Later
Operating style		
Research	More elaborate	Less elaborate
Investigation	Painstaking	More perfunctory
Long-term strategy	More often present	Less often present
Tactics	More innovative	More routine
Exploration of options	More exhaustive	More stereotyped
Cost	Higher	Lower

169 lawyers and the twentieth had 106 lawyers; the twenty firms had a total of 2568 lawyers (*Business Week* 1968). In 1979 the twenty largest firms, ranging in size from 192 to 502, had a total of 4681 lawyers. The average size of the twenty largest firms had increased from 128 to 234 lawyers - an increase of 82 per cent. In the 1979 survey there were 82 firms as large as the top twenty of 11 years before - and there were thirty firms as large or larger than the largest firm of the earlier period (*National Law Journal* 1979).

This growth at (and of) the peak is part of a general shift to larger units of practice. In 1956 units with three or fewer employees made up nearly 90 per cent of the units in the private legal services industry; ten years later this had dropped to 82 per cent and by 1976 it was down to 73 per cent.[5] In 1948 sixty-one per cent of all lawyers in private practice practised alone: thirty years later it was estimated that only one third of a much swollen private bar was in solo practice (Weil 1967, p.18; Cantor 1977, p.26). Larger firms have been receiving an expanding share of expenditures for legal services.[6]

Ordinary law practice is usually restricted in range to a single locality. Mega-law firms and their corporate counterparts are able to extend their geographic reach by access to funds of information and networks of contacts that enable them to identify suitable local counsel and monitor their performance. Increasingly mega-law firms are themselves organised on a nationwide or even an international basis. Twenty years ago the occasional Washington or foreign branch office seemed anomalous (Smigel 1969, p.206). But in 1979 of the twenty largest firms, nineteen had offices in more than one city. (Of the nineteen outside Washington, sixteen had offices there.) The mean number of city locations of the twenty largest firms was five. Of these fifteen had at least one branch overseas. Most branches were moves to the forum (Washington) or to follow favoured clients (Schell 1979). But the genuine multi-city mega-firm had made its appearance (soon to be followed by the multi-city legal clinic serving individuals).

Mega-law firms are not mere aggregations of lawyers who do similar work. A high degree of specialisation is cultivated within such firms.[7] They are ordinarily divided into departments (corporations, banking, real estate, litigation, etc.). They are organised to coordinate the work of various specialists on the problems of the client. In some cases this includes non-lawyer experts - in planning as well as in litigation. The range of specialties cultivated within firms reflects the needs of the particular kind of client:

> Although lawyers are relatively little specialized to doctrinally distinct substantive areas, they do display specialization of a fundamentally different sort. Their specialization is not so much a division of labor as a division of clientele. Lawyers tend to specialize in the representation of limited, identifiable types of clients and to perform as broad or narrow a range of tasks as their clientele demands. (Laumann and Heinz 1979,

p.217; cf. Johnstone and Hopson 1967.)

Clients are served by teams of lawyers. The work of a junior lawyer is supervised and reviewed by seniors.[8] Training is imparted to young lawyers in the course of a prolonged (four to ten year) apprenticeship, normally ended by either promotion to partnership or by departure from the firm.[9] In recent years there has been both a democratisation of manners and a shift to more meritocratic recruitment: law school performance counts for more and social connections for less (Smigel 1969). But at the same time there has been an accentuation of hierarchy within the firm. The number of partners in proportion to all lawyers has fallen dramatically. In the fifty largest firms, according to a *National Law Journal* survey, the number of partners per hundred associates dropped from 100 in 1975 to 63 in 1979 (Lavine 1979, p.35).[10]

The production by shifting work groups of individualised products - sometimes innovative, sometimes routine, often overlapping and interrelated - poses formidable problems of coordination. Large firms try to provide coordination by organisational structures like work teams and hierarchic supervision, by sophisticated systems for storing and indexing documents to avoid duplication of effort, and by such devices as firm lunches, newsletters and retreats.

Although the partnership form is retained, these are modern firms with central direction and rationalised management presided over by full-time professional office managers. Legal services are seen as a product to be sold: clients are charged by the fraction of the hour for the time of each lawyer who works on their matter. The remnants of patrician airs and professional *noblesse* are further dispelled. Lawyers are more businesslike (Schell 1979). As one Chicago lawyer observed 'law firms are becoming more like businesses and less like clubs' (Rottenberg 1979, p.124).

The clients who engage these large firms (or foster similar concentrations of lawyers within their walls) are overwhelmingly corporate organisations and large ones at that. These services are available only to large corporations, to other organisations such as labour unions and government departments, and to wealthy individuals.[11] They are so confined in the obvious sense that they are immensely costly because the product is labour-intensive custom work. These costs do not diminish with the size of the matter at stake so that thorough individual treatment of smaller matters may be forbiddingly expensive.

This kind of thorough custom work is called forth by the complexity and uniqueness of the legal problems which beset these clients. But complexity and uniqueness are not independent of the investment of legal effort:

> ... the discovery of a unique issue is likely to be a function of the amount of time that lawyers devote to a case, and thus of the amount of money that the client spends on lawyers. If the stakes are high, the problems can become very complex; if the client lacks money, his problems are likely to be routine (Heinz and Laumann 1978, p.1117).

Much mega-lawyering, like virtually all ordinary lawyering, is routine and stereotyped. Problems are handled according to pre-fixed formulae (Carlin 1962; Johnstone and Hopson 1967). But mega-lawyering allows more scope for individualised response to the client's problem. The combination of talent, ample resources, and client capacity (or need) to experiment fosters occasional innovations - a new kind of lending instrument, tax shelter or litigation strategy.[12]

Whether breaking new ground or operating in well-trafficked legal settings, mega-lawyering often involves meticulous and exhaustive research, painstaking assembly of data, and generous use of experts. Ordinary lawyering on the other hand, often involves little consultation of legal learning (Ross 1970; Macaulay 1979), more perfunctory investigation, and a fair amount of 'winging it' (Smigel 1964, p.172). One knowledgeable observer of the American legal scene recently concluded:

> ... one of the chief reasons why competent lawyers go into corporate work is precisely that business clients are willing to invest enough in their lawyers to permit them to develop the highest possible levels of professional skill. Indeed it is not far wrong to say that lawyers for the big corporations are the only practitioners regularly afforded latitude to give their technical best to the problems they work on. The rest of the Bar ordinarily has to slop through with quickie work, or as one lawyer put it, make good guesses as to the level of malpractice at which they should operate in any given situation (Hazard 1978, pp.152-3).

Mega-law draws recruits from higher social strata, from higher status ethnic groups, and from élite educational institutions. It provides them with immensely greater rewards. It enjoys more prestige within the profession (and outside as well). Sorting the various specialties by their prestige among other lawyers, Laumann and Heinz (1977, p.197) found

... two mutually exclusive clusters, i.e. higher status specialties with predominantly corporate clientele vs. lower status specialties with small business or individual clients ...

What accounts for the prestige of a specialty? Prestige is associated with the intellectual difficulty of a field. But Laumann and Heinz compared specialists who represent opposed sides (e.g., antitrust plaintiffs or defendants, consumers and merchants, etc.) in the same controversies and presumably encountered comparable intellectual challenges; they found that 'the side that represents the more "established" interest is consistently rated higher in prestige' (p.204). They find (p.202) that:

... the most important feature of a legal specialty in accounting for its relative prestige standing is its pro bono score. The higher a specialty stands in its reputation for being motivated by altruistic (as opposed to profitable) considerations, the lower it is likely to be in the prestige order.

The prestige of work done for corporate or establishment clients and the derogation of altruistic motivation lead Laumann and Heinz to conclude that 'the legal profession is more concerned with the facilitation of business, with "getting things done" than with alleviating human suffering or with helping people.' (p.205).

Although mega-lawyers provide a wider range of services and more individualised treatment, they do not necessarily dominate the relationship with the client. Individuals who use lawyers for occasional or emergency service tend to let the lawyer define the problem and make crucial decisions about expenditures, pace and resolution (see Rosenthal 1974). But corporate clients tend to be in charge. As Joel Handler (1978, p.25) sums it up:

Strong, rich and confident clients direct their lawyers; on the other hand, lawyers dominate the relationship when clients are poor, or deviant, or unsophisticated.

Laumann and Heinz (1977) report that legal specialties serving corporate clients are perceived by knowledgeable observers to have less freedom of action than the less prestigious fields that serve individuals. This may be due to their sophistication and to the monitoring by inside house counsel (Heinz and Laumann 1978).[13]

The absence of autonomy is neither new nor troubling. From its beginnings, the organisation of large firms to serve large corporate actors was connected with the rejection of a style of lawyering that emphasises lawyers' claims of allegiance to public obligations independent of the interests of the client (Schudson 1977; Auerbach 1976; Hurst 1950). The boundaries of client loyalty remain perennial issues for debate, but the great bulk of the profession, fortified by the ideology that all, even great corporations, deserve quality representation and that adversary confrontation will assure just results, eschews moral screening of client interests. This kind of 'hired gun' service orientation is nicely summed up in a remark reported to have been made to a law school audience by a well-connected and powerful Chicago lawyer:

> A good lawyer is like a good prostitute ... If the price is right, you warm up your client (Tybor 1978, p.18).

(For an academic elaboration of this perspective, see Fried [1976].)

Even the most robot-like of hired guns may have interests and commitment which cut across those of his principal. In ordinary law practice devotion to client interest is often subverted by economic pressures which induce lawyers to earlier resolution than is optimal for the client (Rosenthal 1974). Loyalty is often deflected from the one-time client to the forum or opposite party with whom the lawyer has continuing relations (Carlin 1962; Carlin and Howard 1965; Ross 1970; Blumberg 1967). These deviations from client loyalty are facilitated by the imbalance between the knowledge and experience of the lawyer and his client. These deviations are not absent in the mega-law setting, but their presence is attenuated by greater client sophistication, by the continuing relationship between client and firm, and by fee arrangements that do not erode the lawyers' resolve to pursue matters. Nevertheless, some clients detect a decline in the devotion of their lawyers. For example, one business executive expresses dismay at:

> ... the subtle but very real growing unwillingness of counsel in some cases to serve the traditional function of an out-and-out advocate of his client.
>
> Businessmen have many advisers.... The attorney, however, has always had a very special place, because unlike the other people the attorney was an advocate. His function was to present his client's position. He was not to view his client's position objectively or dispassionately, but rather he was to defend it to the death regardless of its popularity. Our lawyer was supposed to represent us and only us (*Business Lawyer* 1978, p.844).

He attributes this change to lawyers' fears that aggressive advocacy might attract suits against them and might compromise their entrée at agencies and thus their ability to retain other clients. In this view, the exigencies of mega-lawyering constrain the lawyer toward an independent position. At least some lawyers thought businessmen needed reassurance that their loyalties were unalloyed. As one lawyer recently told a meeting of his fellows:

> I think that the lawyers have to strive even harder than they have before to get off this pedestal that we like to think we're on to convince the chief executive officers that we're there to help them solve their problems. We have no objectives except their objectives and it's our job to convince them that we are on their side and not part of the problem. (*Business Lawyer* 1978, p.833).

The mega-firm represents its clients not only in courts, but in a variety of other forums, including administrative and legislative ones. It negotiates with actual and potential collaborators and antagonists and with actual and potential regulators. It not only resists incursions and vindicates rights, but it utilises the facilitative opportunities afforded by legal regulation.[14] Mega-lawyering does not merely respond to problems as defined by clients, but attempts to devise advantageous interchange between the client's operations and the legal environment. As one banker put it:

... we want [counsel] ... to do more than simply respond to instructions from our lending officers ...

We want our lawyers to ask almost in a kind of dialectical exchange 'have you thought about doing it this way?' Even when
it might not be an entirely legal issue that's involved (*Business
Lawyer* 1978, p.840-2).

This apparently unslakeable thirst for legal services, reflects the
world in which mega-law appears. Corporate client and mega-
lawyer come together in a setting in which there is an immense
proliferation of law and at the same time an increasing awareness
of its indeterminate and problematic character. New law pours
forth from legislatures[15] and even more is promulgated and administered by an ever-growing array of agencies stimulated by a
general climate of regulatory interventionism.[16] But the regulatory
power is fragmented among various agencies with overlapping
mandates and jurisdictions, compounded by a federal division of
authority. With the waning of belief that determinate answers can
be found within the body of legal doctrine, the scope of legal inquiry expands into new and expensive spheres. Dependence on
extensive marshalling of facts, technical complexity, multiple
sources of law, the absence of systematic codification, widely scat-
tered powers of innovation and interpretation among weakly coor-
dinated and weakly hierarchised agencies - all combine to produce
a situation in which just what the law is and how it will be applied
is often highly uncertain, arduous to ascertain, and somewhat
malleable.

MEGA-LAW AND LITIGATION

A generation ago élite large scale lawyering was mostly an office
practice centred around planning, counselling and negotiating.
But a climate of denser regulation and greater inclination to assert
rights have combined to bring a greater admixture of public
contest into big law.

The increase in litigation is reflected in the organisation of the
mega-firms:

... at Cravath, Swaine & Moore, which has such blue-chip
clients as IBM, CBS, Westinghouse, and Chemical Bank, ten

years ago, litigation was about 20 per cent of Cravath's 'total effort'. Now more than 40 per cent of the firm's manpower is so occupied (Bernstein 1978, p.106).

To enlarge their potency as litigators, mega-firms have departed from norms against lateral recruiting. The search for experienced litigators has led to an increase in mergers and 'raiding'.

Mega-law is most visible in connection with monster litigation and litigation is an increasingly prominent part of mega-lawyering. Nevertheless mega-law does not depart from the American mode of avoiding full-blown adjudication.

The predominant pattern is one of claim and threat, counter-threat (of extended defence), and settlement. Authoritative regulators (police, courts, administrative agencies) may be invoked or tacitly adverted to; their processes may be merely initiated or pursued through intricate and expensive proceedings. But in almost all cases the outcome or resolution is arranged by the disputants rather than imposed by an adjudicator (although in many cases, such as divorce and criminal sentences it takes the form of such an imposed resolution). This is the pattern found in most modest civil matters, which are settled by the opposing lawyers, what Mnookin and Kornhauser (1979) described as 'bargaining in the shadow of the law' (for an elaboration see Galanter 1979).

There are of course realms into which the law's shadow penetrates only dimly - because of the presence of more formidable indigenous controls or because of barriers of cost and ideology.[17] But even where the law is most palpably present, adversary adjudication is transformed into mediation, bargaining and settlement. Full-blown adjudication subjects clients to cost, delay, aggravation and unacceptable risk; it exposes their lawyers to risk and disruption they would prefer to avoid. Organisational pressures, administrative impulses, a zeal to mediate, and impatience with trials incline judges to concur. Arranging mutually tolerable outcomes is facilitated by the great latitude enjoyed by local legal professionals to interpret the complexities of the formal law in terms of their own understandings and concerns. This latitude, in turn, derives from a diffuse structure of authority with weak centralised controls and from cost and information barriers that effect a covert delegation of broad discretion to the local legal culture.[18]

But mega-law does significantly transform this threatening litigating-bargaining complex. Investment of massive amounts of time, relentless investigation, exhaustive research and lavish deployment of expensive experts imposes on the other side corresponding expenditures, endless delays, and costly disruptions of their normal operations. If not everything is an open question, sufficient investment can make almost any matter sufficiently problematic that it takes considerable money and time to lay it at rest. Pursued in multiple forums, with brazen insistence on extracting the last measure of formal entitlement, and offering little hope of respite - such litigation raises the bluster and stratagem of ordinary litigation to lethal proportions. Litigation in the mega-law mode is distinctive in the way that mobile high technology warfare between superpowers differs from the set piece battles of an earlier day.

Such mega-litigation serves as a potent doomsday machine whose ominous shadow induces settlement, more or less amicably, in many disputes. Litigation usually leads to a prolonged clinch and then to settlement. But sometimes it is used outright as a kind of warfare. Thus Braniff Airlines attempted unsuccessfully to eliminate a potential competitor on one of its more lucrative routes:

> Braniff's first line of attack in the early 1970s was to smother Southwest in a flurry of lawsuits - litigation so seemingly endless that Allstate Insurance Co., the Sears Roebuck & Co. subsidiary, shied from financing Southwest's planes. Altogether, Braniff filed five distinct legal proceedings before state or federal regulatory bodies, plus appeals to various courts - all after the US Supreme Court decision affirming Southwest's operating authority. 'Southwest Airlines is now legally free to begin service unless we find another basis for court action', one internal Braniff memo warned, 'Our attorneys have little hope that the (Texas Aeronautics) commission will act, but it is a phase of our continuing court action', according to a second company document, this one sent to Harding L. Lawrence, Braniff's chairman who supervised the legal flurry; Mr Lawrence holds a law degree (Landauer 1977).

Whether clinch and settlement or all-out warfare, this kind of litigation can consume resources on an astonishing scale. The prolonged (1961-73) anti-trust case in which management and bankers tried to wrest control of TWA from Howard Hughes reached a high water mark. Its chronicler (Tinnin 1973, p.6) tells us that:

> The documents numbered more than 1,700,000 single pages, filling 694 feet of shelf space. The pretrial testimony - in which some witnesses spent as long as three months on the stand - filled another dozen or so such volumes.
>
> The abundance of testimony resulted in part from the complexity and breadth of the case. It was also due to the tenacity and ingenuity of the lawyers, who themselves produced a ten-foot-high pile of briefs and counterbriefs. Arguing from diametrically opposed positions, operating on almost unlimited budgets, and aided by squads of assistants, the lawyers fought the case not once but twice through the federal judiciary system from district level all the way up to the United States Supreme Court. At the height of the litigation more than forty lawyers and investigators were engaged in the case at a cost of about $17,000 a day. The legal fees, court costs, and sundry expenses themselves amounted to a considerable fortune - at least $20 million.

When the Supreme Court of the United States finally disposed of it (on grounds that had attracted only 'a few fleeting comments' at oral argument), Chief Justice Burger was moved to label it 'the twentieth-century sequel to *Bleak House*' and to wonder that a single party's 'visible expenses' include '56,000 hours of lawyering at a cost of $7,500,000 ... '. (*Hughes Tool Co.* v. *Trans World Airlines*, 409 US 363, 393 (1972).)

Some of this litigation is so immense that it poses a problem for even the largest mega-firms to weave it into the career patterns of its members. Cravath, Swaine and Moore have experienced difficulties stemming from the IBM case. Associates fear their training opportunities and chances of partnership are constricted by spending virtually their entire apprenticeship in the bowels of a single case. But they are also fearful that chances for promotion might be jeopardised if they chose to rotate off the case. Assurances, bonuses and other perquisites were apparently insufficient to prevent serious problems of turnover and morale (Margolick 1980). A comparable problem was reported among Federal Trade Commission lawyers, frustrated by the lack of trial experience gained in a case in which after five years was still 'in the early stages of pre-trial discovery' (Cowan 1978).

One indicator of the qualitative shift that is involved in this kind of mega-litigation is the emergence of firms of 'litigation support specialists' who find trails across the trackless deserts of paper generated in the mega-case.

The Control Data Corporation has converted its own anti-trust experience into a revenue generating 'litigation service'. The company has sued the International Business Machines Corporation in 1968 and then spent four years in a massive pre-trial discovery process screening thirty million pages of IBM documents, from which it selected and computer-indexed about a million pages.

When the suit was settled in 1973, Control Data was required to destroy the index, which it did. Shortly thereafter, however, Control Data decided that the computer techniques it had developed in the litigation should be useful in other big anti-trust cases. Since 1973, some fifty big corporate clients involved in anti-trust as well as patent, product liability and other types of cases have used the service according to Robert S. Arthur, manger of information services at Control Data. One has paid more than $1.5 million in two years, he said:

In contrast to what Mr Arthur calls the 'medieval technology' of standard methods of copying documents and organizing case materials, Control Data provides paralegal teams which screen millions of documents, select pertinent papers and then index each by content, date and author. The computer cross-references not only the tens of thousands of documents that a plaintiff discovers in a defendant company's files, but also provides access to pretrial depositions. A big case may involve 100 or so depositions, each 200 to 400 pages long, Mr Arthur noted (Kohlemeier 1976).

The elaboration of procedural safeguards and remedial means spawns an increasing amount of what Damaska (1978, p.240) calls 'companion litigation'. A dispute over the composition of a class, the reasonableness of a request for discovery, or lawyers' fees may proceed alongside or even supersede the original substantive controversy. One indicator of the shift in the scale of litigation is the increasing frequency of lawyers retaining other lawyers to represent them in applications for court ordered fees. One lawyer recently counted himself among about forty lawyers specialising in the growing area of fee petitions.

These mega-controversies may involve payments of hundreds of millions of dollars or control of billions of dollars of assets. The prodigious quantities of lawyering that are consumed are overshadowed by the stakes. But controversies about individual persons and their entitlements can be fought in comparable style with comparable consumption of resources. Thus four New York firms divided $3.2 million in legal fees for their work in the complicated nine-year litigation over the estate of abstract expressionist Mark Rothko (Asbury 1979).

The sense of disproportion is accentuated when the troubles of single individuals require lawyering on this scale. Consider the experience of A. Ernest Fitzgerald, the Air Force cost analyst who disclosed the multi-billion dollar cost overrun in the C-5A transport. In the course of winning his six-year fight for reinstatement (with back pay) in his $31,000 per year job, he accumulated lawyers' fees of more than $400,000:

A small army of Government lawyers was sent to work against Mr Fitzgerald - lawyers representing the Air Force, the Department of Defense, the Justice Department, the United States Attorney's Office and the Civil Service Commission. These lawyers delayed hearings, refusing to turn over documents, appealed every concession made, filed motions that required scores of time-consuming proceedings taking up time - and all the while Mr Fitzgerald's attorneys were costing him $125 an hour (*New York Times*, 2 Jan. 1976, p.8).

We began by considering mega-lawyering as a device for the provision of large quantities of diversified legal services to large corporate organisations. But it tells us something about the law as well as about its providers and their clients. It points to legal institutions as part of a world of large intimidating organisations, manned by specialised functionaries, guided by recondite learning, accessible only through imposing intermediaries.

The majesty of mega-law is imparted not by wigs, robes and gibbets, but by files, experts and computers massed in assemblages beyond the span of personal experience and beyond the grasp of personal understanding. The evocation of religion is replaced by the evocation of science.

TRANSFORMATIONS OF CORPORATE MEGA-LAWYERING

Large firm representation of corporate business is the prototype of mega-lawyering. But the mega-lawyering pattern can be stretched and re-shaped in many ways. Two notable contemporary shifts are in the organisation of corporate lawyering and in the kinds of clients who receive mega-lawyering.

Large corporations may internalise some or all of their legal business. Lawyers employed by private industry have been an increasing share of the increasing number of lawyers. Lawyers employed by private industry rose from 5 per cent of all lawyers in 1951 to 7.8 per cent in 1960 to 9.4 per cent in 1970 (US Bureau of the Census 1975, p.416). The number of in-house attorneys, according to one estimate (Gallucio 1978, p.169) increased by 400 per cent in the last twenty-five years. A specialist in searching for in-house lawyers estimated that corporate legal staffs are growing at twice the rate of law firms (*Wall Street Journal* 4 Oct. 1977, p.1, col.5). This trend is powerfully encouraged by continuing cost differentials. One management consultant recently estimated that an hour of work by inside counsel cost $41 compared to $79 for outside counsel (Bernstein 1978, p.104) - a figure which coincides with the estimate of two large corporations that in-house costs are half those of outside counsel (Gallucio 1978, p.176).

Corporate law departments come to resemble the mega-firm outside. They are organised in specialised departments, use modern office management techniques, have a salary structure designed to compete with the mega-firms, utilise large numbers of paralegals, and operate in multiple locations. A 1980 survey identified 108 corporate law departments with 28 or more lawyers (*National Law Journal* 1980).

Increasingly, corporate law departments handle labour matters, securities, and financing matters, and relations with government, along with much minor litigation (Gallucio 1978). But 'big case litigation remains the nearly exclusive domain of law firms which can provide armies of legal specialists in a hurry' (*Wall Street Journal*, 4 Oct. 1977, 1.1, col.5). The increasing prominence of litigation in the mega-firm apparently reflects changes in the location of corporate legal work as well as an increase in litigation.

There are varied and interesting deviations from the prototype in another direction. This style of lawyering may be detached from its original large firm-corporate client base and used by other lawyers for other clients. Thus Myron Cherry, 'a successful anti-trust lawyer with a big Chicago law firm' became a specialist in opposing licences for nuclear plants on behalf of citizen groups. When a utility was unforthcoming with information about a plant near a partner's home, Mr Cherry was dispatched to spend a few days 'making a little trouble' for the utility at a routine hearing on the plant's operating licence.

> He stayed nine months and made lots of trouble. Mr Cherry became counsel for a group of local environmentalists and fishermen who feared that the Consumers Power plant would damage marine life in the area. When federal regulators ruled they didn't have authority over such matters, Mr Cherry changed tack and began raising hundreds of safety-related questions the government couldn't ignore. 'We were determined to drag that hearing out until something was done for my clients,' he says.
> First, he demanded mountains of technical documents from the plant's builders and then used them to challenge the adequacy of the construction; one group of witnesses was kept on the stand nearly three months defending the plant's design ...
> Finally, Consumer Power capitulated, it agreed to install $28 million worth of added environmental safeguards at the Lake Michigan facility in return for an agreement by Mr Cherry's clients to withdraw their opposition. 'We had a $130 million plant standing idle and needed to get it running,' says Mr Selby, the utility's president (Emshweiller 1978).

Other non-establishment groups like religious cults have adapted some of the style of mega-lawyering to formidably aggressive defence of their institutions. The Church of Scientology has since 1970 filed 19 law suits against agencies of the Federal government as well as more than 100 civil suits against journalists, publishing companies, radio and television stations, libraries and outspoken individuals who criticize the church ...' (Bodine 1979b). The formidable legal staff (seven lawyers plus 35 support staff) of Synanon, an unsavoury California cult, provided legal support for a variety of terror tactics.

> ... after a particular beating, lawyers would go over the incident to discuss mistakes so that they could have a better legal posi-

tion on the next occasion (Mitchell 1979).

Law suits were used to harass and intimidate opponents and critics. Encouraged by a $2.6 million settlement obtained from the *San Francisco Examiner*, Synanon attorneys 'proceeded to file a slew of enormous lawsuits against other papers, television networks and magazines that tried to write about the foundation' (Steward 1979). Threats of litigation were wielded to fend off government investigation as well as unfavourable attention from the press.

An approximation of mega-law is found in the occasional criminal defence in which the defendant is wealthy, notorious or has become a *cause célèbre*. The defence will exploit every technical possibility, such as investing in 'scientific jury selection' and other tactics that are far beyond the means of any ordinary individual. There are attempts to institutionalise this style of all-out aggressive defence. Thus the Defender Association of Philadelphia, staffed by 100 attorneys (some specialised in juvenile cases or insanity hearings) 24 investigators, 15 social workers and a psychiatrist, aspires to afford clients 'the same kind of background that a large corporation law firm offers its clients in tax cases' (Anderson 1977). Team Defence, Inc., an Atlanta firm 'supported by private funds and donations', defends poor defendants against serious charges in a self-consciously mega-law style.

> ... Proceedings are challenged every inch of the way as are the racial feelings of judges and prospective jurors. Courts are asked to pay the expenses of experts for testimony on the finest of details. And, as in any well-mounted case, every attempt is made at delay.
> ...They believe that courts and prosecutors can be persuaded to [bargain] ... through the simple expedient of making a jury trial inordinately expensive. In time, they believe, Southern prosecutors will think hard before heading for trial.
> The cost of the Willis case (which is still going through pretrial hearings) to Lanier County will be about $100,000 says county attorney D.W. Slone, and 'it may go higher than that'. This is a county where general tax revenues last year were less than $130,000 ... .
> Anthony Axam, a black member of the defence team (he previously worked for Ford Motor Co.), compares this concept of criminal defense to that of 'a very high-priced corporate law

firm - we're setting up a prototype'. (Maxwell 1977)

In retrospect, the late 1960s-early seventies fights about OEO legal services appear less as fights about whether there should be a large number of lawyers serving poor clients, than about whether they should be organised to enable them to engage in mega-lawyering. The objection to autonomous reform-oriented legal services was summed up neatly by the head of OEO programs in California who, defending Governor Reagan's veto of the California Rural Legal Assistance programme said: 'What we've created in CRLA is an economic leverage equal to that of a large corporation. Clear that should not be' (quoted by Stumpf *et al.* 1971, p.65).

Many other 'law reform' efforts can be seen as attempts to put mega-lawyering at the service of non-established interests - the poor, minorities, consumers, neglected children, the handicapped, inmates of mental institutions and so forth. As a fundraising letter from the Council for Public Interest Law succinctly put it, 'The idea ... [is] to give ... ordinary citizens ... the same kind of legal representation which historically has been enjoyed only by the very rich, the giant corporations and the government'. What is promised here is not just the services of skilled and dedicated lawyers, but something more - operation of a scope and continuity to reap the advantages conferred by mega-law. These include the ability to pursue a long-run strategy by coordinating efforts on several fronts, by selecting targets and forums, managing the sequence, scope and pace of litigation, monitoring developments, and deploying resources to maximise long term advantage (including educational and organisational effects as well as favourable awards).

Ideally the public interest lawyer enjoys the opportunity to pursue his strategy without subordinating it to the distracting exigencies of desperate or injured clients.

> And where, as is often the case with clients of public interest law firms, clients are weakly organized or not organized at all, mechanisms of accountability are attenuated and lawyer autonomy is more pronounced (Rabin 1976, pp.234-5).

To the extent that it is liberated from control by clients, the course of public interest lawyering is shaped by the exigencies of organisational maintenance, commitment to ideological goals, the professional inclinations of the lawyers - each of which involves potential conflict with clients.[19] Public interest law looks like an approximation of mega-law with less ample funding than the commercial variety, but with an extra dose of autonomy. But this freedom is a source of instability, for only a weakly organised group would for long tolerate this kind of autonomy in its lawyers.

In an ironic twist, the public interest law format for mega-lawyering - a tax exempt foundation free of responsibility to the short-term needs of specific clients and free to pursue its notion of the public interest - has been reborrowed by large corporate economic interests. Pacific Legal Foundation, the prototype, was founded in 1973 (Weinstein 1975). In 1978 it claimed 'a staff of 15 lawyers, an annual budget of $1.2 million, [and] had instituted or joined more than 100 major legal proceedings since its founding ...' (Lindsey 1978) and there were at least seven more business-supported firms. All the liberalised rules of standing and innovative new remedies won by a decade of public interest law were available to them. Detached from the interests of specific parties, they were under no pressure to settle to get back to business for, like their liberal counterparts, they are in the law business not the business business. It is of course much more appealing to be cast as the beleaguered entrepreneur trying to free himself from the tentacles of the government octopus which is smothering him with nitpicking regulation imposed by small-minded bureaucrats instead of despoiler of nature or callously indifferent to the health and safety of specific employees or neighbours.

The public interest law format (insofar as it remains unconscripted to the representation of established interest groups) displays instabilities, but it is significant because it suggests the possibility of institutionalising the practice of mega-law outside the precincts of the large firm. As such it is part of a growing periphery in which the mega-law style is separated from the large firm - in corporate law departments, public interest firms, some legal services offices, and a growing number of specialists organised in small 'boutique' law firms.

THE IMPLICATIONS OF MEGA-LAWYERING

Mega-lawyering is not new and it is not the mode. What

characterises the American legal scene is not the replacement of ordinary lawyering by mega-lawyering, but the simultaneous growth of both, a growth in which mega-lawyering, is an increasingly visible and influential part of the whole. In 1979 the number of lawyers in the United States reached half a million - an immense proportion of the workforce compared to other industrial countries.[20] It remains an open question how much of this vast amount of lawyering will be organised in the mega-law style. How many clients can be organised to support it and absorb it? Ordinary lawyering (as practised in the recent past) is pressed by other rivals as well. No-fault automobile insurance and no-fault divorce are joined by other reforms intended to reduce the need for lawyers' services in many routine transactions. The decline of restrictions on advertising and marketing of legal services has given impetus to experiments in delivering legal services by multi-branch legal clinics and pre-paid insurance schemes. These devices borrow some of the elements of mega-law (e.g., specialisation, rationalised management) but they focus on techniques of standardisation and routinisation of discrete transactions rather than on delivery of continuous and comprehensive individualised service to forward the long-term goals of clients.

Many critics have noted the super-abundance of lawyers in the United States. And many Americans seem to share a sense that lawyers have unwarranted and unaccountable power in American society. Yet - apart from some accounts of Washington mega-lawyering (e.g. Goulden 1972; Green 1975) - the growth and engorgement of part of our bifurcated legal profession has attracted little critical scrutiny. Among the observers who decry the excessive legislation of society, the litigation explosion, the overload of the courts and the imperial judiciary, it is rarely thought worthy of notice that the vast batteries of lawyers that flourish in America are organised in a way strikingly different from their counterparts elsewhere.

I submit that this different kind of profession does make a difference. It amplifies the powers of competent players of the law game, accentuating the advantages of those able to invest in continuous service, advance planning, long term strategy and large manoeuvres (Galanter 1974). It enables large corporate entities to enjoy advantages which are withheld from individuals. It points, too, to the possibility of ameliorating these disparities by organising or otherwise aggregating weaker players and devising methods of delivering mega-lawyering to such combinations (Galanter 1976, p.235 ff.).

Beyond this, mega-lawyering reflects the larger contours of law in contemporary American society and the virtues and discomforts associated with it. The growth of mega-lawyering is fostered by the proliferation of law and the consequent multiplication of the possibilities of legal manoeuvre. Using these possibilities, it produces more participation, more formal entitlement, more procedural refinements, which in turn present further opportunities for stratagem and manoeuvre. Thus mega-law is intimately connected with a dual movement of legalisation and disenchantment. On the one hand there is more legislation, more administrative regulation, more litigation; more issues and settings are subjected to legal controls. There is a proliferation of formal rules, accompanied by a heightened consciousness of rights and increased reliance on law and lawyers. On the other hand, as more persons and groups invoke legal institutions, join legal battles and use legal notions, there are more standoffs and compromises. It is a world of bargaining, deals and settlements. As law becomes omnipresent and elaborated, it is exposed as indeterminate, manipulable and political. Mega-law heightens our expectations of legal vindication while it teaches us to despair of their realisation.

ACKNOWLEDGEMENTS

This essay began as a talk to the Conference on Law and the Sociology of the Professions, sponsored by the Centre for Socio-Legal Studies, held in Oxford, 2-4 April 1979. Opportunity to elaborate on my talk was afforded by a Fellowship for Independent Study from the National Endowment for the Humanities, but the Endowment bears no responsibility for the contents of this essay. I would like to express my thanks for the stimulation of a faculty seminar on the history of the legal profession, organised by Robert Gordon and Jack Ladinsky, held in Madison during the Spring Semester of 1979. I am grateful for the helpful comments of Roman Tomasic, for the generosity and constancy of Stewart Macaulay and Frank Palen in their help with sources, and for the capable assistance of Mark Lazarson.

NOTES

1.   On the history of American legal profession, see Hurst (1950); Auerbach (1976).· For comparison of the American with the German profes-

sion, see Rueschemeyer (1973b); with the English, Johnstone and Hopson (1967). Comparative estimates of the presence of lawyers may be found in Galanter 1968-9; Johnson, *et al.* (1979).

2. It is the scale of the innovation that is comparable, not the patterns of professional-client relations that result. In medicine we see the development of echelons of higher specialists who have episodic relations with the diseases of patients, where general practitioners have more enduring relations with the 'whole' patient. In law, this is reversed: corporate organisations get individualised and continuous 'client caretaking' from specialised practitioners while private individuals have episodic contact with generalist and less skilled members of the profession.

3. Many of the features in the mega-law cluster seem mutually reinforcing and one might think of a number of causal links that are plausible. For example firms with a wide range of services would have continuing relations with clients (and continuing relations would foster the elaboration of services); firms with continuing relations would encounter client problems at an early stage; early contact with a problem would be conducive to performance of services in varied institutional settings, and so forth. (Galanter 1973.)

4. This baseline is itself the outcome of a period of growth. Smigel (1964, p.35) reported that the number of lawyers in the twenty large firms in New York that were the subject of his early 1960s study increased by 16 per cent from 1957 to 1962. Seventeen comparable large firms outside New York grew by 47 per cent from 1951 to 1961.

5. US Bureau of the Census 1958, p.3; 1967a, p.19; 1974, p.27. These figures are for employees, so they include salaried lawyers as well as other employees.

6. The market share of firms with gross receipts of more than $1 million increased from 14 per cent in 1967 to 20 per cent in 1972, while the number of such firms increased from 400 to 928. (US Bureau of the Census 1967b, pp.5-5; 1972, pp.4-4).

7. Census data in 1972 showed 56 per cent of all lawyers in private practice were in 'general practice' (defined as receiving no more than 25 per cent of receipts from one area of law). But only 24 per cent of lawyers in firms with annual receipts of over $1 million were in general practice (US Bureau of the Census 1972, pp.4-34, 35).

8. Cf. Bellow 1977:120 on the contrasting absence of hierarchy and peer controls and of on-the-job instruction in legal services officers.

9. Often departure is under the sponsorship of the firm to a smaller firm or to the law department of a corporate client, forming a network of alumni which serves as an important extension of the large firm. On the tendency of corporate legal officers to retain their former firms, see *National Law Journal*, 9 Oct. 1978, p.13.

10. Some large firms have recently instituted a new intermediate rung of 'participating associate', 'non-equity partner' or 'special partner' between associate status and full partner (Bodine 1979a). In some instances this is a step toward partnership: in others it is a permanent nonpartner status. Hoffman's (1973, p.144) perceptive study of New York 'blue chip' firms reported that permanent associates are a dying breed

'... being phased out by attrition at most firms ...' but less than a decade later the institution was re-invented.

11. Subsequent references to clients are abbreviated to corporations but should be understood to include other organisational entities as well.

12. A dramatic instance of the shift from stereotyped to innovative litigation is detailed in Fitzgerald's (1975) account of the Contract Buyers League, a group of Chicago blacks who bought houses on contract at disastrously disadvantageous terms. As isolated individuals they received stereotype lawyering within the scope of their limited resources. Once they had organised and embarked on aggressive action, they were adopted as a cause by élite liberal lawyers who brought a series of innovative suits on their behalf. That even within mega-law there is a patterned distribution of innovative energies is suggested by the continuation of Fitzgerald's account (oral presentation, University of Wisconsin Law School, December 1977). Before they were organised and militant, the buyers had approached thirty Chicago law firms and had been turned away on the ground that their case was hopeless. Subsequently they were taken up by one of the firms that had turned them away earlier. The first time they had been ushered into the real estate department, which said they had no basis for mounting a legal attack. The second time around they were taken to the litigation department which resolved to 'find something'.

13. Formal controls - either by government or professional guild - have always rested lightly on this kind of practice (see Carlin 1966; Auerbach 1976). The disciplinary energies of the guild remain focussed on the sins of the low status and marginal, but recently there has been a move toward significant controls by government, e.g. as an offshoot of regulation of the securities industry.

14. Consider, for example, the extensive use of the Freedom of Information Act (originally touted as increasing citizen access to government) for corporate intelligence-gathering. Weekly listing of FOIL requests by law firms can be found in the *Legal Times of Washington*.

15. One estimate has it that all legislative bodies in the United States pass 150,000 new laws annually (*Newsweek*, 10 Jan 1977, p.43).

16. The *Federal Register* (of administrative orders and notifications) grew from 2411 pages in 1946 (its first full year) to 63 766 by 19 Dec. 1977. In that year an OMB study counted more than 80 regulatory agencies and commissions in the federal government employing more than 100,000 workers to interpret and implement federal regulation (Mullaney 1977).

17. In a fascinating study of lawyers as enforcers of consumer protection legislation, my colleague Stewart Macaulay (1979) portrays the unwillingness of lawyers to invest in developing expertise in this area - an area of great complexity, difficult burdens of proof, and relatively small stakes. They prefer to act as mediators, 'working something out' i.e., taking a matter that the client thinks should be pursued in the adversary mode and translating it into a conciliatory model. (This picture contrasts sharply with Maureen Cain's portrait, in this volume, of English solicitors 'translating' client problems from everyday to legal discourse.) Macaulay attributes the lawyers' reluctance to take an adversary stance

to a combination of protecting their standing with established interests in the community and of ideological distaste for consumer claims.

18.   By 'local legal culture' I refer to a set of understandings and concerns shared by the community of legal actors and significant audiences, and that defines the appropriate style of playing judicial and lawyer roles, the uses of various legal proceedings, appropriate dispositions, and so forth. Descriptions of such patterned local differences in 'legal culture' may be found in Church *et al.* (1978); Jacob (1969); Wilson (1968); Levin (1977).

19.   Cf. Stewart's (1975, p.1772) observation that:

'Public interest' lawyers representing unorganized interests may have a marked personal preference for formal processes of decision, including judicial review, because a considerable portion of the psychological reward which they receive for their work may depend on the high visibility of their efforts, and because dramatic court victories may assist fundraising efforts.

20.   This figure is a projection from the number, 462 000, listed in the US Bureau of the Census, Statistical Abstract for 1978 combined with the fact that roughly 30 000 law degrees are being conferred each year and a majority of the recipients are admitted to practice. Any comparisons of the numbers of lawyers across national boundaries have to be taken with caution because of differences in what lawyers are and differences in who is counted (are judges included, lawyers in private industry, retired lawyers, etc.) For all their roughness, a sense of the difference in magnitude may be gathered from the following estimates of the number of practising lawyers per million population in the mid-1970s:

United States	1406
Canada	714
England and Wales	709
Belgium	510
Switzerland	442
Netherlands	199
France	189
Japan	91

Based on Rhyne (1978); US Bureau of the Census (1979). Comparable disparities are computed by Johnson *et al.* (1979, pp.10-12).

8 Professionals in Bureaucracies: the Conflict Thesis Revisited

CELIA DAVIES

Ten or more years ago, the writing of a paper on professional work in organisations would have been a secure but possibly slightly tedious enterprise. Professions were understood to be distinctive phenomena; groupings of persons (usually male), possessed of a special expertise in a framework removed from the purely self-interested pursuit of economic gain. Organisations, furthermore, were understood to be bureaucracies, devices for partitioning work activities and co-ordinating them through a hierarchy of offices based on a legal-rational pattern of authority and involving hierarchical co-ordination and routine rule following. Profession and bureaucracy were thought to be antithetical both at the level of structural principles for organising work and at the level of motivation and compliance. The attempted insertion of 'professionals' into 'bureaucratic organisations' was a readily recognisable sociological problem. Terms such as 'strain', 'conflict', 'accommodation', 'adjustment' were central.

From the multitude who have written on the topic of professional/bureaucratic conflict, Scott (1966) can be singled out. He offers a clear and succinct formulation of the two as opposing institutional forms. A professional carries out a complete task; he does so on the basis of his special knowledge acquired through training; he is loyal to the company of equal professionals; as a practitioner he has arrived at a terminal status and seeks no higher position within the organisation. A bureaucrat, on the other hand, carries out a limited set of tasks which must be co-ordinated with others; his training is short and accomplished within the organisation; he is supervised by a hierarchical superior and sanctioned if he does not follow the rules. His loyalty and his career are tied to the organisation. From here it is but a short step to postulate conflict and Scott identified four major areas in which this would occur. The professional would be likely to resist bureaucratic rules, bureaucratic standards, supervision and the demand of the bureaucracy for unconditional loyalty. Figure 8.1 below, while not following Scott's terminology precisely, sums up these divergent perspectives.

	Bureaucracy	*Professionalism*
task	partial, interdependent with others	complete, sole work
training	short, within the organisation, a specialised skill	long, outside the organisation, a total skill
legitimation for act	is following rules	is doing what is to the best of his knowledge correct
compliance	is supervised	is socialised
loyalty	to the organisation	to the profession
career	ascent in the organisational hierarchy	often no further career steps in the organisation

FIGURE 8.1   A model of professional/bureaucracy conflict (after Scott 1966)

Thinking such as this has given rise to a considerable volume of empirical work. Doctors, scientists, engineers, accountants, nurses and social workers are among the groups which have been counted professional and thus assumed subject to the sorts of conflicts outlined by Scott (see for example: Corwin 1961; Engel 1969, 1970; Kornhauser 1962; Miller 1968; Scott 1969; Sorenson and Sorenson 1974; Wilensky 1964). Much of this material has focussed principally on dilemmas for the individual, raising questions as to the level of satisfaction professionals enjoy with aspects of their work and the adjustments and accommodations they make in the face of bureaucratic demands. Perhaps it is not surprising that sociologists, not themselves immune to an ideology of professionalism, should be readily sympathetic to apparent problems of an oppressive and restrictive bureaucracy.

Other studies, in no way incomparable with these, have focussed on professional/bureaucratic conflict more from a perspective of organisational analysis. Here the issue was not so much the dilemmas and experiences of the professionals but those of the managers. How could organisations be designed to utilise professional skills? What was the range of possible mechanisms to incorporate these skills and under what conditions did they result in successful organisational performance? Litwak (1961) offered an early and much cited discussion of 'models of bureaucracy which permit conflict'. Scott's (1965) notion of autonomous and heteronomous professional organisations and Etzioni's (1964) classification of full-fledged professional organisations, semi-professional organisations, service organisations and professionals in non-professional organisations were two more of the attempts to specify structural options. The field of industry was the one most intensively studied and the one in which it became clear that various forms of buffering devices were possible. Expertise could be bought in on a consultant basis; experts could be physically segregated from the main chain of command (and R and D labs indeed sometimes were), or they could be organisationally segregated. The 'dual career ladder' received a fair amount of attention (Kornhauser 1962; Goldner and Ritti 1967). An organisation chart which emphasised functional groupings of experts in general could be expected to yield high quality and innovation providing as it did a supportive environment for expertise. An organisation chart which stressed a line organisation or which was product based, bringing in experts intermittently as advisors or attaching them to a product line had, on the other hand, the advantage of speed and cost control (for a good discussion, focussed on an industrial example, see Walker and Lorsch 1970). The task force, the product team, the matrix organisation are some of the more recent devices identified by organisational analysis as ways of harnessing expertise in the service of organisational goals (see e.g. Galbraith 1973).

But both the individual studies and the organisational ones threw up anomalies in terms of a model of institutionalised conflict (see especially Hall 1968). Benson in a recent important review sums up in the following way. First, the empirical data has shown the joint occurrence of bureaucratisation and professionalisation. It would appear that far from being total alternatives these two are in some sense complementary. Secondly, successful accommodations of so-called incompatibilities have occurred. Thirdly, some role occupants occupy with apparent ease and satisfaction combined professional and bureaucratic roles (Benson 1973, pp.378-9).

Faced with this situation, there appear to have been three responses. The first has been to make renewed efforts to preserve the basic model; the second has been to deny at a very fundamental level the theory of institutionalised constraint which is employed; the third has been to remodel that theory with the alteration of some, but not all of its tenets.

The professional-bureaucratic conflict literature is replete with examples of the first. Some suggest that conflict is avoided in contexts where professionalism is not highly developed; we should not group all the so-called professions together but should make distinctions based on the degree of expert knowledge or the type of expertise. In a slightly different vein, others have suggested that there may be sub-groups of professionals particularly oriented to organisational work and interested in organisational careers. Still others have sought to break down the unitary notion of bureaucracy, arguing that only some of its components actually cluster or that only under certain conditions does the full set of bureaucratic features obtain. Benson's (1973) review provides a critical guide to this material. The large-scale research programmes of Blau and his colleagues in the USA (Blau and Schoenherr 1971) and Pugh *et al.* in Britain (Pugh and Hickson 1976; Pugh and Hinings 1976; Pugh and Payne 1977) employ multivariate techniques for measuring structural variables and exploring their interrelations. They have produced a set of findings questioning the utility of simple models of bureaucracy and profession as starting points for understanding the empirical complexities. And while work in this field continues to have its adherents, the professional/bureaucratic antithesis is no longer so clearly at its centre.

The second response, a questioning of the theory of constraint embodied in studies of both profession and bureaucracy reflects a long and respectable tradition of scepticism. With respect to professions it draws particularly from the Chicago school and from the work of Everett Hughes, though more recently there has been an effort to locate studies more directly in the tradition of phenomenology. At the level of the individual the focus is not upon profession as a structure shaping the professional and his work but rather on how the professional 'makes out' in various settings and how, in Dingwall's (1976) term, profession is 'accomplished' in interaction. At the organisational level the stress is on routines as the situated products of social interaction and on order as provisional and negotiated. The work here which directly challenged students of organisations and bureaucracies was that of Strauss and his colleagues (1963) arguing that the hospital was a negotiated order. Bucher and Stelling (1969) followed this with a proposal that professional organisation could be better described not in terms of structural mechanisms, but in terms of role creation, spontaneous internal differentiation, competition and conflict for resources, integration through a political process and a shifting locus of power. A critique of this has recently been advanced by Day and Day (1977) and a discussion of this theme in the hospital context found in Davies and Francis (1976).

The third response provides not a denial of profession and bureaucracy but a critique of the way in which each has been regarded. The work of Freidson (1970a, 1970b) in the USA and Johnson (1972) in Britain first exemplified the new 'power approach' to professions. Both authors turned away from a concern to list attributes of a free profession and to measure cases against the list and began to ask about the circumstances under which claims to occupational status and reward are made and are made successfully. 'A profession', in Johnson's definition 'is not, then, an occupation, but a means of controlling an occupation' (Johnson 1972, p.45). This is a message now frequently reiterated by other writers in both theoretical and empirical work.

There are striking parallels with recent work in organisational analysis. Critics have begun to question the notion of an inner logic of organisational structure and change - be it governed by task, size or by the interrelation of structural variables. They contest the assumption that organisations are reasonably autonomous, stable and equivalent across time and place. Instead they propose that organisations are the outcome of struggles, reflect the social relations of wider society, and are thoroughly permeated by the inequalities and contradictions of that society.

The old project of organisation theory had an overriding concern with the improvement of performance. The new project consists of an effort to locate organisations within political, economic and social structures. This line of approach can be seen in a number of recent writings, most obviously those of Benson (1973, 1977a, 1977b), and de Kervasdoué and Kimberly (1978).[1]

The critique of organisations and the critique of professions thus have much in common. Both challenge the functionalist assumption that these institutional forms are equilibrating and of direct interest to participants. Both go beyond an interpretation of interdependence to one which deals with control and constraint of various sorts. Both see current practice as a precarious compromise reflecting wider social relations. Whether their subject matter is profession or organisation these writers exhibit a determination to locate the phenomena they are studying in the wider social structure.

It is this third response, the attempt to devise new questions about professions and bureaucracies and to see conflict and struggle in new ways which I wish to focus upon here. What does this new enterprise entail as far as use of concepts of profession and bureaucracy (and the derivative notion of professional-bureaucratic conflict) are concerned? Insofar as such concepts are part of contemporary lay understanding they are likely to continue to figure somewhere in the explanatory framework of sociologists, but it may now be the moment, first, to lean much less heavily on unitary ideas of a profession and a bureaucracy and secondly to explore conflict as generated and resolved in very different kinds of ways from those envisaged in the conventional analyses and outlined earlier in this paper.[2] This line of argument will be pursued both in general terms and with recourse to examples drawn from my own research.

It was Talcott Parsons in particular who prised apart the notions of profession and bureaucracy, and argued that the authority of expertise constituted a special problem for the bureaucratic organisation.[3] He had found a starting point for this in that small part of Weber's work which dealt with bureaucracy as an abstract form, and had then developed the notion of a profession in a somewhat similar way as a coherent and equilibrating social form. In his more detailed analysis, professions were contrasted with the business form (Parsons 1954) to reveal the familiar solo practice model of professional and client. It was a model in which participants were motivated and sustained by factors which owed nothing to business principles, a model which coped with the vulnerabilities of both parties in a way that secured the trust and continued interaction of both. Conflict was safely contained; it was not an ever-present reality though it could be envisaged when competing principles were brought together. And later writers did just this; for them more than for Parsons himself the idea of professional-bureaucratic conflict became a kind of functionalist toe-hold on change. Furthermore, as fewer and fewer solo practitioners remained in the various fields of professional activity, concepts of organisational professionals, bureau-professionals, heteronomy, etc. came to the fore as denoting the mixed patterns found in everyday practice.

Let us consider briefly but directly the limited conditions under which an equilibrating solo practice model can pertain (Johnson 1972). There appear to be at least six of these. In the first place, the would-be independent practitioner must be able to amass sufficient resources to set up in practice. Individual capital, that is to say, must be freely available to secure an appropriate training, and appropriate premises and equipment. Secondly, he must be able to deploy his skills more or less single-handedly, offering a reasonably complete service to clients without the aid of specialist colleagues or auxiliaries. Thirdly, individual clients must both have sufficient alienable resources to call on the practitioner and be persuaded of the sense of doing so. Fourthly, clients must not be in a position to unite to force their demands on practitioners nor must practitioners be so few in number or so united as to determine client choices. (The precariousness of this 'perfect market' type phenomenon was made clearly apparent in Johnson's discussions of nineteenth-century professionals in the context of the rise of a middle class market.) Fifthly, the process of updating knowledge for the practitioner should entail sufficiently limited activities that it can be achieved in the interstices of practice. Finally, it is necessary that capital, in the corporate form or in the state form, take no direct interest in developing modes of regulating the practitioner's relationship with clients.

Put in this way, it seems entirely clear that such conditions are rarely, if ever, met. Nineteenth-century Britain provided some of these conditions for medical practice, but as Johnson (1972) has argued and as the historical work of his colleagues has shown (Waddington 1973; Jewson 1974, 1976) the doctors were at a disadvantage in relation to clients and a client-dominated patronage mode was important. Peterson's (1978) recent work calls other elements of the model into question. Setting up in practice not only meant severe financial hardship for some young doctors, but this was exacerbated where there were no family connections to ease the way and render the new man acceptable to the community. And in the twentieth century, the concentration of corporate capital, the increased costs of professional preparation and of equipment and facilities, and the interventionist stance of the state are all factors which have effectively transformed the conditions under which professional work can be delivered. Medicine and law, I suspect, would provide an interesting contemporary contrast in respect of most aspects of the model outlined (cf. Rueschemeyer 1973b; Klegon 1978; and, especially, Larson 1977). Medicine currently has the greater capital requirements, can fulfil learning requirements less easily unaided and has been, in Britain at least, a focus of interest and public expenditure more than for corporate capital.

It now becomes clear that the conventional sociological perspectives on the organisation of professional work are very narrow ones. They concentrate on the point of delivery of services, the immediate setting of work practice and the daily routines in it. Such perspectives play down and sometimes totally obscure the material and ideological conditions for different kinds of work organisation. Thus as we have just seen, questions concerning the capital requirements for solo practice work, the learning requirements, the requirements to develop and sustain the knowledge base remain unasked. There is a sense in which this narrowness has been a feature not only of the more phenomenologically oriented studies of professional-client interaction, but of the more structurally-oriented studies too. Reference back to the work of Scott (see Figure 8.1) bears this out.

Scott deals with hierarchy and specialisation as features of work - he does not refer, however, in this connection to a sexual, class or ethnic division of labour, or deal with the problems of domination and subordination arising from these. He refers to careers, but not to the patterns of social mobility or wider life chances involved. He deals with compliance and legitimation, but only as arising directly from the work in hand. He is silent on the question of rewards and on the work setting as a major sphere in which inequalities are produced and legitimised. Bureaucratic work and professional work are considered apart from other kinds of work activity. If we were to insist on considering say factory work and domestic work, would it be possible to characterise these in this 'inward-looking', restrictive way? Both in terms of their intellectual antecedents and in terms of their use, it seems that concepts of profession and bureaucracy may be limiting.

The empirical part of this chapter now follows. It draws on my research on the history of organised nursing in Britain and the USA,[4] and uses as illustrations some of the points where the idea of professional-bureaucratic conflict seems especially barren as an explanatory framework. The data suggest that our conceptual vocabulary is too time and culture-bound, and too static.[5] The focus in what follows is more on bureaucracy than on professions, but this is a tactical decision and a matter of convenience.[6] Both terms require critical scrutiny if we are to further our understanding of forms of work organisation and their transformation.

CASE ONE

Consider the type of organisation represented by the hospital at the point where nurses began to enter it in increasing numbers for training and for 'respectable' employment.[7] There are some general historical accounts of the development of hospitals (e.g. Rosen 1963) and a number of studies offering detailed analyses of the hospital in Britain in the nineteenth and twentieth centuries (Abel-Smith 1964; Ayers 1971; Poynter 1964). However, there is no large scale study dealing with the participants' understanding of the social groups and goals involved and the bases for authoritative action. It is all too easy to come away with a view of the hospital filtered through modern eyes. The hospital is seen as disorganised and chaotic, its boundaries unclear, its staff unreliable and unattractive. Such a perspective does not help in understanding the hospital in its own terms - in uncovering the form of social order it then represented.

Recent work, however, is beginning to bring aspects of this order to light. In the USA Rosenberg (1967, 1977) has argued that nurses and patients alike were subject to a strict and paternalistic regulation which for both groups limited visitors, gave passes to leave the hospital, required church attendance and so forth; he has also introduced the notion of the 'moral universe' of the hospital (Rosenberg 1979). Vogel (1978), in a brief account of the Boston Children's Hospital in the 1880s has stressed the goal of moral uplift and shown how this resulted in allowing visits from churchgoers but not necessarily from the parents of the sick child. Waddington's (1973) work on French hospitals has done much to clarify the importance of class factors in maintaining medical control over patients, and to remind us of the importance of the point that the middle-classes did not enter the hospital as patients until the present century (Abel-Smith 1964).[8]

The histories of British voluntary hospitals provide further pointers to aspects of the hospital order.[9] Work commitment was not mediated by the cash nexus or by a belief in the value of the work activity *per se*. Staff had a diffuse obligation to the hospital which found expression in a terminology of 'house servants' and 'officers' rather than employees. Much payment was in kind; rations were issued and nurses cooked their food *in situ* for themselves. There were no set hours of work, and living-in was expected. Given that the social distance between nurses and patients was not great, given that specific medical treatments might not be prescribed, given that they had differential access to intra- and extra-organisational resources, it does not seem too surprising that forms of reciprocal exchange grew up between these groups. Close attention to time and to an associated work-discipline, as Thompson (1967) has pointed out, are features which emerge slowly and unevenly as a new pattern in the factories of industrial capitalism. We should not look for them too soon, then, in the hospital.

What we need to understand here is the pattern of inequalities in power, status and material rewards and how this was sustained. Here the relations between those of different sexes and classes and perhaps ages and races too, as found in the family, the locality, the church and the military are likely to be relevant. Attention to these might help us learn more than the simple point that the hospital was not a bureaucracy.

Were there changes in the direction of bureaucracy? When we come to consider the specific changes that matrons sought to implement, we find that they do not fit neatly into the themes either of bureaucratisation or of professionalisation. Certainly, some matrons were clearly trying to reconstitute hospital relations on the basis of aspects of work discipline. Tooley (1906) has recounted stories of matrons' efforts to implement set meal-times, to systematise off-duty times, to allow set periods of 'leave' from the hospital, to employ other staff for heavy cleaning work, etc. A recent study of nursing textbooks begins to suggest too that the constitution of an impersonal, regular and predictable hierarchical order was an important theme. Thus gossip (a traditional, informal, small group control) was sanctioned strongly and the presence of members of patients' families was acknowledged as a problem for the nurse. Those in superior positions, furthermore, were told of their obligations to juniors; they should not, the textbook stressed, use their hospital position to choose idleness for themselves or to avoid the unpleasant aspects of the work (Jarman 1980). The implicit contrast here perhaps was with the understood prerogatives of a social superior and the less well understood rights and obligations of an organisational position. On the other hand, as is well-known, the Nightingale system stressed deference to doctors, close supervision of the whole behaviour of the nurse, a willingness to do any jobs deemed necessary and an unswerving devotion to duty and to hard work. The imagery of husband and wife, mistress and servant, as Gamarnikow (1978) has recently shown, was still much in evidence in the early part of this century as a rationale for hospital relations. Notwithstanding the large amounts of research concerned with the hospital as a bureaucracy, feminist and Marxist writers have argued of late that the contemporary hospital continues to be both class dominated and patriarchal (Ashley 1976; Navarro 1976, 1978).

From time to time, there are glimpses of social and sexual divisions and the way these impinged upon the social order of the hospital. Writing in 1893, for example, one American nurse appeared to be making somewhat veiled allusions to sexual favours and justifying a strong hierarchy amongst nurses as a way of avoiding such arbitrary bases of influence.[10] Of greater potential for the student of the hospital order are the conflicts which occurred and were documented. Abel-Smith (1960, ch.2 and 3) has provided examples of the class conflicts when Nightingale nurses with middle and upper-class backgrounds took up positions in voluntary hospitals and in workhouse infirmaries. Peterson (1978, p.73-88) has recently analysed in detail the public debate conducted in contemporary journals concerning the position of nurses in teaching hospitals. She uses this to argue for the precariousness of doctors' 'professional' authority in the face of a strong gubernatorial system of control which was only just beginning to break down in the 1870s.

All this is to suggest that there is no inexorable logic which turns an organisation into a bureaucracy and constrains an aspiring occupational group to make 'professional' demands which bring it into conflict with the bureaucracy. Guided by concepts of profession and bureaucracy we are likely to find a mixture, or a muddle. At any rate, we are led away from an analysis of the specific features of the hospital order which are and are not being challenged, and the way these relate to other social divisions and ideological positions in the wider society.

CASE TWO

Nurses are employed outside the hospital to do nursing of various sorts in private homes and in the community. Historically, they have worked as individual private practitioners, in co-operatives with colleagues, in association with a register (organised by a hospital, by doctors, by nurse associations or others); they have been employed by charitable associations and by local governmental bodies. These contexts of organised work have been almost entirely neglected by sociologists.

The case to be considered here concerns public health nurses in the USA in the interwar years. Two points emerge. First, as with case one, although the period is now relatively recent, it was no straightforwardly bureaucratic organisation to which nurses were being assimilated. Secondly, the organisational form available was clearly quite specific to the political, economic and social arrangements of the USA - in general and in those particular years.

In the first decades of the twentieth century, public health as an educational and preventive issue had fired the minds of many. It fitted well with the progressivism of the times and the concern over social order in the new cities with their first generation rural immigrant populations (Wiebe 1967). In terms of practical activities, diversity was the keynote. Local programmes were initiated by public-spirited citizens in towns and cities, the philanthropic foundations took an interest and funded various schemes for limited time periods. The Shepherd-Towner Act was an example of federal funds given for a five-year scheme for maternal and child health.[11] Such was the interest that Boards or Departments of Health were often set up at state level. As far as nursing was concerned, there was a vigorous promotive association, the National Organisation for Public Health Nursing (NOPHN). It was composed of nurses and of lay members; it engaged in studies and evaluations of the myriad of public health nurses (Fitzpatrick 1975).

The era was one of opportunity but also of uncertainty for public health work in nursing. Those committed to the work had to orient themselves both to the temporary funding of charitable programmes and to the possibility of public funding and recognition of their activities at state level. The latter was no more certain than the former. Jobs for public health nurses were often political plums, part of a spoils system which reallocated jobs with each change of administration.[12]

Against this background, two features of the organisation of public health nursing work in the period stand out. First, consider the following which is a job description for a nurse working at state level in West Virginia after the setting up of a State Division of Public Health Nursing in 1919. The tasks of the divisional nurse consultant included these:

> the stimulation of health education, the creation of an intelligent public opinion; the increasing of the number of public health nurses, and arranging for their employment; the creation of representative organisations in the community, the country and the state; and the providing of helpful consultation and advisory services through the division (Bond 1957: 97).

What is strikingly clear to English eyes is that this is no job specification for a bureaucratic supervisor. It is a promotive and facilitative role; it has a strong political or advocacy component. Nurses are supposed to be in there with the rest of them, drumming up support, persuading of the relevance of their kind of work. And they are to be doing this not just inside the State public health division, but in the local communities too.

A manual of public health nursing published by the NOPHN in the early 1930s echoed this promotive and expansionist view of the nurse consultant rather than the supervisory one. It also, however, gave a great deal of emphasis to the worker in the field. 'The policy of promotion', the manual stated 'must not in any way be allowed to lessen the dignity or detract from the position of the fieldworker' (NOPHN 1932, p.23). Measures suggested in support of the fieldworker included advocacy of appointing educational directors to promote in-service training, and insistence on a view that there were professional ethics involved in setting up a public health agency and that these must be observed.

Was this merely a brief moment before a stable pattern of bureaucratic employment emerged? The advocacy role of nurse consultants became more, not less important in the face of relief programmes in the early years of the Depression. More nurse consultants were appointed and all found themselves in a position where they both promoted programmes and tried to maintain standards.[13] It is difficult to assess the overall result but one study, published in 1937, suggested that a fair proportion of public health agencies, perhaps one third of the official ones, had made strenuous efforts to follow the NOPHN manual and put its suggestions into practice.[14]

An advocacy role and protection of the fieldworker, however, were not all. Towards the end of the 1930s, criticism of the spoils system became stronger and arguments were advanced for civil service principles and the 'merit system' in state appointments.

Figure 8.2 sets out one interpretation of what was involved; publishing in a nursing journal, the author praised these principles

---

— a sound *recruiting system* based on essential *qualifications* for the work to be done rather than on extraneous considerations.

— a *classification and salary* plan with *uniform titles* for similar duties and *equal pay for equal work*

— *in-service training* for employees

— *a promotional policy* offering a career service to all qualified employees

— a *follow-up system* to prevent ambitious workers from becoming lost in blind-alley positions

— a *removal procedure* which will eliminate hopelessly incompetent employees

— an actuarially sound *pension plan*

FIGURE 8.2   Elements of a merit system (after Lyle Belsley 1937)

as a good way to attract well qualified employees and to promote professional standards in nursing.

The merit system represents a deliberate attack on political and personal favouritism. Each of its tenets is a mechanism to reward the competent, to retain them and to develop their expertise further. It is a model of work regulation which emerged at a different moment from the Weberian model. The model responds (as did Weber's) to a felt need for impersonality; it also responds (as Weber's did not) to a recognition of established spheres of competence and the need to develop these. It remains ambiguous as to how far bureaucratic rules and supervision obtain and as to who decides on entry and promotion criteria. From this point of view it is difficult to say whether or not it is a 'professional' model (see Figure 8.1). It leaves room, however, for the 'advocates' and the 'practitioners' discussed above.

It is perhaps worth underlining, however briefly, the contrasts of such a pattern with the situation in Britain. Certainly there has been no place for an advocacy role comparable to the American nurse consultant and little hint of the kind of fieldwork support and in-service education with which the American nurses seemed concerned. With the separate specialisms of midwifery, district nursing and health visiting there is, indeed, no 'public health nurse' as such. Each of these occupational groups has a separate history and a different pattern of regulation of work activity. And whereas charitable funding has been highly important, especially for district nurses, it involved nursing associations, and, in the shape of the Queen's Institute of District Nursing, a countrywide uniformity of training and practice quite unlike the pattern of private funding of nursing work in the USA. Local Authorities often contracted nursing work out to voluntary associations, but where they did not, experience was different again, given the early establishment in British towns of Medical Officers of Health and the fragmented and subordinated way in which trained nurses were added to the staff of MOH Departments.[15]

Schematic as these remarks are, they point up the questionable utility of concepts such as profession and bureaucracy, understood to involve some immanent set of logically integrated features. To understand the organisation of public health nursing work in the USA we would do better to turn to a consideration of the specific characteristics of the socio-economic settings, the political institutions to which this has given rise and the transformations within them. Recent comparative work on British/American politics has suggested that the American pattern involves greater local autonomy and less central control, multiple and specific local jurisdictions (for education, health, etc.) rather than a strong and unitary local government, an openness to organised pressure groups and a pattern where policies are thrashed out by interest groups rather than parties.[16] If we add to this the propensity for federal policies to take the form of short-term funding for demonstration projects (Alford 1972) and a propensity for formation of mixed professional/lay advocacy groups, we begin to build a picture of a highly distinctive ideological and political setting offering a set of experiences and opportunities for work organisation which will not be repeated in the same form elsewhere.[17]

CONCLUSION

Notions of 'profession' and 'professional work' are common currency amongst laymen and sociologists. Implicitly or explicitly such notions rest on a contrast with the detailed regulation of activity connoted by 'bureaucracy' and on a conflict of principles of work regulation. In this chapter, I have raised a number of questions about the utility of such thinking, which, while it informed a great deal of work in the 1960s, seems now to be less popular. The first part of the discussion focussed on intellectual antecedents and consequences of this form of thinking, the second on some interpretative difficulties which arose in the course of empirical research which was both cross-cultural and historical.

Recent work on professions and recent work on organisations, it has been argued, have taken a common direction in that students are attempting to locate these institutional forms more firmly in their socio-economic and political contexts. Their work represents a challenge to representations of bureaucracy and profession as immanent structures and an effort to see work organisations as everchanging and emergent social forms. The two illustrations taken in this paper, of the nineteenth-century hospital and of public health nursing work in the USA in the interwar years were introduced to underline the need to develop such analyses further and to abandon once and for all notions such as professional-bureaucratic conflict.

NOTES

1   I have recently reviewed this material for its relevance to organisations in the field of health. See Davies (1979b).

2.   In an important new study of professions and professionalisation, Larson (1977) has likewise taken issue with the professional-bureaucratic literature. She sees professions and bureaucracy as having common historical origins and so indeed becoming more compatible with the emergence of monopoly capitalism. While her specific material on conflict, resting as it does on managerial and professional orientations, is disappointing, her concepts of techno-bureaucratic and public service modes of integration into capitalism deserve more consideration. They are not, in my view, inconsistent with the argument developed here.

3.   The starting-point is a well-known and much-quoted footnote inserted by Parsons into his translation of Weber's work. Weber (transl. Parsons) (1964).

4.   The material is drawn from work done with the help of a SSRC grant for a project entitled Occupational Development: a Case Study of Nursing (HR 4465).

5.   Cf. Merton (1968, ch.2) who stresses that middle-range theory should be both time- and culture-free. He cites the theory of bureaucracy, it should be noted, as a middle-range theory, and I am casting doubt on this - at least on the way in which it has been used in recent years.

6.   I focus on bureaucracy, first because the debate is more advanced in respect of professions and anyway I take it that readers are more familiar with it; second, because with empirical material about nursing I would otherwise be involved in a tedious detour about whether or not nursing is 'a profession'.

7.   This can be dated, roughly speaking, from the mid-nineteenth century in Britain and the last quarter of that century in the USA.

8.   One further study which deserves mention and though much cited has not been followed up is Perrow (1963).

9.   There are many such histories and their quality varies. For a useful bibliography, see Gaskell (1964).

10.   Consider the following excerpt from an article written in 1893:

> What, for instance, is the consequence of allowing young interns to choose their own undergraduate head-nurses? The standard of the work is at once lowered by the introduction of the personal element. The pupil nurses are exposed to the temptation of seeking the favor of individuals. Partisan cliques invariably form, whose self-interest may be directly opposed to the best interests of the hospital and its nursing work; and promotion on a true merit basis is utterly and at once impossible (Dock 1949).

The whole article by Lavinia Dock is fascinating on the question of authority, not just between men and women and women and women but between occupational specialisms too.

11.   An interesting discussion of public health nursing in this period on which I have relied can be found in Roberts (1954).

12.   Uncertainty of employment was a key feature. For public posts this comes out clearly in the story of the creation and rescinding of a Department of Health in the State of Ohio in the mid-twenties, Rodabaugh and Rodabaugh (1951). As far as privately funded posts were concerned, one author suggested that a three month guarantee of work was reasonable for a public health nurse (Brainard 1919: 46).

13.   For a brief discussion of nurses in the US Public Health Service see McIver (1940). For material on nurses in relief programmes see Swope (1934) and Woodward (1937).

14.   The study was carried out in official agencies only (Roberts 1954, p.265). Such agencies were increasing in numbers - whereas in 1931 non-official agencies employed around 40% of all public health nurses, by 1940 they employed only 29% (ibid., p.277).

15.   These remarks raise a number of questions about detailed forms of work regulation which have not been brought together in any readily accessible way. It seems to me that we do need to study, for example, local health departments, the County Nursing Association, the Queen's Institute and so on, and the counterpart forms in other countries if we are to understand work organisation better, rather than, as is so common, focussing only on 'the hospital' as 'a bureaucracy'.

16.   There is a growing literature on local politics in Britain and America, though as several writers point out, many more empirical studies are available for the USA than for Britain. Some specifically comparative discussions are: Newton (1969, 1974, 1975); Sharpe (1973). See also Heidenheimer et al. (1975) especially chapters 5 and 9. The differences alluded to in these works are not very firmly established, however, certainly not for the period under discussion in this paper.

17.   One author who has pursued this line of thinking somewhat is Arthur Stinchcombe. Specifically he suggests that organisational arrangements are a 'social technology' and advances the hypothesis that there is a 'correlation between the time in history that a particular type of organisation was invented and the social structure of organisations which exist at the present time' (Stinchcombe 1965; 143). His illustrative data from industries founded in nineteenth- and twentieth-century America suggest some support for this insofar as they do have different labour forces and different patterns of authority. I have myself pursued the notion of comparative analyses with respect to historical patterns of nurse education in Britain and the USA (Davies 1980a).

9 Professionals in Bureaucracies: Solicitors in Private Practice and Local Government

TOPSY MURRAY, ROBERT DINGWALL and JOHN EEKELAAR

The status of an occupation represents the product of an interplay between a variety of possible determinants - its relationship to the organised mode of production, its clustering of tasks and skills, its success at collective organisation and self-promotion or whatever. Of critical importance, though, is the ability to sustain whatever status claims are made in everyday practice, with other occupations, with representatives of sponsoring interests or with clients. Without such recognition, status claims remain essentially rhetorical, indicative of the aspirations of the occupation but otherwise of limited relevance in understanding the constitution of social structures. 'Profession' is one such claim. In the course of advancing and defending these claims, various justifications may be elaborated and become partially objectified, serving as consistent orienting principles for interpersonal dealings. While these justifications may, in theory, be indefinite, they constitute, in practice, a finite set which may be used as reliable guides in social interaction.

This paper begins with an analysis of how lawyers make certain sorts of status claim. We argue that both local government and private practice solicitors assert their standing in similar ways, ways which are, indeed, comparable with those employed by doctors. While we view the relationship between such claims and 'professional' status as problematic, there does, nonetheless, appear to be a difficulty for local government lawyers as a result of their employment in a formal bureaucracy rather than in the fee-for-service setting which is generally held to be a necessary concomitant of professional work.

The data presented in this paper have been gathered in the course of a programme of research on child protection in England conducted over the period January 1977 - December 1979. During the period, the team carried out taped interviews with 14 solicitors in private practice, 9 in the county, described as Shire, where the main fieldwork was done on the study, 2 in a remote rural county, 1 in a northern industrial metropolitan borough and 2 in Inner London. We also taped interviews with 21 solicitors working for 15 local authorities. All but 3 of the solicitors we interviewed were male, so we have adopted a masculine pronoun throughout. In addition, we have observed numerous court hearings, case conferences, informal discussions and the like. Topsy Murray had worked for three years before joining the project as an administrative assistant in the legal department of a local authority.

PROFESSING PROFESSION

In an earlier analysis, Robert Dingwall (1976, 1977) argued for the development of an ethnography of professional claims. Extending Moerman's (1974) discussion of the problems faced by anthropologists in legislating ethnicity by fiat, he suggested that sociological discussions of professionalism had foundered on similar difficulties. In attempting to provide a definition of the term that was objectified and independent of members' usage, they had been unable to arrive at an identification which met minimal taxonomic criteria of unambiguity. Dingwall proposed a line of development based on induction from members' usage in an attempt to determine 'When' and 'How' the term 'profession' was employed in his study of health visiting. It appeared that the term was linked by members in a fairly consistent fashion to the personal qualities of the worker, to autonomy in work organisation, to features of occupational organisation and to relations of superordination or equality with other occupations or workers. That these elements strongly resemble those in the traditional literature, need not surprise us: in so far as sociologists and society members share the same conceptions of social arrangements, then sociological elaborations will be founded on that knowledge.

In the present study, we had hoped to carry further some of these suggestions in considering the ethnography of the term, 'profession', across not only health visitors but also, lawyers, doctors and social workers within and between their respective organisational settings. At the time of writing, however, our analysis of these data is rudimentary. What seems clear, though, is that Dingwall's earlier account was somewhat misled by an insufficient attention to the 'when' part of its question. The word 'profession' seems to be bound to particular contexts, one of which is formally recognised occupational socialisation. Our data appear to show that its usage in everyday work, is slight. While the word, itself, may not be found, however, the claims are, in that certain sorts of statement are made about work which are not actually linked at that point to the term 'profession'.

The theoretical implications of this will require further thought and analysis. One possible approach is to reconsider the line of argument developed by Becker (1970) in talking about profession as a 'folk concept', a line upon which Dingwall sought to build. He pointed out that sociologists' difficulties with 'profession' stemmed from its dual usage: by sociologists pointing to 'an objectively discriminable class of human phenomena' and by members making moral evaluations. He argues that the former endeavour should be abandoned. It may well be, however, that to do so would inadvertently throw the proverbial infant out with the bathwater. While the attempt to point to an 'objectively discriminable class of human phenomena' may be philosophically unsound, plainly sociologists are attempting to generate some sort of a category of their own. Perhaps this should be more properly located within the context of arguments like those of Freidson in this volume for the replacement of the sociology of the professions by a sociology of occupations. Rather than asking, 'How do we delimit a category of occupations called professions?', the proper question might be, 'What sorts of categories of occupations can we delimit?'

In beginning such an enterprise, we have found it useful to return to the work of Parsons. In an account developed from his prewar research on medical practice, he attempts to identify a group of occupations characterised by achievement, universalism, functional specificity, affective neutrality and collectivity-orientation (Parsons 1951, p.343). While he uses the word 'profession' to describe such occupations, he later stresses that lay usage of the term introduces an artificial distinction between traditional professions like law and medicine and modern business (Parsons 1954). The actual referent of his characterisation might be better put as 'organised service occupations.'

These occupations have two faces - one private, directed to the individual client, and one public, looking out to the society in which the occupation struggles for power and esteem. Parsons's description of the public face, summarised above, has often been criticised on empirical grounds. Such criticism, however, misses the point. While Parsons may only be reiterating the occupations' own claims, which may bear a minimal relationship to everyday practice, the account has value as an induction from those assertions. It tells us how such occupations justify to a wide audience their claim to a peculiar measure of autonomy, particular forms of work organisation and a guarantee of economic security, features which are said to enable them to promote communal welfare. Doctors contain epidemic disease, lawyers regulate social conflict, businessmen maximise societal welfare.

Against this, however, we must set the private face of communal service. Autonomy may be a source of weakness as much as strength, since the State is generally reluctant to share its monopoly of legitimated coercion with anyone who is not its direct agent. Economic security and collegial organisation may be congenial but still need to be earned. A monopoly supplier without a buyer is an economic absurdity. The professions may enjoy a certain moral authority but depend ultimately on a voluntary contract with their clientele. In order to attract and retain clients, the professions must, like other service occupations, purport to promise an individualised mode of treatment by fellow-citizens with particular specialised skills, and, given the delicate nature of the work, particular moral standing. Trust is, as Horobin observes in his contribution (p.102) at the heart of the division of labour. The more 'sensitive' the task, the more onerous the requisite display of morality.

From this perspective, many of the alleged failings of these occupations, by the standards of their own public claims, become more intelligible. The literature on medicine provides copious documentation of these 'failings'. Ascribed characteristics seem to be as important as achieved in gaining entry to, and graduating from, medical schools. We find the 'clinical mentality' taking precedence over generalised universalistic judgements and personal experience defeating formal rationality. Medical practice, argue Strong and Horobin (1978), is marked by individualistic contracts between doctors and patients rather than wider collectivity-orientations. Horobin and McIntosh's (1977) account of Scottish general practice illustrates that the role of doctors as a kind of generalised wise man is still prevalent, diffuse rather than functionally specific. The most substantial accounts of doctor/patient interaction (Byrne and Long 1976; Strong and Davis 1977) do stress the surface display of affective neutrality. At a different level of analysis, however, medicine does have a profoundly moral character. It shows us how to interpret *and* evaluate an area of the natural world (Dingwall 1977b).

This contrasting model, of a service uniquely tailored to its recipient and based on the personal experience of its provider, whose authority flows not merely from technical competence but also from social and moral rectitude, represents the face of these occupations presented to private individuals. Obviously this model may lend itself to discrimination and unthinking conservatism. It does, however, seem unreasonable to repudiate entirely the notion that service occupations like these do in fact provide a personalised service simply because we do not always like the kind of service that is offered.

Such contrasts in rhetoric find their organisational counterparts. These are occupations with a marked sense of community and strong collective organisations articulating public claims. In everyday practice, however, where we might expect to find these matched by formal bureaucracies with clear hierarchical lines of authority, we tend to come across collegial forms of work organisation, loose federations of practitioners in their own right. This collegial model enshrines each professional's individual discretion, which is further buttressed by the assumption of the fee-for-service relationship with a client as the 'natural' mode of practice. The client acts as economic man buying that service which is best fitted to his individual needs from the most appropriate purveyor. While this relationship may be clouded by insurance or state financing, it can plausibly be argued that even where nationalisation has occurred few fundamental changes have resulted (cf. Strong and Horobin 1978).

We have then, discussed the Janus character of this proposed category of occupations. On the one hand, it is publicly asserted that they offer impartial, objective and freely available ways of resolving problems of social or natural order, On the other, a private promise is given of a service that is personal, individualised and oriented to the resolution of private problems to the satisfaction of particular rather than general interests.

THE NATURE OF LAWYERING

The preceding attempt to sketch a picture of a particular class of occupations, whether we choose to apply the term 'professions' or not, depended however, largely on empirical data from studies of medicine. From Parsons to Freidson, this occupation has provided the base for the key theoretical debates and its relevance as a typical instance of some wider category has largely been assumed rather than demonstrated.[1] Our first task, then, is to explore this picture's appropriateness for the analysis of law, which we may assert on commonsense grounds constitutes an equally archetypal member of the lay category 'profession'. How far does it help sociologists to talk about lawyers and doctors as if they occupied the same space in a sociological classification of work and occupations? In doing so we have followed the Parsonian description outlined above. Can this sensibly be used to characterise lawyers' work? We shall endeavour to show that it can and, moreover, that similar claims are made by lawyers in private practice and in local government employment, although there are minor differences of detail. Subsequently, we consider the implications of these claims for the structural organisation of local government. Given our earlier observations on the 'natural' mode of fee-for-service, we have chosen to begin with a discussion of the private practitioners.

Ten of the private solicitors worked in small practices, mostly in market towns, with little or no internal specialisation, two worked in larger practices with an established division of labour and two worked for a practice specialising in family work. Three of the solicitors were women and the remainder men. Our interviews were centred on their handling of child protection cases. We were mainly concerned with care proceedings under the Children and Young Persons Act 1969. This procedure was designed to accommodate both criminal and welfare cases on the theory that these represented the same class of children. (In fact, the former parts of the Act, sections 4 and 5, have never been brought into effect.) The consequence, however, is that these are technically proceedings involving the local authority as appellant and the child as respondent, so that they are the only two parties to the case, although the grounds cited may well relate to the parents' conduct. Only parties to the case are entitled, as of right, to play a full role in the court hearing and to be eligible for legal aid. While it might be argued that this is a rather small and unrepresentative part of a solicitor's work, we contend that its very strangeness prompted our respondents to reflect upon matters which would otherwise tend to be taken for granted. Two particular features seemed to be at the root of this: the legal aid position is confused and payment may be uncertain, raising issues about the lawyers' collectivity - orientation to wider ends of justice rather than working only for a fee; and the solicitor may be asked to represent a client, a small child, who is unable to give instructions, with implications for the diffuseness/specificity dimension.

Interviews are, of course, occasions where respondents are likely to feel called upon to give public accounts. Some of our questions invited such general statements of principle. Others, however, were addressed to the handling of specific cases which we were following and, as such, are the nearest proxy to direct observation of their practice which might allow us to make inductive statements about the operational philosophies which influenced their actual, private dealings. We intend ultimately to complement this analysis by an examination of their roles in court hearings, the only direct evidence available to the present study.

Care proceedings are rare events in the life of a private practice solicitor and his response is almost inevitably particularistic, responding to the circumstances of an individual case and then searching the law for guidance on its management rather than having a typified response available to resolve a client's presenting problem.

R.D. ... we're talking in something of single figures over the five years you've been here.

Gabor Yes, probably. One or two a year. Having said that, it's got to April, we've done three this year. Before that, no more than one or two a year.

R.D. Do you find that a problem? That you've got to start from scratch, each time.

Gabor I mean this applies on anything which comes in other than, say, a straightforward conveyancing job or what have you. I mean as it happens there's just been a run of very good articles in the Legal Action Group Bulletin, just before this came up, about care proceedings, and I went through those and so on.

This did not mean that they could not go on to induce statements of general application from these individual cases, the legal equivalent of the clinical mentality.

R.D. ... [Is] there anything that you would really like to elaborate on in the light of your experience of this case as a whole?

Cowper Well, I still think I doubt if this is the right way of going, going about care proceedings, um, whether it's the right court to start them off with in the Juvenile Court as opposed to, say, the County Court ... .

Only one of our respondents found this question impossible to answer.

Bogart No, I don't think so. The situation is fortunately, as far as I am personally concerned, these sort of cases are the exception. Um - certainly a useful experience as far as we're concerned (-u-). The more one does it, the more one would be able to sort of formulate notions of the way in which one should function and approach them.

This 'rational' model of generalisation as a result of inductive reasoning from the scrutiny of a series of cases, was fully developed only by those solicitors who claimed a specialist role in the area. Whereas the other private practitioners used specific cases to formulate general rules, the specialists cited general rules and used specific cases to illustrate them.

Dunaway ... there's always, nearly always something like this on the stocks ... I find it very enjoyable and interesting work because you are concerned, very concerned about lives and I think if you try hard enough you are there to see that the right thing is done. Now I think one of the great problems about most advocates is that they think in terms of winning or losing and this is just not so with this sort of case ... the majority of advocates, who don't do enough of this work - perhaps this is the best way of putting it - still think in terms of winning and losing. I mean in contrast to that [my partner] commented on this recent adoption case he did ... they all wanted to do their best ... it wasn't at all like a lot of jurists in the lion's den.

Throughout our interviews these respondents seemed conscious of speaking for the public record. As experts in this area, they assumed our interest in the underlying legal and philosophical issues and turned the interview on to this level. The other solicitors tended to generalise only in response to specific invitations. While one might need to tie the universalism/particularism dimension to the social distribution of knowledge within the professional group, this material does seem consonant with the arguments above. Universal statements are produced in response to requests or assumed requests for public pronouncements, whether on a 'rational' or a 'clinical' basis, while at least these cases are managed in a particularistic fashion.

Care proceedings are a good area to examine questions of specificity and diffuseness. Technically, legal aid is available only for the child which means that solicitors may have considerable problems in determining their instructions and sorting out the diffuse groups of adult and articulate parents and their, often young and inarticulate, child. This may be remedied in either direction. The solicitor may, in effect, take instructions from the parent as the recognised proxy for the child and follow them through.[2] Both Gabor and Andrews did this, for instance, stressing that their duty was to act solely as the client (i.e. the parent) directed. This stress on technical expertise seemed to be linked with reservations about the credibility of the parents.

Andrews ... having heard the evidence of Dr Matthews and knowing what instructions had been given by the Dickens's, I mean, I immediately felt that the Dickens's were not telling me the whole truth, of course I shouldn't really say that but there it is ... as soon as I heard the medical evidence I was convinced that if I was really acting for the child and no more I ought really perhaps at that stage to have thrown one's hand in ...

One of the achievements of a stress on functional specificity is a distancing of professional and client. This can be particularly useful for the professional when difficult moral issues arise which might attract greater public interest in their exercise of discretion. Moral questions are reduced to technical matters where expertise counts more than citizenship. Specificity defends the professional against public intrusion.

In these cases, however, the solicitor may take the view that his representation of the child required that he should form his own judgement on the child's interests and, in effect, give himself instructions. The separation of child and parents leads to a diffuseness in the solicitor's own role.

R.D. ... the basis of knowledge by which you evaluate this situation was predominantly that of your own experience as a parent.

Harris My own experience as a parent coupled with my experience I think as a lawyer. And for a fairly substantial number of years, probably about six years as a lawyer when I was dealing in a much larger firm on a departmentalised basis with child-related marriage-related problems. Um, so that I've probably got specifically more experience in that than some chaps in general practice might have, y'know. I've had sort of family problems rammed down my throat for six years. It's a very testing thing, um, and I don't think it's a good thing to be in it for all your life. Because you begin, like anything else, if you're only in one thing, it's a departmentalised thing, too long you take a very jaundiced view of it all. You tend to get tunnel vision I think. So, yes, you can say that, but while you can apply general experience, and, of course, I think that when you have to attack it in your profession, any problem, it doesn't matter what it is, you don't just accept what's happened as what's happening, you adopt a more analytical approach to what's going on so that you're looking for things and you're saying ... at the end of the day I've only got my personal views to, um, defend my actions with, if you like, and I didn't feel the child's behaviour was in any way attributable to him having been a recipient of violence from his parents, er, which was primarily why I thought it was unnecessary to go to an independent psychiatrist.

The latter section of this material occurs in a passage of discussion following a question from John Eekelaar about the desirability of, in effect, asking for a child psychiatrist's opinion as a basis for formulating instructions. Harris's argument is essentially that such evidence would only be worth having in support of his own view of the appropriate instructions that he would give himself. Like several of the other respondents, Harris is claiming a broad role as an expert on human life. A solicitor can, in principle, turn his skills as an analyst to any problem which may be brought to him and, in general, find a solution which satisfies at least himself.

Although it might be supposed that a specific concern with a case decreased its affectual charge, there is no straightforward linkage between affective neutrality and specificity. Both Andrews and Harris, for instance, invoked the formula of being an officer of the court to justify their particular actions.[3] Andrews did not believe that the child's parents were telling him the whole truth but felt that his duty to the court required him to test the legal soundness of the local authority's case. Harris took the view that his duty to the court required him to take a broad but detached perspective on the best interests of the child who was being represented. In both cases, however, this reference allowed them to defeat potential lines of criticism: that they had, respectively, been excessively credulous or displaced the parents from their 'proper' status as the child's proxies. We have no direct evidence on the maintenance of this stance in lawyer/client interaction. Although Andrews remarked on the efforts which he had made to detach himself, as the child's representative, from the parents' interests in his dealings with the parents and to explain this to them, Harris avoided any encounter with the child's parents in his case. This may have been because he felt it to be too threatening. He argued that he felt it was best to form a judgement of the child's interests unclouded by contact with either the parents or the local authority staff involved. However, several of the solicitors commented on the aggressive and disruptive reaction of parents, especially when they realised the position about legal aid and representation. They seemed to imply that this was unusual but we cannot regard this as the strongest of evidence.

Most of the solicitors, however, came to acquire some commitment to their client's case. It was, we felt, a matter of professional self-respect as much as anything else. No advocate likes losing, although this was often qualified by an assertion that a care order

was probably the right decision. Since they were relatively unfamiliar with this type of proceeding, the cases were often viewed
on a criminal model, where winning, losing and plea bargaining
were appropriate terms of reference. As Dingwall and Eekelaar
(1979) observe elsewhere, this is an understandable construction
given the serious nature of the moral charge which is involved.
Solicitors, then, acting as both advocates and technical advisers
may find that their dealings with clients take on an affectual charge
which is less prominent in general medical practice where patient
advocacy *vis à vis* hospitals is a much smaller part of the doctor's
role, at lest in the UK.[4] Some of the solicitors did, however, have a
stronger moral stance. Finlay, for example, saw an important part
of a solicitor's duty as defending individual clients against an
oppressive bureaucracy.

> *Finlay* ... I got the feeling that once the County Council, once the
> social services get their claws into a certain set of facts that they
> do tend to make the best of them and I suppose this is typical of
> many branches of authority that, er, for instance the police
> when they decide that they've got the criminal they do all they
> can to see that he gets sentenced or he gets convicted rather, not
> sentenced.

This, of course, links up again to the individualistic version of the
solicitor's responsibilities.

The final dimension of professional claims that we want to
discuss here is collectivity versus self-orientation. It may be that
this is better formulated in terms of altruism and egoism. What
Parsons seems to have in mind is a contrast between actions which
advance the self-interest but which have a wider benefit. He
regards a crucial test of this as the willingness to provide a service
without fee if the client is thought to be in need. It is a feature of
these cases that only the child has a right of audience and, conse-
quently, a right to Legal Aid. In theory, parents must finance
their own representation. A typical sum seems to be about £150.
(In practice, some clerks stretched their discretionary interpretation of Legal Aid rules and issued certificates.) Even on Legal Aid,
this work was said to be unremunerative.

> *Harris* There's a large element in them of helping people which
> you can't do on a production line basis. There's got to be a

human interest factor. You've got to understand the problem and give assistance. It takes experience to disagree with someone without them storming off ... that does need practice. They are time-consuming. But they're never turned away from this office for that reason. Although they do create these massive backlogs of paper.

In the case concerned, Harris was acting for the child and the parents obtained representation from Finlay after Harris had advised them that he regarded the child's interests as separate and could not act for them.

Harris As far as I know, at this point in time, they were not legally aided ... Um, Alex Finlay, though, and it's fortunate that she got to a solicitor like that, adopted the attitude that somebody should never come to us and be wanting in assistance or should want for help purely on financial grounds, and provided we can do it we always do it ... within reason, if we felt that someone had a really genuine case we would act for them irrespective of whether or not we were goin' to get paid for it and y'know there's a certain amount of goodwill got to exist.

Finlay So that we, in fact, have to do this out of, well, frankly out of our own pockets, if you ... I mean, every now and then we do find a case where Legal Aid is not available and so we make it, I think, almost policy of the firm that every now and then we do do a case of this kind where we can't expect to get paid. But I don't know that everybody would take that view, or even why anybody should have to even consider it in something which is so vital ...

There are obvious limits to the charitable activities of any private individual as both these respondents remark. Lawyers, like anyone else, have a living to make and both Finlay and Harris commented on their responsibility to the staff of their practice as a whole. Both respondents also note that one could not always anticipate such a response from other solicitors. Quinn was another who observed:

I'm a bit soft-hearted [laughter]. Both in this area and other areas I've done it. Where, for example, someone has been appointed to represent the child and I know that there is no possibility of getting legal aid as such for the parents, rather than have them go away disgruntled with the legal aid system, even though I've thought on occasion the case was hopeless, I've gone on without fee. Um, just for the good of the image of the profession in court I expect ... I'm not saying it applies to all members of my profession. I can think of some people in this town who are genuinely concerned who'd never do anything for nothing ... .

It may be important that these were mostly small practices, although in both urban and country town settings. The contributions by Galanter and by Thomas and Mungham imply that larger firms might be less accommodating. However, it may equally be that the distancing of our respondents from other solicitors is one way of underlining the private claim to an individualised service. More work seems indicated on this point.

Nevertheless, we regard these data as reasonable evidence for the existence of some wider sense of obligation on the part of some solicitors. This collectivity-orientation is, however, tempted by a sense of its realistic limits in terms of the future of the practice as a whole. In a market society, charity is necessarily finite.

The pattern of responses from the local government solicitors was, for all practical purposes, the same as that described for private practitioners. We shall, therefore, consider the four dimensions discussed above fairly briefly.

As one might expect, the local authority solicitors found it easier to discuss care proceedings in universalistic terms. There was a hearing somewhere in their authority's area most weeks of the year. The solicitors would, then, commonly refer to other cases as guidance for the disposal of the particular matters under discussion. These generalisations followed the deductive model already outlined. It was, however, clearly a matter of experience. Our research in Shire coincided with the introduction of two solicitors into this area of work and there was a perceptible learning curve in their ability to typify cases. This bears out our earlier comments on the link between the private solicitors' particularism and their inexperience.

Even for the local authority solicitor there are, though, still non-routine areas, like appeals which are discussed in a particularistic fashion. Relatively few cases get to the Crown Court because of the procedural hurdles.

J.E. ... Now, it seemed to me that an interesting point emerged at the case conference about Mr Conrad's position because there was talk that he should appeal if he wanted to, but it seems as if he can't because only the child can appeal. Whether the child does this depends on the social services being willing to allow this, because they now have parental rights over the child.

Benchley How clever, very good, No, that's all quite beyond me. I shall have to look it up in the books. If and when it happens, I shall deal with it. ... we can't know all the law. We only look it up when it happens.

Again, however, these limited opportunities shall amount to more experience than the average private practitioner ever gets. The authority saw Conrad as a tactical case and did not press the point. In a later case, Leonard, however, Benchley briefed counsel to oppose the *locus standi* of Evans and Finlay to enter an appeal. The judge threw this out only by elaborate extra-statutory work and appeals to 'inherent jurisdiction' to sustain his view of the natural rights of parents to have the original decision reviewed.

The local authority lawyers seemed more likely to take a diffuse view of their responsibilities both in the sense of diffuseness about their client and about their role. This was related both to the organisational form of their relationship with social services and to their individual experience. We identified two types of social service/legal department relations. In this first, the lawyers tended to act as advocates on briefs provided by social services. The solicitors behaved rather like a barristers' chambers with a courts section in social services evaluating the case, preparing evidence and issuing the relevant notices. Under the second system, the lawyers were involved at an early stage of decision-making, often attending case conferences. Our data suggest some evidence of a move from the first type to the second and it seems clear that where the second type has become established both parties are reluctant to move in the reverse direction. As we show in a later section of this paper, the first type accords more with the traditional relationship between lawyers and other local government departments, where the latter stood in a client relationship and the legal department purported to act as the guardian of the interests of the whole authority. However, this has, to some extent, been undercut by local government reorganisation and the rise of chief executive's departments. Child protection has been one area in which this might be resisted as a result of its high public visibility. In order to protect the authority the lawyers have moved to the second type: which has allowed social services to spread their risk from a case which goes wrong.

We tended then to find the less diffuse views expressed in interviews with solicitors working in authorities of the first type and with relatively inexperienced solicitors, who had not yet come to terms with the wider responsibilities which authorities of the second type had assumed. Calman, for instance was a junior solicitor in such an authority.

Calman ... there can be divergences in professional opinion and I think it's bound to say that that happens. I think it possible that I have a slightly different view of the situation because my brief is somewhat narrow. Is there sufficient for a case, or isn't there? ... .

Calman goes on to stress the uncertainties and muddle that can arise from the wider brief of social and medical workers and their sense of caring and compassion for people in general. This makes them reluctant to come to the point of action and the role of the lawyer is to crystallise this and sort it out. Benchley, the most experienced of the four solicitors we saw in this authority, defined his role in a much broader fashion. Thurber, in the following extract, is the social services' central adviser on child care matters.

Benchley ... My role then is to advise basically as to the law and Thurber as to the merits, but I think as one gets a build-up of experience that the two roles can, in some er way, can be confused. So what I say at a case conference probably doesn't entirely relate to the, to the law.
J.E. Yes.
Benchley I find that having been to quite a few case conferences that I'm probably in as good a position in many respects to advise on the social aspects as well as some social workers. I don't say that in an arrogant attitude.

The diffuseness of local authority solicitors' claims has interesting consequences for the organisation of local government which we explore in more detail below.

There is much the same sort of ambivalence about the degree of affect attaching to these cases. On the one hand, solicitors will take the line that their duty is merely to place the facts before the court and allow the magistrates to decide. On the other hand, their view is not limited to this. If a case is brought it is important to win it. The more neutral formula of 'placing the facts before the court' anticipates defeat and provides for an excuse. Benchley puts this quite clearly in discussing the Conrad case.

Benchley ... I'm saying in any case we have a responsibility if we see a situation that is prima facie a care case and this is prima facie a care case. ... There isn't a lot of evidence. I'm saying we will present this case to the best of our ability, although it isn't the strongest case we've presented by a long way and then it is up to the magistrates ... What we are saying is that it is for the magistrates to decide because it is, anyway, because they are the judge. We are not the judge and jury.

The solicitors' desire to win is partly a matter of self-defence and partly of professional pride. In the interview quoted above Benchley went on to comment on the Wayne Brewer case, where the magistrates agreed to return a child against the opposition of the local authority.

Benchley ... The Council and the magistrates were severely criticised and quite rightly so. All I'm saying is that as a Council we must present the strongest possible case because [otherwise] we are failing in our duty ... our duty to the public, our duty to the court and as solicitors we are officers of the court as well, and therefore we must do our best ...

At the same time Benchley evinced considerable glee over the success of the Conrad application at a subsequent interview.

Benchley ... I think the other side were damn silly ... . The other side's solicitor was very inexperienced, but that's, y'know, we live in a hard world don't we? ... I certainly put our side of it. If they were clouded one way, that's up to him isn't it to do something about that ...

Benchley's choice of words underlines the adversarial nature of the practice of these solicitors. Although they made public claims to neutrality, their vision of the cases embraced two opposing *sides* locked in combat. Cases are *won* and *lost*. Often it is almost a racing metaphor; 'going down' or giving a case a 'run out'.

Finally, we come to the collectivity/self-interest dimension. We have already quoted Benchley's remarks on the public duty of the County Council and this theme recurs quite strongly in the solicitor data. At the same time, the elements of self-interest are quite clear. The argument, however, can go either way. Some of the solicitors took the view that care proceedings with their relatively high level of involvement with a client department and of advocacy work were an important career channel. Unlike some areas of local government, this was an area of expansion and development in both statute and case law. A lawyer experienced in personal social services advocacy was likely to have good prospects. Addams drew particular attention to another benefit: for the lawyer who wanted to leave local government, work with a high level of advocacy provided opportunities to meet private practitioners and get known around the courts.

Other solicitors, however, took what we are inclined to regard as the traditional and majority view: that care proceedings and, indeed, most advocacy was low-status work to be relinquished as rapidly as possible in favour of committee work and administration. These latter provided the key career line for ambitious local authority lawyers. Here, their self-interest led them to play down the work, discourage marginal cases and generally limit their involvement with the client department.

In this section of the paper we have, then, demonstrated the affinity between solicitors in private practice and in local government employment in the ways in which they talk about their work. While there are certain differences of emphasis, these would seem to have more to do with the particular topics under discussion than about the essential nature of the rhetoric. Moreover, the framework which we used was developed substantially from empirical study of doctors. The working conditions of the two groups of lawyers, however, are quite different. Private practice solicitors are in the 'natural' mode of fee-for-service, more so indeed than general practitioners who retain their nominal independence but receive the greatest part of their income from a capitation payment. Local government solicitors are paid employees of a major bureaucracy, with less formal independence than a hospital consultant who has access to an elaborate structure of representative and participatory occupational bodies. How can these claims be reconciled with the possibilities of practice in such an institution? In order to answer this question, we need to understand something of both the concept of a bureaucracy and the formal institutional structure of English local government.

THE NATURE OF BUREAUCRACY

The classic formulation of bureaucracy is to be found in the work of Max Weber (1947, pp.329-41). He views it as the organisational counterpart of the rational-legal mode of authority. This mode provides for the legitimacy of some social order to be founded on an impersonal set of normative rules. Bureaucracy is the institution through which these rules are interpreted and enforced. The impersonality of its procedures is secured by a number of structural arrangements. Office-holders have no personal interests in the organisation and enjoy quasi-property rights in their jobs only in so far as needed to secure their independence, as in the case of judges. Procedures are documented in a permanent, written form to secure impersonal practice through time by the compilation of precedents. The bureaucracy, itself, is governed by a set of normative rules which regulate the scope of each office and the hierarchical relationships between office-holders. Their rights and duties are specified and sustained by disciplinary procedures based on notions of due process. The central characteristic of a bureaucracy is its formalistic impersonality. 'The dominant norms are concepts of straightforward duty without regard to personal considerations. Everyone is subject to formal equality of treatment; that is everyone in the same empirical situation' (Weber 1947, p.340).

Weber observes that bureaucracies can take different forms although they will all share the basic characteristics described above. The bulk of his discussion, and subsequent debates, however, applies only to what he called the 'monocratic' type, subject to the authority of a single head and with a single chain of command. It is, though, important to note that he does, in fact, recognise a second 'collegial' type, although he regards this as a degenerate form (Weber 1947, pp.392-407). While collegiality and the need to achieve consensus favours greater thoroughness in decision-making, it tends not to be conducive to 'the need for rapid, clear decisions free of the necessity of compromise between different opinions and also free of shifting majorities' (Weber 1947, p.336). It also tends to dilute personal responsibility. Weber distinguishes thirteen variants of the collegial bureaucracy but only one is important here, namely, where there are parallel monocratic authorities with specialised functions whose joint consent is required for any decision. Since 'collegial' is now more commonly used to describe the form of organisation characteristic of professional partnerships, we shall designate this as a 'consensual' bureaucracy.

Much stress is often placed on the antithetical character of professions and bureaucracies. We must, however, be cautious about this. It is important to note the parallel development of both institutions in the emergence of the modern capitalist order. Professions and bureaucracies, as we know them today, are both essentially creations of the second half of the nineteenth century. Further, we must recognise, with Parsons (1954), the fundamental continuities in officially-expressed values between professional and bureaucratic forms. It would be as true to say bureaucracies made public claims of promotion by achievement, of universalistic treatment of clients, of functional specificity, of affective neutrality and of collectivity orientation. This is particularly so, of course, when we consider the bureaucracies of the modern State. In his introduction to the 1947 translation of Weber's *Wirtschaft und Gesellschaft*, Parsons toys with a distinction between legal competence and technical competence (Weber 1947, p.58n). Professional practice is based on technical competence, the practical *ability* to carry out a task, while bureaucratic practice buttresses this with the notion of legal competence, the *authority* to carry out a task. Put in this form, it is a weak and unsatisfactory distinction. Professions depend upon the statutory licence and mandate which confers a monopoly of legitimate practice and, thus, the legal authority to perform technical tasks. Parsons does, however, link this equality of technical competence to the equality of collegial practice. As such, we can begin to tie this to our earlier discussion of the private face of professional practice and its role in the production of collegial forms. What Parsons is identifying is one of the features of that model, the discretionary application of individualised experience, rather than the model itself. Where one professional's experience is as good as another's an egalitarian form of organisation seems inevitable.

If we latch onto this element of individualised discretion, then the problem for the local authority lawyer becomes clearer. In order to demonstrate this, we need to discuss some aspects of the organisation of English local government.

LOCAL GOVERNMENT: A PUBLIC BUREAUCRACY

Until 1974, the Chief Clerk's department with its staff of lawyers, generally solicitors, played the key role in co-ordinating the executive branch of English local government. While each of the major Council Committees - Education, Housing, Highways, etc. - had its own parallel executive department, the Chief Clerk's stood in a similar relationship to the Council meeting as a whole to adjudicate between the claims of the various committees. The position of the lawyers derived from the statutory foundation of local government. Authorities are created and regulated by Acts of Parliament, so that they have a continuing need to interpret those Acts to ensure that legal duties are being met and powers are not being exceeded. If money is spent without statutory sanction, for instance, this will be detected by the District Auditor and render councillors personally liable for its reimbursement.

Although the cadre of lawyers constituted an in-house resource for general legal services, especially conveyancing and advocacy, the core of their work was committee administration. It was here that councillors were advised on the legal implications of their acts. The committees and their departments could only act within the limits of the lawyers' interpretations. Although elected councillors can, in the last resort, *direct* officers to carry out their instructions, this is not without some personal risk, as we saw in the surcharging of the Clay Cross Council for refusing to implement the Housing Finance Act.

The 1974 reorganisation had strong similarities to its NHS counterpart. Both were designed, by management theorists, to undercut the hegemony of professional groups in favour of lay administrators trained in management skills. In doing so they moved towards a consensual bureaucracy, deliberately elevating those features which Weber criticised so strongly. Where he saw delay, compromise and political struggle, the management theorists saw rational corporate planning based on an informed and democratic consensus replacing professional autocracy. The allocation of resources would be determined by a collective of heads of service rather than by the profession dominating the division of labour.

The Bains reforms, then, attempted to limit the influence of lawyers by creating separate administrative and legal departments, dividing the interpretation of statutes and general legal services from the development of policy. Lawyers would be reduced to technical advisers within multi-disciplinary teams which would be jointly responsible for decisions. These reforms have had a mixed fate. Many of the administrative posts went to the solicitors who had been doing this work for years and where separate departments were set up they often tended to be small, weak organisations of bits and pieces which did not fit anywhere else.

Shire is fairly typical. The Director of Administrative Services is a lawyer as are his professional staff who provide both administrative and legal services. The Chief Executive, who is not a lawyer, has only a small and rather heterogeneous staff. Formally, Administrative Services looks like a hierarchical department. There is a functional division into sections for environmental and personal services. Each is led by an Assistant Director, a lawyer, with a Senior Assistant and an Assistant Solicitor and a bevy of lay Administrative Assistants. A third group of one Senior Assistant Solicitor and three legal executives dealt with conveyancing, agreements and contracts.

In practice, however, it was still possible for the solicitors to retain sufficient of their former independence for the rhetorical forms we described earlier to remain relevant. This reflected, in part, the organisation of their immediate work setting and, in part, the degree to which they had succeeded in maintaining and even developing their traditional relationships with other departments, as we noted earlier.

The Administrative Services Department operates in a manner which we would recognise as characteristic of a professionally dominated organisation. While the lay staff have a line relationship to the dominant group, that group itself operates on a collegial basis. If we take mistakes at work as an example, then lay staff may be reprimanded by line superiors. The lawyers, however, tend to respond in a manner reminiscent of Arluke's (1977) account of 'death rounds'. Here he shows how conferences to analyse the cause of recent deaths in a hospital became occasions for reaffirming the solidarity of the group through the normalisation of mistakes. Any member in the same situation might make them. Control of work standards through such meetings is, then, at best indirect and a matter for the individual conscience. In Shire, similarly, when the Social Services Department complained about the quality of representation in care proceedings after failing with several applications in a short period of time, the lawyers' response was to meet and examine the general quality of the evidence they had been asked to lead rather than the individual management of cases.

If neither supervision, the positive power of direct work, nor reprimands, the negative power to censure work, are apparent, it seems difficult to justify describing the lawyers as a hierarchical group. This is compounded by the low level of functional specificity seen in a purportedly functionally organised department. Lawyers are, in principle, perfectly substitutable, a view encouraged by a deliberate policy of staff rotation in Shire. Committee work was thought to vary little except in volume and its reallocation required a minimal amount of learning about a new topic area, a task within, and indeed, an indicator of, the lawyer's competence. Similarly, at one time or another, almost every lawyer in the department, except the Director and his deputy, represented the County Council in care proceedings. In such a situation, a 'junior' solicitor may easily become more expert in some area than his titular senior. The distribution of knowledge within the department is fluid and bears no consistent relationship to the formal hierarchy.

Lawyers might, of course, consult and advise each other within the distribution of expertise.

Benchley ... Roger has his caseload and I have mine. However, of course, on complex points or on very serious cases we do talk about them together, rather on an *ad*, not on a planned but on an *ad hoc* basis and ask each other's advice as and when appropriate.

Such hierarchy as there was in the department rested partly on this fragile base, and partly on the accident of acquaintance with prestigious members of the Council. The opportunities for making such contacts depended, of course, in some measure on which committees were serviced by the solicitor, although his choice of social activities might also be relevant. We should stress, however, the essentially sociable basis of these contacts. Councillors, as we have seen, seldom direct lawyers. The representative status of the

former is counterbalanced by the latter's role as keepers and inter-
preters of the organisational charter.

Local government solicitors, then, can be seen to have created
an enclave for themselves which allows them to reproduce many of
the conditions of private practice. Their status and responsibilities
within a bureaucratic structure are diffused through the group to
create an area of discretion which is relatively immune from any
surveillance, whether by colleagues or, indeed, elected Council
members. Given this, it is not surprising that we find them making their occupational claims in a similar fashion to their counterparts in private practice. Moreover, it must be recognised that
both segments have available rhetorical formulae like the appeal to
being 'an officer of the court' which can be drawn upon both to
unify the occupation and to defeat others' claims on its allegiance.
The rule of law is placed against the instructions of private clients
or elected representatives with the lawyer in a mediating role.

We shall pursue some of the consequences for the workings of
local government more fully in future writings. In particular, we
shall attempt to show how the exercise of this discretion constrains
other departments. We noted how the responsibilities of legal
departments were becoming increasingly diffuse. This may well be
related to the attempts to re-establish legal dominance since the
Bains reforms. The lawyers lost some of their position as guar-
dians of the authority's interest to the collective of chief officers
and some of their managerial functions to the chief executive's
department. Bains plainly envisaged a much narrower role for the
solicitors as technical advisers. Their position however as decoders
of the governing statutes could not be displaced. We think that the
increasing penetration of social service decision-making by
lawyers which we observed and on which we commented briefly
earlier in this paper may be one strategy for countering these
pressures. External concerns about child protection could be used
to claim a necessity to survey the legality and public defensibility
of social service decision-making at a level below that of the Director's reports to his fellow chief officers. There are obvious implications, then, for the amount of discretion which social workers can,
themselves, claim in their practice. Although our data are limited,
we think that a similar tendency could be shown in respect of other
departments, a tendency which is being reinforced by spending
economies which are reducing the amount of legal work which is
being contracted out.

OCCUPATIONAL CLAIMS

We have, then, tried to show how certain sorts of occupational claim are made by solicitors, whether in private practice or in local government. These claims are, we suggested, essentially similar in their nature and, moreover, congruent with those proposed by Parsons using data for doctors. All of these groups seem, on the face of it, to share a rhetoric of practice which is, in principle, capable of being described along rather similar dimensions. Further, we have discussed the Weberian notion of bureaucracy and its relevance to the study of local government in England. We showed how solicitors had shaped their place within that organisation in such a way as to create a zone of discretion which allowed them to reproduce features of private practice and sustain the unified notion of the occupation. We could then, suggest that it makes reasonable sense to regard solicitors and doctors as subsumable in a single category of occupations for some sociological purposes. This is not, of course, to deny the observable differences and internal segmentation of both occupations. Nevertheless, both have rhetorical formulae to unify members around certain themes like 'officer of the court' and its medical analogues and both, we have argued, may be seen to share certain overriding ways of talking about their work. How far this may be true of other occupations is, of course, an empirical question.

The question, however, remains as to whether this all adds up to a claim of 'professional' status. A banal answer might be that it does if we choose to employ the term 'professional' thus. A more satisfactory approach might be to suggest that we have the wrong data here to address that question. The fact of the matter is that our lawyers seldom used the word professional except to put down others, especially social workers, as non-professional. It could be argued that they were treating their own status as so 'obvious' as to be unworthy of comment, but it is difficult to warrant any claim by asserting the absence of a possibly-noticeable alternative. If we want to do an ethnography of the term 'profession' then we need to find settings where it is naturally used, settings like organised socialisation and the writings, speeches and lobbying of occupational associations.

One final observation may be in order. We commented on the similarities between the language which Weber, at least in Parsons' translation, used to describe bureaucracies and the language which we derived from Parsons to discuss medicine and law. We noted, too, their common nineteenth-century origins: Weber's model was the Prussian State and both medicine and law were, at least in the UK and North America, radically transformed at about the same period. Is this more than a coincidence of language or do, in fact, bureaucracies and organised occupations have complementary rather than conflicting roles in the modern nation-state? Rather than beginning from *a priori* antithesis, as in the traditional model reviewed by Davies in her paper, would the study of bureaucratic and 'professional' occupational claims not advance our understanding of the nature of the bargain between private and public interests in contemporary societies?

ACKNOWLEDGEMENTS

Earlier drafts of this paper have been read by Celia Davies, Gordon Horobin, Janine Nahapiet and Pam Watson. We are grateful for their comments and encouragement. Robert Dingwall and John Eekelaar are supported by funds from the (British) Social Science Research Council and Topsy Murray by funds from the Department of Health and Social Security.

NOTES

1.   Although Parsons (1954) included an essay on the legal profession, the basic analytic categories are derived from a study of the doctor/patient or, more particularly, the psychotherapist/patient relationship. See also Rueschemeyer (1964).

2.   The issue of proxy rights is discussed at more length in Dingwall and Eekelaar (1979).

3.   The concept of an 'officer of the court' will receive a fuller treatment in a future piece of work. It does, however, exercise a considerable importance as a formula for affirming the fundamental unity of law. Despite the separation between judges, barristers and solicitors in English legal practice, their common duty to the court is seen as something which, in principle, overrides all other commitments, even those of the client paying the lawyer's fee.

4.   Horobin, in a personal communication, notes that GPs may engage in advocacy in relation to other agencies, like municipal housing departments. We may be seeing here both a lesser occupational tolerance for internal dissent, related perhaps to the location of illness in a natural frame of causality which is, hence, open to 'objective' diagnosis and treatment, and a difference between 'one-shot' and 'repeat' players. If a GP has a long-standing and continuing relationship with a particular hospital, he may be reluctant to compromise this by a vigorous pursuit of a single patient's interests.

Part III

Professional Careers

The final group of papers, by Paul Atkinson, Malcolm Johnson and Alan Paterson deal with issues of professional careers. Atkinson reviews the debate on professional socialisation. This played a key role in both Parsonian and Hughesian traditions. The former saw it as the process by which the normative order of the profession was internalised, while the latter was concerned to establish how novices acquired strategies for coping with the experience of work. As Atkinson observes, however, it is a debate which has gone stale. He points to the deficiencies: a narrow focus on training institutions at the expense of extra-curricular settings; an assumed homogeneity of faculty interests; and, most critically, a neglect of the linkage between education and practice. The transmission of knowledge disappears as a topic. Atkinson directs our attention to the vigorous debate around this issue in the 'new' sociology of education, most particularly in the writings of Bernstein and Bourdieu. The influence of extra-curricular factors is the main topic of Johnson's paper. He points to the dearth of biographical research on the professions. What are the typical career pathways and how do people come to pass along them? Using data from a study of UK medical graduates, he shows the interaction between work and non-work elements in this process, drawing our attention to the misleading assumption of the centrality of work as a life-interest. In concluding the volume, Paterson presents data from his study of senior UK judges to remind us that there are beings higher than professionals. (Is our preoccupation with the latter, then, a reflection of our own rivalries, as Strong has suggested?) Judges, he argues, constitute a distinctive occupational group. Although they are solely recruited from lawyers, the change in their work and social location which results from their elevation is sufficient to set them apart. Again we are reminded of the importance of developing an appropriate understanding of practice before moving to classification.

10 The Reproduction of the Professional Community

PAUL ATKINSON

A decade or so ago, one might reasonably have said that contemporary work on 'professional socialisation' (or some such designation) was a major contribution to the sociology of occupations, and indeed to the sociology of education. Nowadays, while recognising the importance of some classics in the field, one would perhaps be rather less inclined to regard it as an area 'where the action is'. Part of my argument will outline the development of the sociology of professional education. In doing so, I hope also to indicate ways in which new life might be breathed into the field. I shall draw heavily on research on health-related occupations: this is the arena in which I have conducted research myself, and is also the best documented and most heavily researched field. I shall also seek to draw on recent work in the sociology of education, as I shall argue that the separation between the study of 'professional' education and the investigation of education at school level has contributed to the stagnation of the former. My argument is not that there is any great intrinsic weakness in recently published research in, say, medical education, but rather that the field has failed to develop to any significant degree, and has tended to recapitulate very similar themes instead of breaking new ground.[1]

It is undeniable that the 1950s and 1960s witnessed the production of a significant corpus of publications reporting research on the education of 'professionals'. The major studies were undertaken in the United States, under the aegis of the dominant American paradigms of sociological inquiry - functionalism and symbolic interactionism. Those occupations commonly designated 'professions' were taken as particularly apt exemplars in functionalist theorising: Parsons's (1951) remarks on medicine are a notable case in point.

From the functionalist perspective occupations such as medicine and the law were marked by a high degree of homogeneity and consensus - constituting, in Goode's (1957) famous formulation 'communities within the community',

> whose members share identity, values, definitions of role, and interests. There is room in this conception for some variation, some differentiation, some out of-line members, even some conflict; but, by and large, there is a steadfast core which defines that profession, deviations from which are but temporary dislocations. (Bucher and Strauss, 1961)

Various theorists thus attempted to identify and list such core characteristics or 'traits'. In practice, this exercise proved to be a troublesome one, when it was not simply an uncritical reiteration of 'professionals' statements of pious hopes and self-interests.[2]

The functionalist position necessarily led to an emphasis on the socialisation of 'professional' trainees. From this point of view, it is the process of socialisation which reconciles the opposition between the functioning of the social system and the action of individual members of society. The core values are *internalised* via this process: in this way a homology is assured between the system norms and values and the subjective meanings of social actors.[3]

In the 1950s, then, such interests led to a focus on 'socialisation' into the 'professions'. At the same time, as Merton (1957) has noted, there were more practical considerations which pointed in the same direction. Merton instances rapid changes in professional knowledge, implying as they did a revision of training programmes. Merton's remarks apply specifically to medical education, in which, he suggests, there was a renewed recognition of social factors in the origin and management of illness and of the potential contribution to be made by the social sciences. He notes, too, a commitment to the 'scientific' analysis of education, and a systematic comparison between the objectives of innovatory programmes and their actual outcomes.

Merton's comments were made in the context of one of the classic functionalist studies of professional socialisation, undertaken by a Columbia University research team. Although reported in the form of a number of separate, more or less self-contained studies, there was a unifying theme. In keeping with their underlying theoretical perspective, Merton and his colleagues assumed a distinctive set of roles and values as the *terminus ad quem* of medical education:

> (Medical students) are engaged in learning the professional role of the physician by so combining its component knowledge and skills, attitudes and values, as to be motivated and able to perform their role in a professionally and socially acceptable fashion. (Merton *et al.* 1957, p.41)

The Columbia research acknowledged the importance of the medical school as a socialising agency. It was acknowledged that there might be some discrepancy between various values and norms and that stress and anxiety in students could be an unintended consequence of the socialisation process. But, in practice, the tenor of the research reflected the unquestioned assumptions of their theoretical commitments. On medical schools Merton remarked:

> It is their function to transmit the culture of medicine and to advance that culture. It is their task to shape the novice into the effective practitioner of medicine, to give him the best available knowledge and skills, and to provide him with a professional identity so that he comes to think, act, and feel like a physician. It is their problem to enable the medical man to live up to the expectations of the professional role long after he has left the sustaining value-environment provided by the medical school. (ibid., p.7)

The major alternatives to the functionalist view of socialisation were inspired by the Chicago school of symbolic interactionists. Whereas the functionalists tended to see 'professions' as a special category of occupations, the latter saw them as essentially similar to other occupations. Gouldner (1962) summarised the difference between the two 'schools' in this way:

> ... the former [functionalists] are more respectful of the medical establishment ... they are more prone to view it as a noble profession. [Chicago sociologists] however, tend to be uneasy about the very idea of a profession as a goal for study, believing

instead that the notion of an 'occupation' provides more basic guidelines for study, and arguing that occupations as diverse as the nun and the prostitute, or the plumber and the physician, reveal instructive sociological similarities.

For those of this latter persuasion, then, the search for criteria which define a 'profession' as such is quite misconceived. 'Profession' is itself seen as a lay term with no precise denotation: it is a title which is *claimed* by occupations under certain conditions and at particular times. It is therefore a symbolic label which some occupational groups lay claim to, and which they may be granted by others. Despite the wealth of connotations attached to the title, there is nothing inherent in the work, training, values or whatever, which marks out the occupations so designated.

By the same token, there can be no assumption of consensus within the occupation. On the contrary, the 'Chicago' perspective opens the way for the recognition of differentiation and conflict as a normal state within occupational groups. In the classic formulation of this view Bucher and Strauss (1961) remark that, 'the assumption of relative homogeneity within the profession is not entirely useful; there are many identities, many values, and many interests'. They use the term 'segments' to refer to coalitions of interest and outlook within an occupation. The essentially static view of functionalists and 'trait' theorists was replaced by one which saw occupations as - potentially at any rate - in a constant, processual state of flux. Not only do occupations strive to attain 'professional' status, and to maintain their positions, but segments are also engaged in pressing their particular interests.

The functionalists had tended to reproduce the 'professionals' own claim, suggesting such high-flown ideals as 'service' and 'collectivity' orientations. The interactionists, on the other hand, more cynical, perhaps, focussed on the mundane aspects of 'professional' work. Writers in the Chicago vein have studied how members of occupations operate pragmatically and survive amid conflicting pressures in the everyday performance of their work. The moral concerns of this latter school lead them to celebrate the 'underdog' while rebunking the rhetoric of superordinates.[4]

These perspectives account for the interactionists' distinctive approach to education. In line with their interests in day-to-day survival, Becker and his collaborators (1961) in their study of the

Kansas medical school, stressed the immediate experience of medical students, playing down the relationship between 'socialisation', and future 'professional' practice. Rather than assuming the assimilation of a repertoire of roles and values, they concentrated on how students 'made-out' - how they got through medical school.

This emphasis therefore directs attention to what the interactionists call 'situational learning', or 'learning the ropes'. Initiates are faced with immediate practical problems of getting by in novel situations and must find ways of coping with them. Collectively they work out 'perspectives' to organise their experience and develop survival strategies:

> Newcomers in any social situation go through an initial process of learning the ropes: finding out who the other people in that situation are, where they are located, what they do, what they expect the newcomer to do, and how they want him to do it. We seldom dignify this process by calling it learning. (Miller 1970)

It was precisely this aspect of 'learning' which was seized on by the interactionists - ultimately, as I shall argue, with limiting effects.

Central to the study of the Kansas medical school is the notion of 'student culture'. Within the relatively self-contained institution of the medical school a distinctive sub-culture develops among its students. Its content derives (at least as regards academic matters) from the pressing problems faced by students in organising their work and allocating their limited resources of time and effort. (It is in keeping with their overall view of 'professions' and occupations that the Chicago researchers should have drawn explicitly on perspectives and findings from industrial sociology - on workers' attempts to control their own level and direction of effort.)

The Columbia-based research too had focussed on something akin to student culture, and the contrasting portrayals of student life - and especially students' status - encapsulate the overall difference between these two major approaches. The Kansas study emphasises the subordinate status of the students, who are cast in the role of 'underdog'. There is a marked social barrier between students and faculty. The training period is characterised as a 'trial by ordeal'; student culture is a sort of underground resistance movement. In this, medical students are portrayed as really no different from other students: substantially similar results were reported by the same group of researchers in a study of liberal arts students (Becker *et al.* 1968) in which they again focussed on the collective negotiation of academic effort.[6]

The picture presented by the Columbia group was radically different. The relationship between student culture and faculty orientations is seen as complementary rather than conflict-ridden. The student culture is described as a 'little society', whose function is to maintain the communication network of the school, clarifying standards and controlling behaviour based on norms which are shared by staff and students alike. Students were described as being treated as 'junior colleagues' who were being groomed and sponsored towards full professional status and partnership with their mentors.

The interactionist critique provided an excellent counter-balance to inadequate views of 'socialisation' implicit or explicit in many studies of training (including the functionalist view, as well as more atheoretical social psychological approaches). This was developed by Olesen and Whittaker (1968) whose work on student nurses was, broadly speaking, interactionist, though more obviously influenced by existential phenomenology.[7] Commenting on the 'image of man' implicit in much of the sociological literature they remark that students have often been portrayed as empty vessels ready to be filled with approved knowledge and values - unformed social actors who are rendered competent by the training process. This perspective, they suggest, is appealing in the sense that it suggests simple before-and-after research designs, obviating the need to flounder in the 'broader complexities of role ambiguities and cultural transmission' (Olesen and Whittaker 1970).

Interactionism, then, directed attention firmly towards the process of training. There was no sense in which the training institution could be treated as a 'black box' (not that the functionalists necessarily took this extreme view either). Hence attention was turned towards the organisation itself, and it was, in itself, treated as problematic. Rather than taking its goals, values and culture on trust, the interactionist typically looks for the 'hidden curriculum' which informs the actual daily practices of teachers and students.

I have dwelt at some length on those two major approaches to professional education - familiar ground though it is - in order to outline the sort of debate which has characterised and dominated subsequent work in this field. And it is undeniable that more recent work has been so dominated. This is not to imply that no further research of any value has been conducted. Rather that the original classic studies and their theoretical and empirical obsessions have continued, to a considerable extent, to define the parameters within which development has taken place.

Two of the major monographs (Miller 1970; Mumford 1970) in the field - on interns rather than medical students - explicitly recapitulate the two earlier studies of medical schools. Miller, in particular, offers what is, in effect, a faithful version of *Boys in White* applied to junior doctors. Bloom's (1973) study of the medical school at New York's Downstate Medical Centre is also located within the same tradition. Shuval (1975a, 1975b), in her research on Israeli medical students, is constrained to explore the applicability of the 'boy in white' and 'junior colleague' typifications. True, she shows that these characterisations cannot be applied in a blanket fashion: the students experience a tension between the two, and their self-perception depends on context within the medical school. In a similar vein I too attempted to show that the medical school was itself a more segmented arena than it had originally been portrayed - and did so in terms essentially derived from the original debate (Atkinson 1977a). In 1978, Coombs produced an addition to the literature on medical students which is remarkable only for its almost total lack of originality. He reiterates, from a socio-psychological viewpoint, much of the conventional wisdom on the effects of medical education, and students' adaptations, adding little or nothing, substantively or methodologically, to the work of the sixties. Recently too a group at McMaster have been working directly in the interactionist tradition, in examining medical students' coping strategies (Haas and Shaffir 1977).

Of course, there is some novelty in the more recent research reports. There is bound to be: even the most slavish replication will usually turn out looking slightly different from the original model. Concepts have been clarified, and useful data added to our stock of knowledge. Nonetheless one is forced to acknowledge that overall the field has gone rather stale.

In the first place, the interactionist view of socialising agencies and institutions has tended to over-emphasise their discreteness. Goffman's (1968) ideal type of the 'total institution' could almost have provided the model for such studies. The position of a novice in, say, *Boys in White* is in many ways remarkably similar to that of the 'inmate' in Goffman's *Asylums*. No doubt some socialising agencies are of this sort and many of the 'total institutions' which Goffman describes have socialising functions anyway. Dornbusch's (1955) description of a military training academy is a case in point. Although predating the publication of Goffman's book, Dornbusch anticipates many of its features. He stresses the extent to which recruits are segregated from the world outside, subjected to degradation ceremonies, and plunged into the distinctive ethos of the academy. From this perspective, then, it would be reasonable to view the socialising setting as a sort of total institution. But Dornbusch's own account goes further. He uses the term 'assimilation' to capture the process whereby the cadets become incorporated into the military ethos. By assimilation is meant a

> process of interpenetration and fusion in which persons and groups acquire the memories, sentiments and attitudes of other persons and groups and, by sharing their experience and history, are incorporated with them in a common cultural life.

There is, however, a tendency in the interactionist view for the enclosed, total institutional picture to be stressed, at the expense of 'assimilation' (or something like it) into a larger culture or occupational group.

The limitations of too narrow a focus on the institutional context of training have been commented on elsewhere. Olesen and Whittaker (1968) for instance, employ the notion of 'lateral role socialization' to refer to issues of enculturation not strictly limited to the student role, but which nevertheless impinge on 'professional socialization' - for instance adult gender roles and nursing students. Dingwall (1977a) refers to similar considerations in his study of health-visitor students: he draws attention, for instance, to the tension between their status as students and as adults - a tension heightened by the traditional ethos of nursing education. In a rather different way, Malcolm Johnson's work in the present volume points to 'extra-curricular' influences on medical careers.

A second limitation is the fact that, paradoxically, the interactionists tend to portray the socialising agency as internally homogeneous (though this is a failing shared with studies under different theoretical auspices). Here again the 'total institution' seems to furnish an implicit model. As I have remarked elsewhere there has been little attention paid to professional segmentation within the medical school, or in other comparable settings (Atkinson 1977a).

Bucher (1970) has been alone in addressing this topic directly, though only faculty perspectives are investigated. Bucher notes that members of the medical school claim 'professional' autonomy in the conduct of their work, and exercise that autonomy in the light of their segmented allegiances and interests. Their work in the medical school thus reflects their specialised bodies of knowledge, a view of their specialist segment's place in the order of things, and a view of the relationship that should pertain between themselves and members of other segments. Kendall too refers to some aspects of segmentation in American medical schools - referring to conflict between physicians who are in practice in 'the community' and those who work full time in the medical school.

By and large, however, this has remained an under-developed area, and it is ironic that the Chicago-school interactionists (with the exception of Bucher), despite their recognition of 'segmentation', should not have followed such a line of enquiry. That they did not do so is readily explicable, however. It derives from their emphasis on 'situational learning', and their desire to treat the educational experience as divorced from issues of 'the profession' in a wider sense. One has little sense, for instance, that the medical school has anything ultimately to do with any other aspects of the occupation of medicine.

In the last analysis the obsessive concern with the immediate, situational features of educational settings leads the Chicago theorists and their followers to an almost absurd position. After the two major studies reported in *Boys in White* (Becker *et al.* 1961) and *Making the Grade* (Becker, Geer and Hughes 1968), Becker and Geer (in Geer 1972) turned their attention to occupational learning in different contexts. Rather than mounting yet another study of a single institution, they directed a number of small, related projects (mostly undertaken single-handed by junior colleagues). These were deliberately focussed on topics other than 'professions': a barber school; apprentice high steel workers; learning door-to-door selling; a county jail school; workers learning new jobs in an electronic plant. Becker provides a concluding chapter (pp.89-109), and one paragraph is worth reproducing:

> Students do not learn what the school proposes to teach them. Colleges do not make students more liberal and humane ... nor do they have any great effect on students' intellectual development and learning ... . Medical school training has little effect on the quality of medicine a doctor practices ... . Actors considered expert by their peers have seldom gone to drama school ... . The spectacle of elementary and secondary education gives credence to Herndon's ... wry hypothesis that nobody learns anything in school, but middle-class children learn enough elsewhere to make it appear that schooling is effective ... .

The title of Becker's piece sums up his argument: 'School is a Lousy Place to Learn Anything'.

Now I am sure that Becker is deliberately and self-consciously engaging in hyperbole - trailing his coat. But he is clearly in danger of adopting a nonsensical position - one which is only a slight exaggeration of the interactionist stance. There have from time to time been stories of individuals operating as successful and apparently competent doctors, dentists and so on who turn out to have no formal qualifications. Commentators never overlook the irony of such revelations. But it would nevertheless be quite absurd to extend the argument - as Becker appears to - and suggest that medical students do not learn medicine in medical school.

It is undoubtedly true that students do not 'learn medicine' in any absolute sense. They certainly do not assimilate a package of knowledge and skills which they then proceed to apply throughout their subsequent working lives as medical practitioners. There is no ideal 'medicine' which exists absolutely and independently from the practicalities of day-to-day practice in actual medical settings. On the other hand there can surely be no doubt that medical students do learn medicine - or at least some version or versions of medicine - and it may seem banal and even bizarre that one should need to emphasise the point in this context.

If Becker can be taken to mean that 'medical school is a lousy place to learn medicine', then one assumes that he has some idealised view of how medicine could and should be, and how it should be taught, and that present educational practice falls some way short of that. A corollary of that might be to argue that 'medical school is a place to learn lousy medicine'. That is certainly a view worth canvassing. But here again Becker's overall position would preclude such a view, since he and his interactionist colleagues foreclose any principled exploration of the relationship between training and work.

In effect this issue boils down to the interactionists' failure adequately to cope with problems of knowledge and to produce a sociology of the curriculum. This in fact is a point of departure where later developments in the sociology of education diverge from earlier interactionist influences. For a direct consideration of school knowledge has become a major strand in the so-called 'new sociology of education'.[8] It was a legacy of both the functionalist and interactionist approaches that there should be a concern with the latent functions of education and aspects of the hidden curriculum. These were both, in their way, 'demystifying' - stripping away the rhetoric of educational provision in order to disclose its actual practice. But in the process the manifest function of education - the transmission and management of knowledge, the manifest curriculum - became overlooked. I want to argue that such a reappraisal is necessary in the context of 'professional' education, without necessarily abandoning the insights derived from the interactionist ethnographies of educational settings.

What is implied by my remarks so far is this: despite the apparent cleavage between the two major schools in this field, there have in fact been convergences - both in terms of what has been done, and what has not been done. Fundamentally, both positions treat 'the profession' as unproblematic. The functionalists do so by taking on trust the characteristics the professions claim, and assimilating their view of education to that perspective. The interactionists effectively treat it as un-problematic by default, since they fail systematically to question the relationship between education, practice and the organisation of occupational groups.

In effect, then, what has been lacking is an adequate treatment of cultural transmission and knowledge management in the reproduction of the professions. Yet this is odd, as all observers are moved to remark on the extent to which 'professions' are potent self-replicating collectivities. We have been in danger of abandoning 'socialisation' only to leave ourselves with no room adequately to cope with issues of cultural reproduction.

Taking a leaf from the book of educational sociology, then, I want to suggest that we should treat educational knowledge as a central topic in our analyses of 'professional' training. This will go far beyond a simple exercise in 'curriculum studies' such as may be undertaken by learned bodies, Royal Commissions, faculty review committees and so on (though such deliberations are important sources of data). Rather, our concerns will be those outlined by Bernstein (1971, p.47):

How a society selects, classifies, distributes, transmits and evaluates the educational knowledge it considers to be public ...

Hence the production and reproduction of knowledge - legal, medical, religious, educational and so on - will become the *leitmotiv* for a sociology of professional education.

We must recognise that all educational knowledge - be it that of primary schools or universities - is in a sense *arbitrary*. There is no absolute, pre-given corpus of knowledge which self-evidently presents itself as a 'curriculum', and which is inherently endowed with order, sequential organisation and so on. The curriculum is a device whereby knowledge is classified and combined: it is a cultural imposition. There is no ideal 'law', 'medicine', 'theology' or whatever 'out there' to which the curriculum corresponds as a mere reflection or copy.

Educational knowledge separates what is thinkable from what is unthinkable; it identifies what is deemed important and attempts to distinguish it from what is trivial; it marks out what is introductory from what is specialised and advanced; it may construct an essential 'core' as opposed to the peripheral or optional. In the course of setting up and legitimating such definitions of knowledge curricula portray the essentially arbitrary as *natural*: natural, that is, in that they appear to reflect a given order in the domain of knowledge and in the world of work. Hence its status as a cultural artefact remains hidden. (Though this is not to deny that there may be occasions on which some conscious questioning may take place).

Bernstein's own major contribution to the field is based on his notions of 'classification' and 'framing' of knowledge of which he says: 'Classification ... refers to the degree of boundary maintenance between contents 'and' ... frame refers to the degree of control teacher and pupil possess over the selection, organisation and pacing of the knowledge transmitted' (1971, pp.49-50). Building on the Durkheimian concept of boundary-maintenance, Bernstein identifies two ideal-typical modes of curricular organisation, based respectively on principles of 'collection' and 'integration'. These knowledge 'codes' imply differing modes of social organisation and control in educational institutions. Despite a characteristic elusiveness, Bernstein's ideas in this context have proved highly suggestive, particularly in view of contemporary change in the organisation and content of secondary schooling in Britain. Arguably they can and should be applied with equal value to higher education - and to professional education in particular.

Armstrong (1977) has attempted to account for some general features of medical education in the light of Bernstein's theoretical framework. He argues, for instance, that typically the preclinical phase is informed by principles of strong classification between subject contents - and hence a collection code - while the clinical phase is marked by a shift towards an 'integrated code': while the former is characterised by more explicit bases for authority and control, the latter is based on implicit orders of meaning and control. His paper is a starting-point, perhaps, but it cannot encompass the variety of medical curricula. Armstrong is forced to present an over-simplified view of medical education in order to apply Bernstein's somewhat schematic ideas. (His identification of clinical instruction as corresponding to the 'integrated' model is contentious in any case.) Nevertheless he does enough to suggest how fruitful such an approach might be. He underlines how strongly boundaries have been maintained in medical education: how strongly disciplines have been classified, and subject loyalties fostered: how the 'sacred' knowledge of the profession has been segregated from profane, mundane knowledge.

One further line of development in such a direction is suggested by the work of Pierre Bourdieu, an influential sociologist of education, whose work is based on Marxist and structuralist principles - and has a number of points of convergence with Bernstein's version of structuralism.[9] Bourdieu's arguments are directed at the education system in general, and are not specifically concerned with higher or professional education. Bourdieu suggests that education is marked by a system of *violence*: not the open, palpable violence which the term normally connotes, but symbolic violence. This operates through the imposition of meanings and definitions such that the real relations of power and interest are hidden. Education promotes a consensual view of the legitimacy of certain varieties of knowledge, while masking the social differences it serves to promote and reproduce. For Bourdieu 'cultural reproduction' does not refer simply to, say, the functionalists' copying of the taken-for-granted social order. Cultural reproduction serves to preserve the appearance of neutrality while legitimating sectional interests. Bourdieu's position is captured in the aphorism: 'culture classifies - and classifies the classifiers'. Hence the social organisation and transmission of educational knowledge furnishes a *cultural code* whereby the social structure is reproduced.

Through the educational system what Bourdieu calls 'cultural capital' is differentially distributed, in a manner which parallels capital of a material sort. A key but elusive concept here is Bourdieu's notion of *habitus*. This refers to the distinctive 'modes of perception, of thinking, of appreciation and of action' associated with any given collectivity. The habitus thus defines the 'taste' of a group - its characteristic, taken-for-granted view of the world. In the world of education the habitus which defines successful schooling remains implicit, Bourdieu argues. The education system *assumes* that its pupils are possessed of the necessary cultural competence, the character of which is never made manifest. The (middle class) student already versed in the mysteries thus appears much more readily to be 'naturally' gifted. In this way the essentially social distribution of cultural capital appears to be a natural distribution of personal qualities.

We cannot, in Bourdieu's terms, identify a single habitus in professional education, nor even in a single professional school. But one very common component of the habitus can be indicated. That is, the emphasis on 'personal knowledge', 'personal experience' and 'personal judgement'. Jamous and Peloille (1970) are rare in having provided a systematic account of this feature of professional knowledge and its reproduction, in terms of its historical development and its significance for inter- and intra-professional process. (Their account is developed primarily through an examination of medical education in France.) Some studies of professional education have—documented such features of knowledge transmission, and on the basis of such work in medicine, Freidson (1970a) has identified them as characteristic of the 'clinical mentality'. But all these approaches have tended to treat such matters as 'training for uncertainty', as Fox (1957) called it, in terms of individual psychology and adaptation. While there certainly are problems in coping faced by individual novices, we have - building on Jamous and Peloille - elsewhere attempted to show that the issue goes far beyond this. The definition of 'indeterminate' knowledge and its preservation is part and parcel of the politics of professional knowledge and professional power. It is a crucial claim in the quest for autonomy. Yet the implications even of this issue remain but poorly examined.

Incidentally, 'indeterminate' personal knowledge cannot be seen as *the* habitus of professional education. It is, as my colleagues and I have argued, often a contested definition (Atkinson *et al.* 1977). As Jamous and Peloille suggest, there is a tension between the 'tacit' and the 'technical' (often expressed as 'scientific'). Bourdieu's habitus, then, cannot be understood in any simple all-embracing sense for any given educational setting. Indeed, it is its very contested nature which gives such an analysis its cutting edge in an investigation of professional process and conflict.

The issue of 'indeterminate' knowledge in professional education does, however, illustrate Bourdieu's contention that the habitus may remain implicit, while its mastery is treated as the realisation of natural talent. Competence as the tactic knowledge of, say, medical diagnosis is, as Jamous and Peloille put it, regarded as a personal 'virtuality' of practitioners - and hence of successful recruits. Bourdieu uses the notion to account for the differential distribution of educational success within education systems. In the context of professional education we are dealing with internal differentiation (e.g. as between specialties) *and* with methods where by exclusivity - and the appearance of professional 'community' - is assured. (This may, in part at least, account for the notorious propensity of such occupational groups to self-recruit: there is a sort of 'mythological charter' that such candidates have already assimilated much of the profession's oral tradition and habitus - though it is not expressed overtly in such terms of course.)

The curricula of professional training exemplify a further point which Bourdieu makes most forcefully (though not uniquely). That is, curricula, as socially organised knowledge, appear to embody what is self-evidently the best available knowledge, and rationality. They promote the appearance of consensus while actually enshrining sectional interests and perspectives. With this in mind we should return to the interactionists' insistence on professional segmentation. For curricula must be seen to incorporate - while often masking - intraprofessional interests, as well as reproducing the esoteric expertise which is held to be the preserve of the profession as a whole. Relatively little attention has been paid to this aspect of professional curricula.

In general terms it has been pointed out that curricula embody and legitimate partial versions of professional work and interests. For instance it has been argued that medical education serves to perpetuate and reproduce a particular view of medicine. It promotes what Celia Davies (1979a) has termed the hospital-centred version of medical care. I have also attempted to show how the practice of clinical instruction reproduces the characteristic empiricism of the discipline, and the distinctive approach to disease and doctoring of hospital-centred medicine (Atkinson 1977b, 1981). Likewise, in an unpublished thesis, Margaret Reid (1980) has examined in some detail how academic general practitioners have tried - with some success - to establish and legitimate their own area of specialised expertise, and incorporate it into the curriculum of medical schools. Such developments have been integral to the collective attempts by general practitioners to enhance their standing within medicine.

In the context of legal education Bankowski and Mungham (1978) have pointed out that the private practice of law is 'overrepresented' in the law school curriculum. These authors have also offered a rare contribution to the political economy of professional education. They argue that debate over the content of professional education in Britain can be shown to coincide with one or more of the following three factors: professional expansion leading to the creation of new centres of education, or the transformation of old ones; threats to the material base of the profession; demands for access to professional services from previously disenfranchised groups. They argue that these factors operate on the legal profession at the present time, and can be related directly to concern over the form and content of legal education. Bankowski and Mungham suggest that 'contemporary arguments about the character of legal education have many of their roots deep in the shifting material base of the profession'. Hence the study of the professions and professional education will be focussed on the same recurrent issues: 'a political economy of legal education can usefully function as a prolegomenon to a political economy of the legal profession itself'.

During periods of change in the organisation and composition of professions, then, it may be possible for new 'missionaries' to emerge, and to stake out claims for new territory, or to re-colonise abandoned ecological niches (Bucher and Strauss 1961). To extend Bourdieu's metaphor of cultural capital we should recognise that those who control the capital and its distribution may themselves be competing in an academic market. Some particular innovations have received attention - particularly the recent emphasis on social and 'behavioural' science in medicine and the law, or the early introduction of 'clinical' work (Bankowski and Mungham 1976; Rees 1975; Sheldrake and Berry 1976). But even these innovations remain under-analysed for the most part, and we lack adequate frameworks to locate such innovations. Sociologists have apparently been more concerned with the practicalities of implementing them.

To conclude, I have tried in this paper to indicate how and why the sociology of professional education has - in my view - failed to develop and keep abreast with the sociology of education in general. I have attempted to point to some directions in which development might fruitfully take place. In doing so, I do not want to seem to imply that *no* work of the sort I am advocating has been undertaken. I have tried to provide examples of such contributions. But I do want to suggest that a more vigorous and systematic development of such work is needed. We need further examination of the social organisation of curriculum and knowledge transmission, both as a general concern, and in the context of specific occupational groups.

NOTES

1.   In the following discussion I am not absolving myself from the criticisms raised. I must however exempt Robert Dingwall from many of the strictures I make. He has taken a rather different tack from the one I advocate below: e.g. *The Social Organisation of Health Visitor Training* (1977a).

2.   See, for instance, Roth (1974, pp.6-23).

3.   Cf. Dawe (1970, pp.207-18). Coser (1978) has recently remarked on both the Freudian and Meadian influences contributing to a preoccupation with 'internalisation'.

4.   This view is perhaps most clearly articulated by Becker (1967).

5. The same view is advanced in Geer, Haas, Vona, Miller, Woods and Becker (1968), pp.223-8.
6. In the absence of independent criteria it is hard to tell whether the apparent similarity between medical and liberal arts students at Kansas was anything more than an artefact of the interactionists' preconceptions. It is, however, more than likely that the close similarities in the accounts are products of shared emphases and strategies in the two research projects.
7. Their main research monograph is Olesen and Whittaker (1968).
8. The title 'new sociology of education' has been applied to a somewhat diverse collection of theoretical approaches and empirical studies, variously inspired by phenomenology and Marxism. The main programmatic statements can be found in Young (1971). A useful review is Demaine (1977).
9. The major source for these ideas is Bourdieu and Passeron (1977).

11 Professional Careers and Biographies

MALCOLM JOHNSON

Within the sociology of professions and occupations the concept 'career' has had a chequered history (Stebbins 1970). At some stages in sociological development the plotting of career development patterns was a paramount activity, whilst at other times careers have been chopped up into interesting phases (apprenticeship, internship, career plateaux) or merely forgotten in favour of more appealing political themes.

In this paper there will be an attempt to draw together these approaches by looking briefly at the career of 'career' and observing in current studies a relative lack of concern with continuous processes and interrelationships between the different careers and individual pursuits in life biographies. A case will be made both theoretically and empirically, for the development of the biographical approach as a method which can offer more than just life histories. Indeed it will be suggested that biographical studies which centre on occupational careers can provide vital data and material for analysis which is generally uncollected or ignored. Material from the Medical Careers Study will be used to illustrate and substantiate these observations.[1]

As this paper is presented within a collection broadly concerned with the legal profession, some attempt is made to relate to the position of legal practitioners. However, as the studies from which the conceptual tools are drawn lie in the fields of medicine and ageing, and the empirical findings from research on doctors, the references to lawyers will be largely indicative and suggestive.

DOCTORS AND THE SOCIOLOGY OF MEDICINE

Medical practitioners have attracted much sociological attention for as long as there has been interest in the professions and in healing. With the rise of a formal sub-discipline of medical sociology, in recent decades, this attention has intensified. Yet inevitably the questions have changed over the years (Freidson 1970a; Johnson 1972). In the early post-war period the questions were broadly concerned with: Who are they? quickly followed by a lengthy period of asking: How does medical education and training transform individuals into doctors?

It might be said that these earlier concerns were born of a sociological desire to provide explanations for an accepted social phenomenon, i.e. that physicians held a special and unchallenged status in society which carried high esteem and commensurate rewards. Although the research which resulted from these questions was critical of doctors, the criticism tended to be about the organisation of the profession and the sophisticated systems of patronage and reproduction which appeared to sustain its ascendancy in health care and in the wider community (Bloom 1973).

Only at a later stage when studies of doctor-patient relationships (now referred to in the more neutral phraseology of healer-client interactions) began to focus on the conflict element in dealings between professionals, did the more overt attacks on doctors begin to emerge (Zola 1972; Illich 1975). Thus in the late 1960s and into the seventies, the thrust of medical sociology became more politically aware and more concerned about the methodologies available to do the sort of interactional studies that the climate of knowledge and opinion demanded (Robson 1973; Navarro 1978).

In this movement from social survey to small scale analysis and the shift from essentially descriptive studies, the attention given to doctors moved away from issues like careers. This may have been due to the attraction of the seeming 'relevance' of patient related studies. It certainly had something to do with the corporate state of the sociology of knowledge at the time, which almost demanded that the aware social scientist should be engaged in critical studies of what Eliot Freidson (1970b) summed up definitively in the term, 'professional dominance'.

Within medical care itself, particularly in Britain, the experience of severe restrictions on the growth of services and the emergence of vigorous industrial action by doctors, nurses, paramedical, scientific and support staff has reinforced interest in the politics of health. Studies of the conflicts which arise from the professionalising efforts of nurses, physiotherapists, scientific workers and administrators and the bargaining for more autonomy and status by other groups (e.g. ambulancemen), have made the medical profession more of a comparative than a primary focus (Stacey 1976; Stacey et al. 1977). The doctors' traditional territory is being assaulted and plundered by the claims of their co-workers (previously their 'helpers'). Current discussions reflect the sense of disruption of the established social order resulting in a stream of analytical comment and investigative research (Barnard and Lee 1977; Atkinson et al. 1979).

Commentators and researchers alike have continued to employ a body of taken for granted knowledge and assumption about the established professions in the analysis of contemporary issues. Closer examination of how doctors (and I would guess, lawyers) feel and are behaving in relation to the changes being imposed upon them in their professional lives reveals a diversity of attitudes, responses and plans which are not wholly in accord with accepted models of professional behaviour. Indeed there is evidence from our study which indicates increasing concern with non-clinical and extra-professional activities as ways of gaining greater satisfaction, rather than seeking status and money rewards offered within medicine.

We are encouraged by the literature to see professional life as presenting a series of competing career paths which once entered upon, demand adherence to patterns of qualification, experience, commitment and work habits which lead to advancement, rewards and recognition. All of this activity takes place within the work setting and non-work factors are all but ignored. In medicine this view has emerged for two main reasons. Firstly, most of the career/development studies have been non-sociological and using simple survey techniques have sought to plot careers through job lists. Usually associated with this data is a series of personal and professional characteristics which are correlated together.

To consider medical careers, or indeed any occupational careers, taking special note of non-professional influences on decision making would seem fairly obvious. Yet remarkably little regard has been paid to them either in sociological research or in manpower planning. When account has been taken of them it has been in search of extraneous factors which may have distorted the manpower planning models. Butler *et al.* (1973) showed clearly the dominance of family reasons and locality links for the failure of the Designated Areas Policy to create geographical movement amongst British General Practitioners; whilst Klerman and Levinson (1969) drew attention to the dilemmas faced by US psychiatrists in weighing professional and personal factors when offered promotion. The widely held notion of the professional 'ladder' in hospital (if not in all specialties) has created an impression deeper and more durable than the evidence can sustain. It is, of course, an observable, but not the only, model for doctors' careers.

Secondly, sociological studies have tended to be about stages or phases of medical careers, leaving us with a fragmented picture which denies the continuing processes at work although process is not neglected within the stages themselves.

As a result of the approaches adopted in this body of research, it may be that some of our theorising and empirical data will need revision if doctors turn out not to be wholly the sorts of people we believe them to be. However before putting forward some alternative formulations, it is necessary to sketch an outline of the main strands in physician studies.

CAREER STUDIES IN MEDICINE

Much of the groundwork in the sociology of professions was done using medicine as its laboratory. Moreover this work has proved to be of more than just descriptive or comparative value. Merton *et al.* (1957) and Becker *et al.* (1961) staged one of the more noteworthy post-war methodological encounters through their studies of medical schools and the processes of translation from lay person to man or woman of medicine. Along with the pioneering work of Everett Hughes (1956) and Parsons's (1951) chapter on medicine in *The Social System*, these studies established the medical profession as a productive field of analysis and theoretical speculation. Paul Atkinson's contribution to this volume discusses this material in more detail. *The Student Physician* and *Boys in White* drew attention to the first stages of medical careers in which the would-be doctor is trained in clinical skills, educated and inducted into a new social position.

Career analysis in medicine in the 1950s and early 1960s was heavily influenced by these two studies. This had the effect of centring much of the research effort on the medical school phase, as in the work of, for example, Sam Bloom (1973) and Judith Shuval (1975a, 1975b).

These medical school studies were conducted within a growing literature which was concerned with a much wider span of career development. Everett Hughes (1956), Oswald Hall (1948) and Bloom (1963) all wrote influential papers which mapped out the careers of medical graduates in stages. It is perhaps significant that these wider-ranging attempts to classify the progress of doctors in their professional lives, were constructed on the basis of very little evidence about the post-qualification period. Indeed, nearly twenty years later there are very few similarly large scale sociological studies of what happens once the doctor is in practice.

Despite the lack of empirical material, the writings of people like Hughes demonstrated a real concern for the whole range of professional experience. In his seminal paper, *The Making of a Physician*, he comments: 'One of the problems in the study of a profession is to discern the career lines of people who follow it. This in turn requires identification of the significant phases of careers and the sequences in which they occur'. So from an early point in the work on doctors there was significant support for processual studies which would illuminate the whole experience. Yet we had to wait until 1970 for Emily Mumford's study of *Interns* to take us a stage further in the process. At this point sociological interest divides off into the many facets of professional organisation and behaviour within the profession, within health care and with patients. The results can be assembled and distilled into a picture of how medical careers are shaped and how they move, but there is, so far as I know, no major study of medical careers *per se*.

From within medicine there is a substantial body of literature about the careers of its members. It too tends to be specific to statuses or to specialisms or to time spans. It looks specifically at such issues as specialty preferences, geographical location choice, job satisfaction, mobility, intra-cohort comparisons etc. The work of John Last (1968) for the Royal Commission on Medical Education generated a sustained interest in how career preferences are influenced and change over time, which has taken up many subsequent pages in *Medical Education*. Similarly that journal and its American counterpart the *Journal of Medical Education* have in almost every issue contributions which plot the progress (and further progress) of the Ogston's (1971) cohorts of Aberdeen graduates, Shaw's (1979) women graduates of St Mary's, Flynn and Gardner's (1969) graduates of the Royal Free, Conrad Harris' (1974) Manchester cohorts and similar studies of consultants (Coghill *et al.* 1970), women psychiatrists (Brook 1976) and so on. There is similarly an abundance of studies on medical manpower which seek to utilise the product of this career research. Notable amongst this literature is the work of Parkhouse (1977; 1978(a) and (b); 1979). A few large studies exist which deal with a broader spread of interests and of time, like Lyden, Geiger and Peterson's *The Training of Good Physicians* (1968) and Fredericks and Mundy's (1976) ten-year longitudinal study of one graduating class. Yet, like these studies, this literature tends to be directed to manpower planning and policy issues.

So career analysis applied to the medical profession is abundant in supply and has many uses and purposes. Its drawback for the student of professions is that it is highly fragmented and episodic. Indeed in some ways it neglects career as a concept in favour of taxonomy and classification of occupational experiences. This is curious in the light of its history and the fact that Hughes's intellectual progeny - Becker, Strauss, Roth, Goffman, *et al.* - have done so much to elaborate the concept, career, as it is now applied to patienthood, illness, deviance, dying and other areas of status passage.

There are therefore many reasons why accounts of professional careers should exist and the rest of this paper deals with a biographically based enquiry which attempts to develop a more dynamic view of the relationship between doctors' professional and other life careers. But the study is, we hope, not only a gap filler. It espouses the sort of wider concerns about the nature of profession and its accomplishment and the more structured and political concerns which were mentioned earlier as prevailing in medical sociology. For it is not just the study of professional careers that is important, but what it reveals about the nature of society as a whole. Or as Wilensky (1960) put it: 'I believe that ... in the study of links between economic order and life-style, with attention to change in the biography of persons and the history of structures lie some of the most fascinating clues to the shape of modern society'.

MEDICAL CAREERS STUDY – CONCEPTS AND METHODS

For this SSRC funded study conducted in collaboration with Mary Ann Elston, the complete qualifying classes of five English medical schools, ten years apart, were selected. Those who qualified from Leeds, Liverpool, Bristol, The London Hospital Medical College and St Mary's Hospital Medical School, London in 1954 and in 1964 were identified as the study population, giving a total of 700 doctors.

Thus there are two cohorts with similar medical school experience for each school and so comparisons can be made between schools and between years, e.g. in terms of the different conditions in the medical profession when the two groups qualified, i.e. in the mid-fifties and mid-sixties. More importantly, the 1954 graduates will almost certainly have reached the highest points in their professional careers. (It is likely doctors in this older cohort will be similar to the typical solicitor or barrister or the typical manager in the same age group as seen by Pahl and Pahl (1971); as 'having come to terms with himself, and his sense of career and personal identity will be fixed'. At the time of the data collection many of the 1964 group were still moving up the ladder so far as consultant posts are concerned and their careers are still in a state of flux. Thus it is possible to see the medical career at two points in time, at its peak and in process, simultaneously.

The methodology is somewhat along the lines of a triangulation procedure outlined by Denzin (1970). Firstly, from published sources and interviews with key figures in the medical schools of our sample, e.g. past deans, we have constructed a picture of the climate of medical education and the state of the medical profession over the appropriate period in order to locate our data on the individual's career development. Secondly we constructed a massive postal questionnaire which covered the doctor's education and background, medical school experiences, medical posts held, details on family development, involvement in medical politics, extra-medical activities and view on aspects of medicine. Respondents were asked to identify career contingencies and the relative weight of various factors such as finance, and family commitments in job decisions at various stages in their lives. Questions were also directed to the influential figures in their career development. In this way we are able to examine the forms in which, and the extent to which, patronage operates in the medical profession, from the point of view of individuals' career progress. The literature on the professions makes frequent reference to the autonomy of the professional, to his power to control his work situation. There are very few studies of how this power is exercised and by whom within the profession. One way in which this autonomy is exercised is through professional 'political' organisations, such as the BMA. We hope to identify who in the profession becomes involved in medical politics, what their values are and how a career in medical politics relates to careers in clinical medicine. In addition a carefully selected sub-population were subjected to full life history interviews.

This three-pronged attack corresponds in part to the three dimensional conception of career put forward by Stebbins (1970). He distinguishes between 'career patterns', 'individual objective career' and 'subjective career'. Individual objective career represents the observer's view (and the observer can be the individual in question) of an individual's progress through the series of stages which constitutes a career pattern. Career patterns are the sequence of stages provided by social institutions and they may be as clear cut as that in the hospital doctor or nurse case, or open to bargaining and negotiation as in the case of TB patients (Roth 1963). An individual's progress through these stages may also be the result of achievement of relatively clear cut statuses, e.g. 'A' level passes to go to university. Subjective career is 'the actor's recognition and interpretation of past and future events associated with a particular identity and especially his interpretation of important contingencies as they were or will be encountered'. In presenting this set of propositions Stebbins argues that all three elements are somehow of equal worth. This seems to be at odds with recent research findings, which, although upholding the reference group model of 'normal career', demonstrate the many ways in which dissonant performance can be counted as 'success'. Nonetheless, his conclusion that the subjective approach is valuable because of its ability to demonstrate modifications of behaviour from what would be predicted on the basis of objective approaches, remains valid.

In the study we derived the career pattern or line for the English medical profession as an objectivated and typical sequence of stages mainly from the relevant literature, available historical data on matters like manpower distribution and from discussions with members of the medical profession. We traced the individual's objective career by the questionnaire and their subjective career from the interviews and biographies as well as by some sections of the questionnaire.

The question still remains as to what counts as a career and we hope to show the value of extending the concept beyond its normally rather restricted application to a subset of occupations. A literature search produces many discussions of careers but few of 'career'. There are three main categories of literature.

First, that of career guidance and occupational choice which will not be discussed here except to note that it may be sometimes appropriate to treat the choice of a particular specialty within medicine as being on a par with occupational choice in a wider sense. The second category is that of large-scale studies of the occupational experience of workers in those occupations which are seen as having a 'career structure'. Occupational experience in this case means achievement on a hierarchical ladder and is normally compared with other attributes, such as father's occupation, level of education, length of marriage etc. The orientation is towards the articulation of these occupational careers with the social environment and with the manpower demands of society. Examples include studies by Cotgrove and Box (1970) of scientists, Fogarty *et al.* (1971) of *Women in Top Jobs* and managers by Pahl and Pahl (1971). Most of these writers recognise that careers are meaningful to those who have them though the relationship of this meaningfulness, the sequences of career stages and the individual's progress through them remains problematic in many cases.

It is in this group of studies that the fullest discussions of the distinction between subjective and objective aspects of career is found, e.g. Goffman points to the essential two-sidedness of a career and like other interactionists he concentrates on the subjective and/or moral aspect. 'The moral career of a person of a given social category involves a standard sequence of changes in his way of conceiving of selves including importantly his own' (Goffman 1968).

It is unnecessary here to go over the work of Goffman, Roth, and Becker and others in detail. The use of concepts like career contingency, timetabling and bench marks are of particular importance for this study for they stress the interaction of different areas of life. Involvement in an occupational career carries implications for family life, etc. and these subsequent commitments become constraints on choices and action in the occupational career. Whilst they may sometimes be complementary, they are just as likely to be a source of tension. Equally, in employing the career notion it is important to recognise as Roth does, the temporal aspects of passage and the way the progress of time might lead to false impressions that all careers can only advance. In reality time itself is differently perceived by different individuals; though we must all face the irreversibility of the passage of time. What is reversible in careers is whatever might be seen as success or advancement. Occupational careers (like illness careers) can, and do, suffer setbacks resulting in loss of status, prestige or pay. Yet the term career is generally reserved for those occupations which provide for formal advance in skill, status or rewards.

Careers like medicine and the law are characterised in the non-sociological research as incrementally advancing along scales of authority and autonomy, leading to principal in general practice (in law or medicine) or to consultant status in medicine and its legal near equivalent, Queen's Counsel. Students of these professions know otherwise. Doctors who wish to be neuro-surgeons may end up 'falling off the ladder' and becoming general surgeons, gynaecologists, GPs, psychiatrists or anaesthetists.

Contingencies which bring about such changes in career paths might be structural and externally defined - like a shortage of posts in a chosen specialty or repeated failure of a key examination like FRCS which would remove the possibility of becoming a surgeon; or as a result of the individual's own choices and actions - marriage, the arrival of children or a geographical move to be near to relations.

These observations about career as a concept and occupational careers in action do not exhaust the proper discussion about their relationship. Similarly what is said below is only a summary statement of my thesis about the linkage of occupational careers to other careers within a whole biography and their joint utility in the sociological study of ageing processes. These thoughts have been expressed at length elsewhere (Johnson 1976, 1978, 1979).

CAREERS AND BIOGRAPHIES

The justification for setting an occupational career study into whole life biographies, rests on well established criteria. If we wish to fully understand an event or series of related events, we usually do so in two ways. The first is to look for an internal logic which might provide an explanation of its own. The second is to examine the broader context in which the events took place in case the explanation more properly lies in the social environment or in an historical analysis. Occupational careers do have plausible and useful internal explanations; but they can be given greater depth and often radically different meanings when set more broadly. For this reason the Medical Careers Study collected information in three independent stages, so that the general health scene, the occupational career path and the concurrent life careers are available for separate and joint analysis. Only in the forty full life-history interviews were these three fused together in tellers' oral accounts.

Methodologically, biographies are justifiable in the same manner as all historical accounts and suffer from similar drawbacks. The validity of some aspects of a personal account cannot be verified from the point of view of internal consistency, or from other available sources. Yet it has a validity of its own - even if factually incorrect - for it represents the individual's own sifting of the facts and explanation of them.

Biographical studies do not take every statement as being factually true. (But then it would be naive of the user of any methodology to believe that his enquiries produced 'factual truth'.) They are more concerned with the meaning of social events as seen through the eye of the self observer. Like all observers, his or her view will be selective and subject to interpretation. Yet this very selection tells us much about the way individuals see themselves as products of the past. What emerges from biographical accounts is the distilled view people have of themselves and what has happened to them, which has survived through life and will provide the basis for the future.

This summary of life past is the basis of self-esteem and self-image. As Robert Butler (1963) has indicated, reminiscence and life review are important aspects of psychological health. Glaser and Strauss (1971; Strauss 1978) also draw our attention to the constant need to reconstruct our self images and personal histories in the light of recent and current happenings. Thus personal biographies are possessions which we all have and tend to keep in good repair. The wealth of material received both as written comment on the questionnaires and in the life history interviews is a testimony to these claims.

CAREER INFLUENCES – SOME ILLUSTRATIVE FINDINGS[2]

Of the 704 doctors approached 499 (70.6 per cent) returned completed, the thirty-two page printed questionnaire, which itself was biographically shaped and employed a variety of information eliciting techniques. It dealt with early home life, education, medical school, post-qualification experiences and qualifications, job sequences and evaluations, marriage and family, career influences and wider ranging sections on attitudes to contemporary health care, working abroad, other preoccupying activities, political involvement and plans for the future. There were some special sections relating only to women. The forty interviews were conducted subsequent to the survey. Thus the interviewer already had a great deal of relevant material to hand which could be cross checked and elaborated. The interviews (carried out by the two investigators) were focussed, but not structured, tape-recorded and transcribed in full.

Within the setting of this paper it is possible only to provide some illustrative findings which relate to the central theme of the arguments presented earlier. Influences on career choices have been chosen because (i) they demonstrate the very large extraprofessional element and the interaction of life careers, (ii) because the consequences of the results are very significant for the models of how doctors behave in career decision making and (iii) because they raise important questions for medical manpower planners.

Of the 497 who returned usable questionnaires 400 were male and 97 (19.5 per cent) female. Ninety-two per cent of the total were British. Responses from the ten graduating classes ranged from 62.8 per cent of the Leeds 1964 group to 81 per cent of the Bristol 1954 group. For all five medical schools, the response was higher from the 1954 cohort than from the 1964 graduates. Eighteen per cent had doctor parents and 30 per cent of those with doctor fathers went to the same medical school. There were 30.4 per cent who went to public schools, 14.5 per cent to direct grant schools, 47.7 per cent to grammar schools. All but eleven were still engaged in medical work.

These items of basic data indicate only the broadest parameters of the study population but they serve to show that the doctors are fairly representative of their time and their career choices are not likely to be atypical. However no claims are made about statistical representativeness for the profession as a whole. Indeed as each cohort experiences a changing set of environmental factors it

TABLE 11.1   Career influence: percentage rating

	1954			1964		
	Great	Some	None	Great	Some	None
Bristol						
Family	28.9	42.2	28.9	32.4	32.4	35.1
Teacher	—	15.0	85.0	—	37.8	62.2
Friends	—	22.5	77.5	2.7	2.7	94.6
Doctor	9.1	43.2	47.7	5.4	24.3	70.3
Leeds						
Family	28.9	42.2	28.9	22.5	50.0	27.5
Teacher	7.7	12.8	79.5	5.0	25.0	70.0
Friends	5.6	19.4	75.0	2.5	15.0	82.5
Doctor	14.6	31.7	53.7	15.0	20.0	65.0
Liverpool						
Family	25.5	34.5	40.0	20.4	44.9	34.7
Teacher	—	23.8	76.2	8.2	28.6	63.3
Friends	4.9	22.0	73.2	2.0	24.5	73.5
Doctor	15.4	39.6	50.0	16.3	18.4	65.3
London						
Family	30.0	36.7	33.3	42.0	36.0	22.0
Teacher	8.5	21.3	70.2	2.3	37.8	65.9
Friends	4.0	24.0	72.0	2.3	34.1	63.6
Doctor	22.0	24.0	54.0	13.3	33.3	53.3
St. Mary's						
Family	30.3	41.9	27.9	29.3	29.3	41.5
Teacher	12.9	19.4	67.7	2.4	40.5	57.1
Friends	11.5	30.8	57.7	2.4	11.9	85.7
Doctor	8.3	58.3	33.3	16.7	21.4	61.9

would be unreasonable to attempt to encapsulate the whole profession in this way. Both in the mailed questionnaire and in the interviews, questions were raised about how career choices materialised and what influences came to bear. Here the decision to enter medicine and decisions about specialty choice first as undergraduates and then after doing registration house jobs are briefly examined.

Entry to medical school and thus the choice of medicine as a career was determined largely through family influences. As Table 11.1 shows family was the greatest factor for all ten graduating classes (especially those with medical parents), with doctors of their acquaintance coming a fairly poor second, although in the 1964 group school-teachers became much more prominent as influencers. All three of these groups tend to remain as influences as the medical career progresses, though inevitably spouses gain an ascendancy once they appear on the scene. For some students becoming a doctor fulfilled vicariously a parental ambition to enter medicine. For others it was a significant event which affected the decision. In the 1954 group more than half had completed compulsory military service and whilst this merely deferred medical school for most it provided others with the unexpected impetus and means (i.e. special grants for ex-servicemen) to embark on medical training. Personal experience of illness or that of a relative, or of a relative's death were important influences for about 10 per cent of entering students.

In response to questions about significant events and their influence on specialty choice (see Table 11.2), marriage headed

TABLE 11.2   'Significant events' and career choice by sex (%)

	Influenced entry to medicine		Affected choice specialty		No effect		
	M	F	M	F	M	F	N
	1.2	1.2	47.7	86.6	50.5	12.2	415
Children	0.3	0.0	34.0	91.9	65.7	8.1	380
Own illness	14.9	9.4	12.0	28.1	73.1	62.5	207
Finance	1.6	1.5	37.6	20.6	59.2	77.9	387
Economic/ political	1.7	1.7	22.9	10.0	74.7	88.3	357

the list for men (47.9 per cent) and whilst important for women (86.6 per cent) was outstripped by the arrival of children (91.9 per cent) (Elston 1980). Money and the economic and political climate as it affected medicine also figure as important but lesser determinants of career choice - factors which manpower planners tend to assume as paramount.

These responses to direct questions are of interest and have a value of their own. However respondents were frequently likely to write comments on the questionnaires which expressed their opinions more forcefully. Below is a transcript of the spontaneous comments on significant life events which influenced specialty choice for the 1954 Liverpool cohort. Of the twenty statements, thirteen involve family; only a small number relate to work experiences or to medical school.

31256	Decision to emigrate to New Zealand.
31259	Married sooner than would have in order to get a job in general practice. Financial matters gave some anxiety and unbalanced concentration on the job.
31260	Having young children of my own was a tremendous help in my career as a young family doctor.
31263	Availability of government grant - ex-service.
31267	See previous comments re disappointment in professional maladvice and disgust with declining patient service in NHS and bulldozing attitudes of politicians e.g. Mrs Castle and Sir George Godber.
31269	Difficulties in marriage delayed career and probably reduced potential.
31271(F)	Would probably have managed own single-handed practice, but it was available when I was admitted for major surgery, so passed to others.
31284	My first wife became involved with drugs and alcohol and when we divorced in 1972, I had to stay on a high income to pay off alimony.
31293	Parental encouragement.
31294	General practice was very difficult without a wife twenty years ago.
31298	I married during my first house job and was keen to settle down as quickly as possible in general

	practice.
31304(F)	Father died six months before qualification and I have never been free of financial and emotional support for my mother.
31303(F)	Marriage.
31311	Marriage prevented me from going on for further qualifications, and own illness prevented me from taking on extra responsibilities in general practice.
31312	Looking for complete job satisfaction.
31316	Uncertain of the reason - always wished to be a doctor.
35318	Marriage and children made me more content and determined to make a success of general practice. Political interference is the one thing I find irritating.
31322	Birth of children in America led to reappraisal of situation, and priorities resulted in a return to England as we did not wish our children to suffer from being brought up in an English home in another country.
31323	Marriage before entering university. Increasing State planning and control over medical organisation.
31325	Dr Charles Bryan (Uncle Bryan to me from an early age). General practitioner and surgeon (FRCS) to cottage hospitals in the Rhondda Valley. Trained in America on money earned as a mortician; never doubted I would be a doctor.

Of the respondents, 209 commented on the people who had influenced them in career choices, 99 cited a family member, 32 a doctor (other than a relative) 20 teachers, 9 friends and 49 other sources of influence, often a war-time acquaintance.

Questions about influences on specialty choices during the final undergraduate year reflect the expected impact of medical teachers, especially those in clinical fields. In scores of brief testimonies there are accounts of particular individual senior doctors whose enthusiasm, efficiency, authority, kindness, ability to teach or sheer stature in the medical community, have marked the lives of impressionable students. What is fascinating about these influences is their total unpredictability, their range and the great variety of consequences for the subsequent career routes of students. A number of cases described 'Damascus road' conversions to specialties hardly known about or valued previously. In this way recruits were magnetised into the less prestigious aspects of medicine like pathology, geriatrics, forensic medicine and anaesthetics. Some examples drawn at random:

> Senior lecturer in physiology who acted as devil's advocate, making me sure that my choice was right, despite drawbacks.
> Dr Helen Mayer (Obs & Gynae) in London had the most constructive influence on my career - both at the student and post-graduate level. As a teacher she inspired me, and as a chief she developed my self-confidence.
> Dr Williams Evans, Cardiologist, stimulated my interest in cardiology. I attended his open ward rounds throughout my clinical years.
> I wanted to specialise in surgery because I admired my surgical professor at the time I was a student. He was very good both as a surgeon and a teacher.
> The uncongenial attitudes of the medical students and doctors I met, confirmed my preference for psychiatry.

Such comments as these suggest a powerful but uncontrolled set of influences emanating from the medical school which bears little relation to the conception of it as a socialising agency. The effects of individual teachers can be as negatively strong as they can be positive. In examining the many references to figures involved, the study identified three main categories which are well supported in the data but still require full verification. The most prominent clinicians of the medical schools, often achieving world-wide reputations and knighthoods or peerages, we had identified prior to the survey and interviews. These were termed *Stars*. They were however seldom overwhelming career influences being too remote, and often too frightening, for the young student or houseman to know, and, because of their eminence, often away from their duties. Yet for those who served under such men later in their careers they could prove great influences and powerful patrons. Lord Moran at St Mary's and Lord Cohen at Liverpool are good examples.

The second type of influence observable in respondents' reports we termed *Imprinters*. These were often well known in the medical schools as individualists either of personality or practice. Their personal approach to the specialty they exercised or taught was characteristic and presented with great effect. Good communicators of well respected ideas, these Imprinters were able to exercise influence over more people than those they worked with directly and their specialties tend to be disproportionately represented in early career preferences. It was as though they were able to imprint their views and enthusiasms on impressionable minds. Not all imprinting was positive and some were firmly turned against career options by some Imprinters.

Whilst Stars and Imprinters were 'public' figures in their different ways, the third category, termed *Role Modellers*, were drawn from the whole range of teachers and colleagues. They were typically the good craftsman, the enthusiastic or diligent teacher, the caring practitioner and the encouraging and supportive head of a firm. Usually these doctors whose 'ways of doing' medicine were such excellent models were of senior status, but quite frequently we were given accounts of registrars and senior registrars who had this effect.

At the post-registration stage medical and family influences come more into balance at what is a testing and realistic choice making period. For after house jobs are completed, the decision, to enter general practice or seek a hospital training post, is crucial. The wrong choice of Senior House Officer jobs, i.e., in an inappropriate specialty or in an inferior hospital firm, could effectively block any further progress in the chosen field. Below is a further randomly selected page of comments from the Leeds 1964 group. They illustrate the variability of dominant influences, professional and non-professional.

22212	Wife and family - I have tended to choose my career in a way that gave the family greater stability as I saw it.
22213(F)	In a negative way - none of my chiefs have obstructed my progress. All have been helpful with references. All decisions and choices were mine.
22219(F)	Restriction of career because of husband and 4 children.
22222	I came to the teaching hospital where I now work in Canada, as senior resident (= 3-4 years Registrar). The Professor (Head of Dept) here greatly assisted

my study, techniques of exam passing and self concept, in a way no-one had ever done before. In the UK as long as you fill in a service grade, consultants really couldn't care less about you. 'Sorry you failed the Primary old chap. Hard luck'. Why not look closely at the candidate and try and find out why he's failing?

22223   Dr W.B. Smellie - advice regarding the choice of practice, and then by his experience and his teaching.

22225   Professor Goligher - taught me by example. Mr R.A. Hall - retired consultant surgeon at York. Clearly established in my eyes the superiority of a good district general consultant.

22229(F)   I married at the end of my second pre-registration job and as my husband went into general practice in his father's practice I joined him.

22232   My wife's health.

22234   My wife and subsequently my two daughters. I felt that I should be able to spend as much time at home as possible. Having served six years in the Royal Navy during which time there were many separations, my family life assumed even greater importance.

It should be noted that this is the stage at which the newly qualified doctor is faced with the task of evaluating his or her prospects of succeeding in a given specialty against the available competition and the known supply and demand factors (e.g. neuro-surgery, highly prestigious, highly competitive, long delay before achieving seniority but good financial rewards. Obstetrics and gynaecology, respectable, less competitive but fairly popular, demands less surgical skill, can expect consultancy earlier, etc.) Thus we may see the physician market as enormously complex and predictable only if the gross variables are taken alone. If we look at the private modes of decision making about career specialty, it is clear that we need more sophisticated models than those currently employed by manpower planners and economists, anxious to provide carrots and sticks to ensure that currently unfilled posts in 'shortage' specialties have enough recruits. This point was recently acknowledged by Maynard and Walker (1978) in their medical manpower forecasts for the Royal Commission on the National Health Service.

CONCLUSION

What we have not been able to do here is fully to demonstrate the dynamic relationship of occupational and other life careers, because space does not permit. However, the choice of career decision making has provided a focus for examining the biographical approach and its potentialities in the study of careers of all kinds.

In reviewing previous research and literature it was suggested that particular methodological issues, theoretical debates, funding policies and sheer chance, have played their part in denying us a complete view of the ways medical careers progress. Indeed there are few such studies in any of the professions. Despite this the sociological apparatus for doing biographical studies is well developed through the extension of the concept career beyond its conventional boundaries.

Throughout the discussion and the presentation of findings there has been a concern to re-examine common conceptions of who doctors are and how they behave as professional people. The Medical Careers Study has the potential not only to provide more detailed information about the formative factors in the dynamics of careers in medicine, but also to make a contribution to the sociology of the professions. It is demonstrable from the data available that stereotypical conceptions of doctors (and no doubt other professionals too) as individuals whose occupational careers are the dominant careers in their lives, are open to serious challenge. Of course there are doctors who behave in that way but the data frequently indicate that other life careers (especially marriage) suffer as a consequence. More commonly, there are compromises at strategic phases in career development.

Perhaps more striking than these observations are the results of doctors' accounts of the increasing trade-offs many are making between clinical work, money and the opportunity to engage in non-professional activities. Individual responses to social changes in family roles and to the changing political economy of health care, have made the medical profession more volatile and less predictable than many commentators are aware. The consequences of these changes and formerly unseen processes are significant not only for our understanding of professional careers, but for the whole notion of profession.

NOTES

1.   The Medical Careers Study, from which this paper is drawn, was funded by the Social Science Research Council and conducted from the Nuffield Centre for Health Service Studies, University of Leeds. The author wishes to make special acknowledgement to Mary Ann Elston who was Research Fellow on the study and whose work and ideas have contributed significantly to what is written here. He also wishes to thank Anne Edwards for preparing the typescript for publication.
2.   The results reported in this section are drawn in part from the End of Grant report prepared for the SSRC (Johnson and Elston 1979).

12 Becoming a Judge

ALAN PATERSON

In writing this paper I was faced with an initial difficulty. Whether one adopts a functionalist view of professions, concentrating on their core values and attributes, a 'trait' model, a professionalisation approach, a folk concept notion, or even if one rejects all these perspectives on professions regarding them instead as abstract classes of occupations (as Professor Freidson argues in this volume), it is not clear that judges[1] in the United Kingdom constitute an occupational group to which the label 'profession' has or can be attached.

True, judges have considerable power. Superficially at least, they have occupational autonomy - judicial independence is a fundamental attribute of being a judge - and occupational control in the sense of defining producer/consumer relations. They do have a monopoly of certain functions in our society, though not of esoteric knowledge or even skill. Furthermore an attenuated career structure does exist for judges, though in practice one can only commence a judicial career when one has reached the age of forty (or fifty in the case of most senior appointments).

On the other hand there are limits to their occupational autonomy - a senior judge who flaunts his prejudices, political biases and his willingness to take bribes is likely to be subject to more sanctions than ostracism by his colleagues, including the possibility of removal - a process which lies in the hands of Parliament. Unlike the United States we have no code of judicial ethics, no requirements of financial disclosure and our formal disciplinary structure is minimal.[2] Though there are shared understandings concerning the role of a judge and many informal modes of discipline the occupational group has no monopoly of these. Thus fellow Benchers of the Inns of Courts and members of the Bar can and do apply sanctions to aberrant judges, in fact in Scotland a recognised part of the role of the leader of the Bar - the Dean of the Faculty of Advocates - is to rebuke judges who have transgressed in their conduct towards members of the bar. Neither are assessments of technical competence entirely in the hands of the occupational group - again barristers and Benchers form part of the larger community in which assessments of merit are made. There is no professional association of judges,[3] no professional schools or formal training, and though there are *rites de passage* there is no credentialing process except perhaps by fiat. Competence is assumed from appointment. It is not a service oriented occupation except in the most general sense - judges have no clients, and it is in a sense axiomatic that they have none. Judges may not take sides, show partiality or take fees from litigants. Judicial notions of service to the community in the abstract contrast starkly with a reality which defines judicial time as more important than litigants' and which often contains little or no emergency service, e.g. where protective injunctions are required by battered wives. Finally, I can find no evidence that judges in the UK or any of the groups with whom they interact, regard the occupation as a profession. Judges do not seem to desire that label - to want to 'accomplish' profession. Thus it is interesting that the drive in this country for judges to become more 'professional' by introducing training for judges in sentencing seems to derive not so much from the spontaneous awareness of the occupation of its shortcomings, but more from bureaucratic pressure located outside the occupation. As the recent Working Party on Judicial Studies and Information (1978) reported, its:

> provisional proposals that a three to four week 'training course' should be undertaken ... by all new judges before sitting, attracted (quite apart from the dislike of the word 'training') a heavy preponderance of adverse comment, particularly, but not exclusively, from the judiciary and the Bar. The primary objection advanced was that a period of three to four weeks would be too long. Many felt that it would be difficult to maintain interest for such a period and that for persons of the intellectual calibre of judges, who can be expected to absorb knowledge quickly and to become equally disenchanted with anything less than the best use of their time, short and intensive periods of study are likely to be both more effective and more

acceptable than longer and more leisurely ones. (para. 3-13)

It is almost as though to become a judge is to attain a status that is higher than that of a profession. If this is so it suggest a three tier model of the occupational world, viz: occupations, occupations with a certain status (professions would fall in this group) and occupations of even higher status (consisting in part of individuals who have graduated from the middle stage). From this perspective the Bar is a school of professionals from whom some will graduate to the judiciary. Similarly Bishops, statesmen or even 'box-office stars' of the screen and stage can be seen to have transcended the status of priest, politician and actor respectively. In reinforcement of this argument one can point to certain continental legal systems which have a career judiciary which is entered on leaving law school. Individuals embarking on such careers are sometimes described in this country as entering a profession but they are not perceived in their own country or here as having as high a status as a judge in the United Kingdom. Space does not permit me to elaborate further on the three tier model, though hopefully it will be of interest to those who respond to Freidson's call for a switch to the sociology of occupations.

It follows from the argument which I have been advancing that the study of the process of becoming a judge is not so much one in professional socialisation as a study in occupational recruitment (including the socialisation of the individual entrants). Yet the literature on professional socialisation is of more than passing relevance and the general framework adopted in this paper is partly derived from a work on the professional socialisation of nurses (Olesen and Whittaker 1968) which focussed on three levels of the socialisation process, the environmental, the relational and the inner. Similarly this paper will cover the institutional structures involved in becoming a judge, the interaction process of role acquisition and the individual adjustments of self, consequent on the transition from barrister or solicitor to judge.

THE INSTITUTIONAL STRUCTURE OF THE APPOINTING PROCESS: SHARED AND NOT SO SHARED UNDERSTANDINGS

Figures 12.1 and 12.2 contain simplified models of the judicial hierarchy in the United Kingdom.[4]

In some respects appointment to the higher judiciary in the United Kingdom and to the Federal Bench in the United States are quite similar. In each case the appointment is in the hands of a member of the executive who not infrequently delegates the task, and in each case the appointment only takes place after an elaborate process of consultation. To adopt Harold Chase's graphic analogy - the appointment of these judges can be likened to a baseball game. Although there is a well defined set of rules and players it is safe to say that no two games are exactly alike. Judicial appointments are made pursuant to law and custom largely from a 'lineup' of individuals who occupy prescribed positions. Yet the 'players' interact within the normative framework differently each time. This is not to suggest he adds, 'that there are no established patterns. Rather the point is made to stress that the "play" which is involved in each appointment is *sui generis*' (Chase 1972, p.3).

The established patterns and expectations in the UK have only gradually become public knowledge. In practice appointment to the higher judiciary in England is in the hands of the head of the judiciary, the Lord Chancellor, who is curiously also a member of the executive and thus a political appointee with a limited security of tenure. The consultation process varies with the appointment to be made. In the case of a vacancy in the High Court Bench he first consults his Permanent Secretary (Coldstream 1959, p.41) for the appointing process is, in a sense, continuous (p.43) and each new Lord Chancellor's ideas of suitable candidates are merely fresh inputs into a complex machinery. (Under the Permanent Secretary the Lord Chancellor's Office maintains a list of qualified candidates who may be considered for judicial appointment and detailed records of all counsel who have applied to the Lord Chancellor to become QCs, which are continually updated in an elaborate card index).

Sometimes he consults the Law Officers or other senior members of the Bar but there is no expectation that he should do so. In this area much depends on the relationship between, and the personalities of, the individuals concerned.[5] On the other hand he invariably consults the Heads of Division, i.e. the Master of the Rolls, the Lord Chief Justice, the President and the Vice-Chancellor, and they expect to be so consulted.[6] In the words of Lord Hailsham LC (1975, p.254), at these meetings;

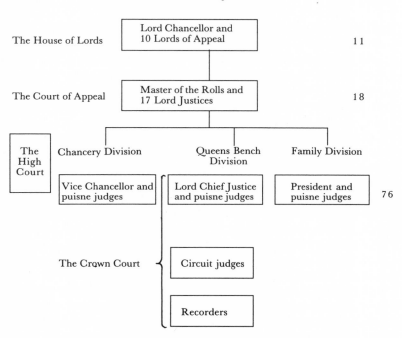

FIGURE 12.1   The judicial hierarchy in England and Wales

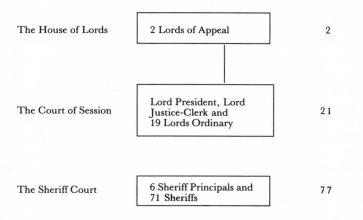

FIGURE 12.2   The judicial hierarchy in Scotland

A number of names is always discussed. There is never a vote, but a consensus is usually arrived at, at which, not unnaturally, the President of the Division in which the vacancy has occurred carries more weight than the others ... . I never remember a case in which the decision, when made, was not in fact a collective one.[7]

In Scotland, by contrast High Court appointments are almost at the gift of the chief Law Officer, the Lord Advocate, who frequently nominates himself, and it is only rarely that the Secretary of State will reject a Lord Advocate's nominations. As one ex-Lord Advocate said recently 'I appointed myself and a jolly good appointment it turned out to be too'. The appointing process to the US federal Bench contains elements of both the English and the Scottish approach but is largely dominated by indigenous factors, and under Carter's administration it became even more complex. The initial suggestions may, as in England, come from the executive's records of likely candidates (compiled in the US by the Justice Department) but considerable attention is paid to names proposed by senators of the State (if they belong to the President's party), names which themselves may derive from a nominating commission, and to those proposed by party leaders. (For circuit court judgeships President Carter set up his own merit selection panels.) The candidate who emerges from this must be passed by the ABA Standing Committee on Federal Judiciary, survive a thorough investigation by the FBI, avoid a senatorial veto, and be confirmed by the Senate Judiciary Committee and the Senate.

WHO ARE MADE JUDGES?

The criteria for selection which are stipulated by law are minimal in the United Kingdom. Five, ten or fifteen years as a barrister or, for some posts, as a solicitor, is all that is required. The formal criteria in the US are even less. The most minimal criteria apply to the Lord Chancellor who requires no legal qualification at all. However these constitutional minima have been greatly enlarged by tradition and practice. Neither solicitors nor academic lawyers may aspire to high judicial office in the UK with any hope, although they may in the US. Such posts in the UK are almost exclusively the preserve of successful QCs (or existing judges) and since even the better barristers do not take silk until their twelfth to fifteenth year at the Bar, in practice much greater standing at the Bar is insisted on than the minimum qualification. This means that the field for recruitment to the High Court (76 puisne judges - although not all are vacant at once) consists of about 400 active silks; and in Scotland 30 practising QCs compete for 27 senior judicial posts. In the US neither the Justice Department nor the Senate insist on substantial experience as a court lawyer in a candidate, though the ABA Committee requires fifteen years of significant legal experience if a candidate is to obtain a good rating, and the ABA pressed without success for the standards and guidelines under the Omnibus Judgeship Act 1978 to require a candidate to have substantial experience as a trial lawyer.

In the UK the pool for selection is further curtailed since in the general run of appointments, moral considerations, physical and mental attributes, legal expertise and political experience may all be considered by the appointers.[8] Thus at one time divorcees were excluded from the Bench. Times have changed now, so that even in presbyterian Scotland divorcees have been appointed to the Court of Session - indeed one of our latest appointments has been divorced twice. It is still likely, however, that a Dean of Faculty who was married to a judge's daughter and consorting with another lady, as one in the 1940s was, would be denied judicial appointment. Candidates who have been accused or convicted of a serious criminal offence or professional misconduct, gone bankrupt or become involved in a scandal are likely to find advancement difficult either in the UK or the US.

On both sides of the Atlantic judicial candidates are expected to be in good health,[9] and in the case of Circuit judges in England this is expressly required by statute.[10] The practical importance of this can be seen from the fact that it is not uncommon now for litigants in the UK who are involved in a lengthy proof to insure the life of the judge for sums up to £250,000 to protect themselves from the expenses involved in a re-trial should the judge die while hearing the cases.

The age of candidates is also important. No High Court judge has been appointed in the United Kingdom in the past 25 years who was aged 40 or less and very few under 45. The average age of such appointments between 1944 and 1970 was 53 and under Lord Elwyn-Jones it rose to 54. On the other hand no High Court judge in the past 25 years has been over 65 on appointment. In the United States the ABA Committee does not favour first appointments to the judiciary if the nominee is 60 or older. Such age limits again reduce the pool for selection.

Lord Chancellors look for candidates with a judicial temperament, i.e. impartiality, common sense, patience, politeness and ultimately the ability to make up one's mind (Goddard 1959, p.131; Kilmuir 1964, pp.302-3). Ideological factors also play a part, for the virtual irremoveability of senior judges once appointed does much to engender a spirit of caution in the appointers. As Abel-Smith and Stevens (1968, p.177) argue, 'It is probable that either too 'advanced' or too 'reactionary' political views could prevent appointment.' This is not an invariable rule however for candidates with relatively extreme political views - left and right - have been appointed, as have some with extrovert or unorthodox opinions on other matters. Indeed one of the arguments used by those who oppose the introduction of judicial selection commissions either in this country or in the US is the allegation that committees tend to produce nominations that are 'too safe' and hence lead to a mediocre judiciary.[11] Certainly the ABA Committee has been criticised in the past for allowing ideological factors to influence their ratings of candidates (Goldman and Jahnige 1976, pp.51-3: Chase 1972, pp.155-64). Whatever the truth of the matters Senators and Presidents have unquestionably demonstrated a concern with the ideological outlook of their nominees - but usually their interest has been to ensure that the ideology squared with their own rather than to ascertain whether it was too extreme (Goldman and Jahnige 1976, pp.59-63).

As far as political involvement is concerned appointments to the Bench in the UK as a reward for party political service are now very largely a thing of the past (Paterson 1974, pp.120-6; Shetreet 1976, pp.67-76). Political experience while no handicap, no longer confers the advantage that once it did, except that is, in Scotland. Only 9 per cent of the higher English judiciary are former politicians or candidates whereas in Scotland 52 per cent of the higher judiciary have been involved in party politics. Yet, to be fair to Scotland, Lord Advocates have frequently appointed judges from the other party. In the US, federal judicial appointment as a reward for party service has not died out and prior to the Carter administration over 90 per cent of appointees to the federal judiciary adhered to the party of the President (Abraham 1975, p.71).

Finally Lord Chancellors, the ABA Committee and the Senate all look for legal competence in a candidate, and success as an advocate and the experience gained from a large practice are also valued (Kilmuir 1964) though intellectual calibre on its own will not suffice.

While the foregoing remarks have outlined the general criteria applied in the appointing process it is important to note that in particular appointments more specific considerations may arise. For instance the vacancy may require to be filled by a QC with a particular specialisation. It is not just that a Queens Bench judge is normally replaced by a common law counsel - the vacancy may require a commercial or an Admiralty specialist. The Lord Chancellor may also be considering whether there are sufficient younger judges of first instance of the calibre required to staff the Court of Appeal and the House of Lords in the future (Kilmuir 1964, p.302). Or the pressure of business in the relevant division may put a premium on appointing a man who is likely to be expeditious in his handling of cases (Coldstream 1959, p.43).

In conclusion then it can be seen that the institutional structure of judicial appointment in England is one that leaves the judiciary with considerable occupational autonomy. Appointment is largely in the hands of the head of the judiciary who takes advice from other élite members of the occupation. Similarly, the qualities sought in candidates are largely the product of the same actors' perceptions of occupational requirements. On the other hand in Scotland and even more so in the US the occupational group has less autonomy in these areas.

INDIVIDUAL AND INTERACTIONAL ASPECTS OF BECOMING A JUDGE

From the perspective of an individual, 'becoming a judge' involves several elements - occupational choice, socialisation, career pattern and self/role adjustment following appointment. There is a body of literature on occupational choice - but there are only a handful of studies on why people become lawyers (Warkov and Zelan 1965; Mercer 1970; Erlanger and Klegon 1978) and I have been unable to trace any study on why certain individuals become judges. In the remainder of this paper I shall refer to some of the models contained in the literature which we have, but unfortunately until such time as the necessary fieldwork is undertaken it is difficult to assess how apt a description the models provide of the process of becoming a judge.

We know from judicial biographies that some individuals do decide at a very early age that they want to be appointed to the Bench. (Macmillan 1952, p.141; Hailsham 1975, pp.97 and 125; Birkenhead 1959). But whether these judges are representative of judges as a whole is impossible to say. Certainly it has traditionally been asserted that appointment to the High Court bench is the pinnacle of a career at the Bar. Since it is not unusual for those embarking on a career to contemplate the potential rewards which that career has to offer it is perhaps reasonable to surmise that many of those called to the Bar will have given some consideration to the possibility of a judicial appointment at a later stage. Indeed the proliferation of lesser judicial posts and the shortage of candidates to fill them at the present time ensures that any barrister of average ability who survives the Bar for ten to fifteen years can expect to get a post as a Circuit Court judge or a Sheriff in Scotland, if he so desires. When all is said and done it is difficult to be more specific about the timing of an individual's definite determination to become a judge. Ginzberg's (1951) assertion that occupational choice 'is not a single decision, but a series of decisions over a period of years' seems to apply to becoming a judge, not least because one cannot embark directly on a judicial career. Since appointment as a senior judge takes fifteen to twenty years longer than, say, appointment as a medical consultant it is likely that any firm decision to become a judge will be taken much later than the decision to become a consultant. In America (and for all we know, in this country) even the decision to do medicine is typically made much earlier than the decision to do law (Thielens 1957, p.181).

There are a wealth of studies of the social background of senior judges in the UK.[12] All of them have come up with similar results. Over 75 per cent of our higher judiciary have been to public schools and Oxbridge (a pattern which has held remarkably steady for the past 100 years) (Tate 1975, pp.24-31). Over 75 per cent of the higher judiciary for the past 100 years have come from the upper and middle classes. (Quoted in Justice 1972, p.79.) Such evidence as there is indicates that in the past 25 years the percentage of appointees with lower social origins has in fact been decreasing. Judicial appointments in Scotland (Willock 1969) to the Circuit Court (Cecil 1972) and to the American federal Bench (Goldman and Jahnige 1976, pp.66-9) are also dominated by white males of élite social origin and/or educational background though to a lesser extent than appointments to the higher judiciary in England and Wales. In short the status of this occupation remains as much ascribed as achieved - a state of affairs which seems at least in part attributable to the organisation and structure of the Bar. In theory entry to the Bar, like the Ritz Hotel, is open to everyone. In practice the problems of getting started, i.e. obtaining finance, a pupillage and a tenancy in chambers all systematically discriminate against those without private means, professional connections or an élite education. Maureen Cain (1976, pp.237-8) has pointed out that the ability to 'get on' with the senior members in chambers, and to share their world view are considerable assets for a pupil or a junior and that such abilities are likely to come more readily to a candidate with a similar background to the senior members. Individuals from other social backgrounds who intuit that this is so may well have to resort in true Goffman (1959) style, to presenting images of themselves that harmonise with the prevailing background expectancies in the chambers.

Women in particular are discriminated against in obtaining tenancies but a woman from a working class background will have very considerable problems. Even as late as 1969 the Bar Council was to be found telling the Monopolies Commission that,

> The fact has to be faced that the profession of barrister requires the masculine approach (however fallacious it may be) to reasoning and argument, and women only succeed in such activities if they have a masculine disposition. (Quoted in Kennedy 1978, p.158.)

With only 9 female QCs practising in England (there are about 450 male ones), and only 10 women Benchers out of 500 or so, the female cause has far to go in its quest for parity.[13]

Judges in the UK receive no formal training before their appointment.[14] Many of today's judges did not study law at university and those who did are unlikely to be much influenced in their judicial behaviour by what they learnt thirty years earlier -

even supposing that the course contained anything of value for potential judges. Since much of the literature on professional socialisation has concentrated on the processes of enculturation and acculturation taking place while the student is undergoing institutional schooling, it is of limited value when one is considering the occupational socialisation of a judge. On the other hand some researchers have stressed the importance of a neophyte's interaction with practitioners and with his peers during and after apprenticeship, for the negotiation of the content of his occupational role. Such researches do seem applicable to the Bar, for evaluation by barrister colleagues and by sitting judges is an everyday feature of life at the Bar.

Even at this stage in the acquisition of an occupational identity barristers are very different from medical graduates, for they lack the neat stepping stones of residencies, house jobs, registrar rotations, senior registrarships and then consultancies. Not for barristers the in-house training, the phased and controlled confrontation with problem cases of the medical graduate. Instead pupillage gives way to trial by error with the occasional assistance of sympathetic judges or more senior counsel. The skill of the legal craftsman is not systematically acquired. Medical graduates in their post-university training have the opportunity to savour a variety of specialisations before deciding which if any they wish to pursue. Barristers who wish to specialise may have to choose to do so at an earlier stage in their career, i.e. at the commencement of pupillage, than medical students, and with less information. Alternatively, the barrister may follow the specialisation, if any, of the chambers in which he gets a tenancy. Given the extreme shortage of tenancies at present, the temptation is strong for barristers to accept any tenancy they can get and thus to accept the specialisation, if any, accompanying that tenancy. In Scotland where advocates do not operate in chambers, the size of the practising Bar (140 or so) and the flow of available work does not encourage specialisation. In England most barristers particularly in the provinces, are generalists working in common law chambers. Lincoln's Inn is the home of Chancery chambers (dealing with trusts, tax, settlements and company work) but there are more specialist chambers in commercial law, patent law, planning law, tax law, admiralty law and defamation.

This process of occupational socialisation for potential judges is unlike medical socialisation in a further respect - for they are not being trained for the position which they may ultimately achieve, namely a judicial post, but to be something quite different, that is, a successful advocate. Moreover their specialisations as advocates may be irrelevant to the judicial posts which they ultimately attain. Despite this, as other researchers have shown (Becker and Carper 1956) it is not unusual for occupational choice to involve some kind of anticipatory socialisation, and this undoubtedly occurs amongst barristers. Members of the Bar have clear ideas about what is and what is not acceptable judicial behaviour, within and without the court. Bencher QCs in particular, who work and lunch with judges throughout the week have ample opportunities for assessing the requirements of the judicial role.

CAREER PATTERNS AND ROUTES OF JUDICIAL APPOINTMENT

A marked feature of several of the studies of professional socialisation is the way that would-be professionals intuitively divide techniques of survival that smooth the transition from layperson to professional. Such techniques are available to the would-be judge. As we have seen 'getting-on' in chambers is something that can be worked on. Fifty years ago junior counsel who were ambitious did not touch divorce cases for 'divorce work was considered inferior and unpleasant' (Denning 1980, p.187). Today there are still certain cases which counsel should avoid if success is desired (Hazell 1978, p.134). Counsel who only handle criminal cases for the defence and never prosecute do their chances of promotion little good. In Scotland it has been made clear to QCs who have no criminal practice that if they wish to be considered for appointment to the High Court Bench (where they will hear criminal cases) it is in their interests to become part-time prosecuting counsel (advocates-depute) for a year or two. This advice has not been ignored - in future the Scottish Bench will have fewer members who are innocent of criminal work but rather more who have only experienced criminal cases from the viewpoint of the prosecutor. Undoubtedly there are career patterns which constitute quicker routes to the Bench. The Bar, like other professions, is segmented (Bucher and Strauss 1961, p.325) and some segments offer better chances of advancement than others. The relative paucity of practising Chancery QCs means that statistically their chances of High Court appointment are higher than those of common law QCs (except perhaps those of QCs practising in the commercial specialist chambers). At one time, in fact, promotion of Chancery QCs appears to have been done on a 'cab-rank' basis (Faulks 1978, p.114). Being a barrister politician used to constitute a major short cut to advancement, but not any more. In the words of Bucher and Strauss (1961, p.324), 'the fate of individual careers is closely tied to the fate of segments and careers that were possible for one generation may not be repeatable for the next.' What then are the routes to the Bench now? Having served in the Law Commission seems to be one. Both in England and Scotland barristers who have served a stint in the Law Commission are being promoted to the Bench, indeed there is some evidence to suggest that as an incentive for the leading barristers to go to the Commissions they are given undertakings of judicial advancement. Serving as a member of the Bar Council (the professional association of the Bar) and particularly service as a vice-Chairman of it, seems to be another route to advancement, for most recent Chairmen of the Council have been appointed to the High Court. In Scotland the Lord Advocate is not the leader of the Bar as the Attorney General is in England. The leader is the Dean of the Faculty of Advocates and he is elected by all the advocates annually. Since 1900 all but four Deans have been promoted to the Bench. And one of those four who was not, was the philanderer mentioned earlier. Some regard this route as an ideal method of judicial appointment since it is both elective and appointive in character. Benjamin Franklin recommended its introduction in America, remarking that under the Scots system you could guarantee that the Bar would elect the best man to be Dean because when he was elevated to the Bench they would be able to share his practice amongst themselves.[15]

Perhaps the least discussed route in England is the one that has received the greatest official recognition and encouragement. It is by serving as a temporary or part-time judge while still at the Bar. The appointing authorities are aware that some good advocates in the past have been unable to make the role transition from partisan to umpire on their elevation to the Bench. Accordingly, before the Beeching reorganisation of the Criminal Courts in 1971, the Lord Chancellor's Department would frequently 'invite' potential judges to sit as a Commissioner of Assize for a month or two, in order to ascertain whether they had the qualities to make the transition. Such 'invitations' were in fact nearer to orders and were ignored only at the candidate's peril. A surprising number of such Commissioners who were sent out 'on sale or return' seem to have foundered.[16] (Faulks 1978, pp.115-17) Nowadays potential candidates are 'encouraged' to become part-time Recorders in the Crown Court (serving for one month a year). Sir Neville Faulks (1977, p.201) records that he did not apply to become a Recorder,

> But when a ghostly and unidentified voice from the Lord Chancellor's Department told me by telephone that it had been asked to find out why I hadn't applied, I surrendered and did so. For once, it is believed, you flout the Lord Chancellor's Department you have 'had' it, and although I had not thought of the Bench I didn't want to be foolish.

Curiously, while those seeking appointment to the Circuit Court or as a Recorder are officially encouraged to apply for the posts, with suitable references, applications for higher judicial appointments, though not infrequently made, are generally not sympathetically received (Shetreet 1976, p.51). Thus aspiring High Court judges should apply to become a Recorder but not for the post they are actually seeking.

THE ULTIMATE DECISION

Another aspect of becoming a judge that has been neglected by academic writers is the final decision by a candidate whether to become a judge or not. It might appear from much of what has been said that judicial posts are so much sought after that they are invariably accepted. This is not always true. A famous silk once summed up the Bar's attitude to judicial promotion with the comment: 'The Bench is like Heaven. Everybody wants to go there but not yet!' (Bowker 1961, p.247). Ultimate occupational choices of potential judges it seems, turn as in other occupations on an assessment of the rewards and penalties of the new job.

After ten to fifteen years at the Bar, senior juniors will have to decide whether to apply for silk and become a QC with the risk of reduction in income that may involve.[17] Alternatively, he might decide to apply for a post as Circuit Judge (or Sheriff in Scotland). Individuals caught in this situation can approach the appropriate authorities for advice as to their chances of obtaining silk or judicial appointment, but in England this is not always done, perhaps because of the candidate's ignorance of the possibility. If the barrister takes silk and fails he may then decide to apply for a lesser judicial appointment. But if he becomes a successful QC his earnings may be substantial. The average QC in England in 1976/77 was earning £19,500[18] and those at the top anything up to £60,000. High Court judges only received £18,675. So the offer of a judicial appointment will almost certainly involve a considerable drop in salary for a QC - and this has long been the case (Bowker 1961, p.54; Maugham 1954, p.334). This, together with some other drawbacks in becoming a judge which I shall come to shortly, makes it likely that some QCs will refuse appointment or be rather loath to take it up. And this is exactly what happens. Disraeli described the salary of a Lord of Appeal as sufficient to make a Scotsman's mouth water - but the first two Scots offered the post refused it and many Scottish judges since have followed suit, declining to leave their roots in Scotland. Various judges have declined to become Lord Chancellor or Master of the Rolls and not a few barristers have declined to be elevated to the High Court Bench including most Attorney-Generals since 1946. Of course it is true that most QCs would not consider rejecting such preferment (after all it confers prestige, it offers peace after the strenuous life of a top QC and it guarantees an index-linked pension), but no study of judicial recruitment is complete which ignores those who have declined appointment.

PROBLEMS OF TRANSITION – SELF/ROLE ADJUSTMENT

New judges encounter a number of difficulties on appointment which are if anything exacerbated by their relatively advanced age when taking up the fresh career, and by the paucity of the training which they receive to assist them to make the transition from Bar to Bench. The few seminars on sentencing (which is all the new appointee in England receives[19]) or on sentencing and on managing one's caseload (which the new Federal judge receives in America) (Cook 1971, p.253) have only a limited impact. Temporary service as a judge before appointment is rarely available to Chancery QCs, and even for the other QCs who have experienced it, it offers no panacea for the problems facing the fledgling full-timer.

In the first place the new judge encounters the problems of what Everett Hughes (1958, p.120) called 'a marginal man' - having to play the new role before one feels completely identified with it or competent to carry it out. As one High Court judge put it, in an interview with the author,

> One has got to develop a much more flexible mind to a point. As an advocate you have a role to play, a line to take and having worked out your best way of presenting that line, your task is then to hang on to it rather like a bull terrier and make sure that it's not whipped out of your grasp. You therefore start as a judge with this deficiency - when you feel X is the right line I think you are initially far less likely to leave hold of that point than you should be.

This danger of reverting to the role of the advocate has frequently been stressed by judges. Sir Gordon Slynn remarked in a radio broadcast in 1978,[20]

> If one has a court practice ... one spends a long period of one's working life ... trying to speak well and usually rather a lot. But the minute you are put on the Bench the great quality is silence, and if you try to talk too much, you immediately find yourself subject to criticism.

The transition creates other difficulties for self/role adjustment as Mr Justice Pain pointed out, in the same broadcast,

> All of a sudden people begin to make a fuss of you. It can go to your head. You've got to learn that the job is important but that you're just the same ordinary bloke when you're off the Bench.

The second problem facing the neophyte judge is the change in the work that he does from what he did at the Bar. His specialisation at the Bar is frequently not taken over to the Bench. Few QCs specialise in Family matters but recruits have to be found for this division of the High Court. At one time appointment to the Probate, Divorce and Admiralty Division (now the Family Division) was considered less attractive than to the Queens Bench and candidates who were offered posts in it (who might have little divorce or Admiralty experience) would stay only for a few years before transferring to the Queens Bench.

Such transfers are no longer common and some defamation or commercial specialists have settled into the Family Division very happily, in part because it has fewer circuits than the Queens Bench. Morris Finer, however, a highly successful commercial QC, appointed to that Division in 1972, described the move to *The Sunday Times*, as follows:

> It is menopausal. After breaking your back as a busy, high-paid Silk for many years, this is a total change. You start again. Not many professions let you do that ... . I have had very little to do with real life for many years, not looking at cases worth less than five million pounds to the parties. At the commercial bar, one didn't care too much who won, the insurance company or the bank. But in the Family Division you suddenly see that 98 per cent of cases are not like that at all. Here it is all about real life. There is very little law involved, it is all up to your discretion. It can lead to boredom, because the challenge is not intellectual. But it is very real and important work.[21]

Finer's experience is not unique - in Scotland the staple diet of any new Court of Session judge is undefended divorce, which he will not have dealt with for many years. In 1971 Mrs Justice Lane in an Admiralty case confessed that she was navigating in unaccustomed waters and took comfort in the knowledge that her decision could be reviewed in the Court of Appeal (Shetreet 1976, p.300). Litigant satisfaction is not likely to be increased on discovering that in the Court of Appeal the position may be little different. Marven Everett QC once remarked in an interview with the author that one of the things that struck him when arguing in the Court of Appeal was how dependent Chancery judges with no common law experience were on senior counsel to guide them through the law in common law appeals.

Finer's comment about judicial boredom also has support from other quarters. Mr Justice Eveleigh confessed in 1978

> By and large I think judging is a pretty boring job, quite honestly. There is an Act of Parliament which says that no one should do any sketching in Court. I offend against that every day of the week.[22]

In the words of Lord Summer, 'judging is always a stodgy job'

(Macmillan 1952, p.145). Yet new judges complain of quite different causes of fatigue. As one High Court judge observed with feeling, in an interview with the author,

> The judge's day in court is much more tiring than counsel's because he's got to concentrate all the time. As a member of the Bar you do your bit and then you sit back with an eye or half an eye on your opponent depending on who he is - perhaps with both eyes on him. But it's not the same degree of concentration - you don't have to write the stuff down.

In the previously-quoted broadcast, Sir Gordon Slynn also emphasised the physical aspects of the change:

> One transition that I found not entirely easy was having to sit still for periods of two and a half hours every morning, and not far short of that in the afternoon. I am afraid that there were times in the early days, when I seized on the slightest opportunity to adjourn for ten minutes, just so that I could walk to my room and walk back again.

ANCILLARY PROBLEMS

Commentators have frequently observed that some roles e.g. that of a priest or a policeman are more all embracing than others. In a sense such role-players are never off-duty. Clearly the role of the judge is such a role. In consequence the problems experienced by new judges extend beyond the work sphere. For instance the considerable drop in salary which most QCs undergo in becoming a judge can pose severe tax and other financial problems for them. Many have to draw on capital and a few have undoubtedly experienced hardship.

Again the all pervasive nature of the judicial role has a considerable impact on the social life of a judge. Several eminent judges, e.g. Lords Denning, Devlin and Hailsham have recently denied that judges are lacking in social awareness - yet it is difficult to argue that many judges and indeed QCs do not lead relatively sheltered lives. In the words of Justice Burton, his transition from the Senate to the US Supreme Court was like 'going direct from a circus to a monastery' (Berry 1978, p.27). Morris Finer's account to *The Sunday Times* of the effects of judicial preferment was equally graphic:

> Undoubtedly you get cut off. For years you were in a common room with many colleagues. Suddenly you are in a very small circle. There is a great *esprit de corps*, between people who in a real sense are the victims of a strange condition. They are bound to cling together. You cannot lunch in a pub because you might be sitting up at the bar with someone you will be seeing in court. You cannot have rows in shops, you can't shake a fist if someone cuts you out at the traffic lights, you have to watch your invitations. All this is necessary mainly because others expect it. The lay public imposes restrictions on judges which they might not impose on themselves.

The last comment has received support from Shetreet (1976, p.323) who discovered in his interviews with judges, barristers and laymen that,

> On the whole, non-lawyers and the legal profession, including leading counsel who in a year or two may sit on the Bench, hold stricter views on the standards of judicial conduct than do the judges themselves.

This may suggest that there is room for negotiation as to the content of a judge's role between the judges and their publics.

In the light of these problems it would not be surprising if some judges tried to resign their calling. Such behaviour is permitted in the United States but in the United Kingdom it is regarded as unacceptable. The cult of the robe forbids it. Several judges tried to resign and to return to the Bar on financial grounds when Churchill was Prime Minister but he refused to permit it.[23] A county court judge resigned in 1892 after six years to become a Liberal parliamentary candidate[24] but this was unique until 1970 when Sir Henry Fisher resigned from the High Court Bench after two years, to become a merchant banker. This event provoked considerable adverse comment and Lord Hailsham, then Lord Chancellor, indicated that in future he would tell all new judges 'that they should approach the Bench with the enthusiasm of a bridegroom approaching marriage, or of a priest approaching priesthood'.[25]

Apart from a 'pep-talk' such as that, which every new judge receives from the Lord Chancellor, little official assistance is offered to the judicial fledgling. His Head of Division will keep an eye on him and he can discuss problems with his colleagues and in cases of doubt go to his Divisional Head or the Lord Chancellor. Some training in sentencing is available to him as we have seen and this will increase if the recommendations of the Working Party on Judicial Studies and Information (1978) are implemented. One of the greatest assets of a new judge however, operates at a less conscious level to reduce the impact of his new isolation upon himself (though enhancing it on others). It is the elaborate pharaphernalia of robe, wig and ritual which accompanies a judge. It may be that uniforms and rituals like these help occupants of newly acquired roles to cope with the psychological, social, physical and economic risks in learning and doing their job as Everett Hughes (1958, pp.90 and 96) has suggested, by acting as risk spreading devices. For it is arguable that the trappings of judges encourage notions of their interchangeability and equal competence, in the eyes of beholders - thus negating their subjectivities and enabling the individual judge to obtain collective absolution by transferring part of his sense of guilt for his errors from his own shoulders to those of the larger company of his colleagues. But on this matter as on many that have gone before, any pronouncements must be treated with caution until someone undertakes the necessary fieldwork on the problems and processes of becoming a judge.

NOTES

1.   Unless otherwise indicated, references to 'judges' in this paper exclude the lowest tier of the judiciary - magistrates and district court judges who are largely laymen and to whom different considerations apply.
2.   Considerable doubt exists as to the procedures for the removal of the superior judiciary both in England and Scotland. Judges at a lower level are removeable by the Lord Chancellor or, in Scotland, the Lord President and Lord Justice Clerk, for inability, neglect of duty or misbehaviour. Alternatively, the judge may not be assigned any cases. Both of these sanctions are rather extreme. For a comprehensive discussion of the formal and informal disciplining of judges in the United Kingdom see Shetreet (1976).
3.   Such associations exist in the United States and amongst magistrates.
4.   As at February 1980.

5.   Because relations between Lord Gardiner and his Attorney-General, Sir Elwyn-Jones were cordial, he was often asked for his advice on judicial appointments. Sir Reginald Manningham-Buller (Attorney-General 1954-62) was actively involved in the process of judicial appointments. See Faulks (1978), p.115.

6.   Confirmed by Lord Gardiner in a letter to the author dated 16 May 1978. See also Hailsham (1975), p.254, and Elwyn-Jones (1975), p.45.

7.   Earl Jowitt, the Lord Chancellor in 1947 recorded that he had 'never appointed a judge without getting the willing approval and concurrence of my brother judges who sit in the staff of the particular division to which I am going to appoint the judge'. If this actually occurred in 1947 the enormous expansion of puisne judges since then must surely entail that it does not represent the current practice of Lord Chancellors now.

8.   Easily the most comprehensive account of the attributes sought in judicial candidates is contained in Shetreet (1976), pp.54-78.

9.   A High Court judge has told me that the Lord Chancellor's Office now insist on a candidate obtaining a medical certificate attesting to his state of health, prior to his appointment being announced.

10. The Courts Act 1971 s. 16(4).

11. I have heard this argument put forward by an official in the Lord Chancellor's Office as a justification for ignoring the suggestion contained in the Justice sub-committee's report on *The Judiciary* (1972, p.30), that a judicial appointment committee should be set up in the UK. The evidence from other countries, he said was that such commissions tended to go for compromise candidates who were sound and unadventurous. See also Senator Adlai Stevenson's (1978) attack on judicial commissions in the US for similar reasons.

12. For a recent summary of these see Griffith (1977), pp.24-31.

13. There are no women Law Lords or Lord Justices, only two female High Court judges, seven female Circuit judges and eight female Recorders. For a discussion of this see Helena Kennedy 'Women at the Bar' (1978) and *Women in the Legal Services* Evidence of Equal Opportunities Commission to the Royal Commission on Legal Services (1978).

14. Some judges feel that one cannot be trained to be a judge. See e.g. Radcliffe (1968), p.274. Others feel that such training would be an unacceptable intrusion on the independence of the judiciary. See e.g. Devlin (1979), p.52. Although the last Labour Government accepted the recommendations of the Working Party on Judicial Studies and Information (1978), that decision does not bind the present Conservative administration.

15. Debates of the Constitutional Convention, 5 June 1787.

16. It may be that QCs invited to serve as Deputy Judges now are also being 'tried out' in the way that Commissioners once were.

17. Sir Neville Faulks (1977, p.150) records that in his time most London QCs were bachelors or persons with independent means because married barristers disliked the risk involved in taking silk. While this is probably a slight exaggeration his general point seems to be well taken.

18. After paying personal pension premium. Survey carried out by the Bar Council for the Royal Commission on Legal Services, 1978.

19. See Working Party on Judicial Studies and Information 1978.
20. Hugo Young, 'Talking about the Law', broadcast 12 Aug. 1978 and reported in part in the *Listener* on 17 Aug. 1978.
21. Interview with Hugo Young. *The Sunday Times*, 5 Oct. 1975.
22. Quoted in 1978 *Journal of the Law Society of Scotland* 469. See also Faulks (1978, pp.130-1).
23. 525 H.C. Deb. 1063 (23 Mar. 1954).
24. The *Law Times* 9 Apr. 1892, p.404.
25. 312 H.L. Deb. 1314 (9 Nov. 1970).

Bibliography

Abel, R.L. (1980) 'The Sociology of American Lawyers: A Bibliographic Guide', *Law and Policy Quarterly*, 2, pp.335-91.

Abel-Smith, B. (1960) *A History of the Nursing Profession* (London: Heinemann).

Abel-Smith, B. (1964) *The Hospitals 1800-1948* (London: Heinemann).

Abel-Smith, B. and R. Stevens (1968) *In Search of Justice* (London: Allen Lane).

Abraham, H.J. (1975) *The Judicial Process* (New York: Oxford University Press) 3rd edn.

Abrams, P. (1968) *The Origins of British Sociology, 1834-1914* (Chicago: University of Chicago Press).

Alford, R. (1972) 'The Political Economy of Health Care: Dynamics Without Change', *Politics and Society*, 2.

Anderson, D. and W. Sharrock (1979) 'Biasing the News: Technical Issues in Media Studies', *Sociology*, 13, pp.361-85.

Anderson, H.B. (1977) 'Public Lawyers Group Gives Poor Defendants a Big-firm Advantage', *Wall Street Journal*, 1, col.1 (21 Sep).

Arluke, A. (1977) 'Social Control Rituals in Medicine: The Case of Death Rounds', in R. Dingwall, C. Heath, M.E. Reid and M. Stacey (eds), *Health Care and Health Knowledge* (London: Croom Helm) pp.107-26.

Armstrong, D. (1977) 'The Structure of Medical Education', *Medical Education*, 11, pp.244-8.

Armstrong, D. (1979) 'The Emancipation of Biographical Medicine', *Social Science and Medicine*, 13A, pp.1-8.

Asbury, E.E. (1979) '13.2 Million Fee to Law firms in Rothko Case', *New York Times*, B-1 (21 Feb).

Ashley, J.A. (1976) *Hospitals, Paternalism and the Role of the Nurse* (New York: Teachers College Press).

Atkinson, P.A. (1977a) 'Professional Segmentation and Students' Experience in a Scottish Medical School', *Scottish Journal of Sociology*, 2, pp.71-85.

Atkinson, P.A. (1977b) 'The Reproduction of Medical Knowledge', in R. Dingwall, C. Heath, M.R. Reid and M. Stacey (eds), *Health Care and Health Knowledge* (London: Croom Helm) pp.83-106.

Atkinson, P.A. (1981) *The Clinical Experience: the Construction and Reconstruction of Medical Reality* (Farnborough: Gower).

Atkinson, P.A., R. Dingwall and A. Murcott (eds) (1979) *Prospects for the National Health* (London: Croom Helm).

Atkinson, P.A., M.E. Reid and P.F. Sheldrake (1977) 'Medical Mystique', *Sociology of Work and Occupations*, 4, pp.243-80.

Auerbach, J.S. (1971) 'Enmity and Amity: Law Teachers and Practitioners, 1900-22', *Perspectives in American History*, 5, pp.551-601.

Auerbach, J.S. (1976) *Unequal Justice* (London: Oxford University Press).
Ayers, G.M. (1971) *England's First State Hospitals and the M.A.B. 1967-1930* (London: Wellcome Institute).
Baldwin, J. and M. McConville (1977) *Negotiated Justice: Pressures on Defendants to Plead Guilty* (London: Martin Robertson).
Bankowski, Z. and G. Mungham (1974) 'Warwick University Ltd, (continued)', *British Journal of Law and Society*, 1, pp.179-84.
Bankowski, Z. and G. Mungham (1976) *Images of Law* (London: Routledge and Kegan Paul).
Bankowski, Z. and G. Mungham (1978) 'A Political Economy of Legal Education', *New Universities Quarterly*, 32, pp.448-63.
Barker, R. (1980) 'Straight from the Horse's Mouth', *The Times Higher Education Supplement* (4 Apr) p.12.
Barnard, K. and K. Lee (eds) (1977) *Conflicts in the National Health Service* (London: Croom Helm; New York: Prodist).
Barry, D.D. and H.J. Berman (1968) 'The Soviet Legal Profession', *Harvard Law Review* 82, pp.1-41.
Baumann, Z. (1976) *Socialism: The Active Utopia* (London: Allen and Unwin).
Becker, H.S. (1967) 'Whose Side Are We On?', *Social Problems*, 14, pp.239-47.
Becker, H.S. (1970) 'The Nature of a Profession', in H.S. Becker *Sociological Work* (Chicago: Aldine).
Becker, H.S. (1972) 'School is a Lousy Place to Learn Anything', in B. Geer (ed.), *Learning to Work* (Beverly Hills: Sage).
Becker, H.S. and J. Carper (1956) 'The Development of Identification with an Occupation', *American Journal of Sociology*, 61, pp.289-98.
Becker, H.S., B. Geer and E.C. Hughes (1968) *Making the Grade: The Academic Side of College Life* (New York: John Wiley and Sons).
Becker, H.S., B. Geer, E.C. Hughes and A.L. Strauss (1961) *Boys in White* (Chicago: University of Chicago Press).
Bellow, G. (1977) 'Turning Solutions into Problems: The Legal Aid Experience'. *NLADA Briefcase*, 34, pp.106-25.
Ben-David, J. (1963-64) 'Professions in the Class System of Present-Day Societies', *Current Sociology*, 12, pp.247-330.
Ben-David, J. (1964) 'Scientific Growth: A Sociological View', *Minerva*, 2, pp.455-76.
Ben-David, J. (1971) *The Scientist's Role in Society. A Comparative Study* (Englewood Cliffs, N.J: Prentice-Hall).
Ben-David, J. (1977) *Centers of Learning: Britain, France and the United States* (New York: McGraw-Hill).
Bennion, F. (1971) 'The Plight of the Professions', *Law Society Gazette*, 68, pp.87-91, 168-70.
Benson, J.K. (1973) 'The Analysis of Bureaucratic-Professional Conflict: Functional Versus Dialectical Approaches', *The Sociological Quarterly*, 14, pp.378-9.
Benson, J.K. (ed.) (1977a) *Organisational Analysis: Critique and Innovation* (London: Sage).
Benson, J.K. (1977b) 'Organisations: a Dialectical View', *Administrative Science Quarterly*, 22.
Bernstein, B. (1971) 'On the Classification and Framing of Educational

Knowledge', in M.F.D. Young (ed.), *Knowledge and Control: New Directions for the Sociology of Education* (London: Collier - Macmillan) pp.47-69.

Bernstein, P.W. (1978) 'The Wall Street Lawyers are Thriving on Change', *Fortune*, 97, (13 Mar) pp.104-12.

Berry, M.F. (1978) *Stability, Security and Continuity* (Connecticut: Greenwood Press).

Birkenhead, Lord (1959) *F.E.* (London: Eyre and Spottiswoode).

Bittner, E. (1963) 'Radicalism and the Organisation of Radical Movements', *American Sociological Review*, 28, pp.928-40.

Bittner, E. (1965) 'The Concept of Organisation', *Social Research*, 32, pp.239-255.

Bittner, E. (1975) 'Florence Nightingale in Pursuit of Willie Sutton: A Theory of the Police', in V. Herbert (ed.), *The Potential for Reform of Criminal Justice, Vol. III, Sage Criminal Justice System Annuals* (Beverly Hills: Sage).

Blatch, W.D. (1966) 'It is an Ill Wind', *Law Society Gazette*, 63, p.29.

Blau, P.M. and B. Schoenherr (1971) *The Structure of Organisations* (New York: Basic Books).

Bledstein, B.J. (1976) *The Culture of Professionalism* (New York: Norton).

Bloom, S. (1965) 'The Process of Becoming a Physician', *Annals of the American Academy of Political and Social Science*, 343, pp.77-87.

Bloom, S. (1973) *Power and Dissent in the Medical School* (New York: Free Press); first printed as 'The Medical School as a Social System', *Milbank Memorial Fund Quarterly*, 49, 2, Part 2, (1971).

Blumberg, A.S. (1967) *Criminal Justice* (Chicago: Quadrangle Books).

Bodine, L. (1979a) 'Law Firm Ladder Gets a New Rung', *National Law Journal*, 1, (12 Mar).

Bodine, L. (1979b) 'The Church that Sues Like Hell', *National Law Journal*, 1, (9 Jul).

Bolton Law Society (1974) 'Instructional Advertising', *Law Society Gazette*, 71, p.589.

Bond, D.H. (1957) *A Half-Century of Nursing in West Virginia* (Charleston, W. Va: West Virginia State Nurses' Association).

Bourdieu, P. and J.C. Passeron (1977) *Reproduction in Education and Society* (London: Sage).

Bowker, A. (1961) *A Lifetime with the Law* (London: W.H. Allen).

Brainard, A. (1919) *Organisation of Public Health Nursing* (New York: Macmillan).

Bridges, L., B. Sufrin, J. Whetton and R. White (1975) *Legal Services in Birmingham* (Birmingham: University of Birmingham, Institute of Judicial Administration).

Brook, J. (1976) 'Women Registrars in Psychiatry: Background and Career Intentions', *British Journal of Psychiatry*, 128, p.599 et seq.

Bucher, R. (1970) 'Social Process and Power in a Medical School', in M.N. Zald (ed.), *Power in Organizations* (Nashville: Vanderbilt University Press).

Bucher, R. and J. Stelling (1969) 'Characteristics of Professional Organisations', *Journal of Health and Social Behavior*, 10, pp.3-15.

Bucher, R. and A.L. Strauss (1961) 'Professions in Process', *American Journal of Sociology*, 66, pp.325-34.

Bulgakov, M. (1976) *A Country-Doctor's Notebook*, (London: Fontana).

Burrows, R.J.F. (1964-65) Law Society *Annual Report*, 12.

Business Lawyer (1978) 'A Businessman's View of Lawyers: A Program', *The Business Lawyer*, 33, pp.817-45.

Business Week (1968) 'Why Law is a Growth Industry', *Business Week*, 13 Jan, pp.78-9.

Butler, J.R., J. Bevan and R.C. Taylor (1973) *Family Doctors and Public Policy* (London: Routledge and Kegan Paul).

Butler, R.N. (1963) 'The Life Review: An Interpretation of Reminiscence in Old Age', *Psychiatry*, 26, pp.65-76.

Byrne, P.S. and B.E.L. Long (1976) *Doctors Talking to Patients* (London: HMSO).

Cain, M. (1976) 'Necessarily Out of Touch', in P. Carlen (ed.), *The Sociology of Law* (Keele: Sociological Review Monograph 23).

Cairnes, J.E. (1887) *Some Leading Principles of Political Economy Newly Expounded* (London: Macmillan).

Campbell, C. and P. Wiles (1976) 'The Study of Law in Society in Britain', *Law and Society Review*, 11, pp.547-78.

Campbell, D., P. Smith and P.A. Thomas (1980) *Annotated Bibliography on the Legal Profession and Legal Services, 1960-1978* (Cardiff: University College, Cardiff Press).

Caplow, T.A. (1954) *The Sociology of Work* (Minneapolis: University of Minnesota Press).

Carlin, J. (1962) *Lawyers on their Own* (New Jersey: Rutgers University Press).

Carlin, J. (1966) *Lawyers' Ethics* (New York: Russell Sage).

Carlin, J.E. and J. Howard (1965) 'Legal Representation and Class Justice', *UCLA Law Review*, 12, pp.381-437.

Carr-Saunders, A.M. (1928) *Professions: Their Organisation and Place in Society* (Oxford: Clarendon Press).

Carr-Saunders, A.M. and P. Wilson (1964) *The Professions* (London: Oxford University Press); first published Frank Cass 1933.

Cecil, H. (1972) *The English Judge* (London: Arrow Books).

Chase, H. (1972) *Federal Judges: The Appointing Process* (Minneapolis: University of Minnesota Press).

Church, Jr, T., A. Carlson, J. Lee and T. Tan (1978) *Justice Delayed: The Pace of Litigation in Urban Trial Courts* (Williamsburg, Va.: National Center for State Courts).

Coghill, N.F., R.W. Revans, F.M. Ulyatt and K.N. Ulyatt (1970) 'A Study of Consultants', *Lancet*, (8 Aug) pp.305-8.

Coldstream, Sir George (1959) 'Judicial Appointments in England', *Judicature*, 43, p.41.

Collins, R. (1975) *Conflict Sociology: Towards an Explanatory Science* (New York: Academic Press).

Conveyancer (1972) 'Leader', pp.81-2.

Cook, B.B. (1971) 'The Socialisation of New Federal Judges', *Washington University Law Quarterly*.

Coombs, R.H. (1978) *Mastering Medicine: Professional Socialization in Medical School* (New York: Free Press).

Corwin, R. (1961) 'The Professional Employee: a Study of Conflict in Nursing Roles', *American Journal of Sociology*, 66.

Coser, L. (1978) 'American Trends', in T. Bottomore and R. Nisbet (eds), *A*

History of Sociological Analysis (London: Heinemann).

Cotgrove, S. and S. Box. (1970) *Science, Industry and Society* (London: Allen and Unwin).

Council of the Law Society (1968) *Memorandum of Evidence by the Council of the Law Society to the Monopolies Commission into the Supply of Professional Services* (London: The Law Society).

Council of the Law Society (1969) *Memorandum on the Road Safety Act 1967* (London: The Law Society)

Council of the Law Society (1972) 'Memorandum of the Council of the Law Society on Conveyancing Remuneration', *Law Society Gazette*, 68, pp.386-7.

Cowan, E. (1978) 'Attorneys Quit F.T.C. Oil Case', *New York Times*, D-1, (26 Jun).

Crouse, T. (1974) *The Boys on the Bus* (New York: Ballantine).

Daheim, H. (1973) 'Professionalisierung. Begriff und einige latente Makrofunktionen', in G. Albrecht, H. Daheim and F. Sack (eds), *Soziologie: René König zum 65. Geburtstag* (Opladen: Westdeutscher Verlag) pp.232-49.

Damaska, M. (1978) 'A Foreign Perspective on the American Judicial System' in T.J. Fetter (ed.), *State Courts: A Blueprint for the Future* (Williamsburg; Va: National Center for State Courts) pp.237-2.

Davies, C. (1979a) 'Hospital-Centred Health Care: Policies and Politics in the National Health Service', in P. Atkinson, R. Dingwall and A. Murcott (eds), *Prospects for the National Health* (London: Croom Helm) pp.53-72.

Davies, C. (1979b) 'Organisation Theory and the Organisation of Health Care: a Comment on the Literature', *Social Science and Medicine*, 13A, pp.413-22.

Davies, C. (1980a) 'A Constant Casualty: Nurse Education in Britain and the USA to 1945', in C. Davies (ed.), *Rewriting Nursing History* (London: Croom Helm).

Davies, C. (1980b) 'Making Sense of the Census in Britain and the USA', *Sociological Review*, 28.

Davies, C. and A. Francis (1976) 'Perceptions of Structure in NHS Hospitals', in M. Stacey (ed.), *The Sociology of the NHS* (Keele: Sociological Review Monograph 22).

Dawe, A. (1970) 'The Two Sociologies', *British Journal of Sociology*, 21, pp.207-8.

Day, R. and J.V. Day (1977) 'A Review of the Current State of Negotiated Order Theory: an Appreciation and a Critique', in J.K. Benson (ed.), *Organisational Analysis: Critique and Innovation* (London: Sage).

Dell, S. (1971) *Silent in Court* (London: G. Bell and Sons. Occasional Papers on Social Administration No. 42).

Demaine, J. (1977) 'On the New Sociology of Education', *Economy and Society*, 6.

Denning, Lord (1980) *The Due Process of Law* (London: Butterworths).

Denzin, N.K. (1970) *The Research Act in Sociology: A Theoretical Introduction to Sociological Methods* (London: Butterworths).

Désrosières, A. (n.d.) 'Elements pour l'histoire des nomenclatures socio-professionelles', in F. Bédarida *et al.*, *Pour un Histoire de la Statistique*, Vol. 1, (Paris: Institut National de la Statistique et des Études Économiques) pp.155-94.

Devlin, Lord (1979) *The Judge* (Oxford: Oxford University Press).

Dingwall, R. (1976) 'Accomplishing Profession', *Sociological Review*, 24, pp.331-49.

Dingwall, R. (1977a) *The Social Organisation of Health Visitor Training* (London: Croom Helm).

Dingwall, R. (1977b) *Aspects of Illness* (London: Martin Robertson, New York: St. Martin's Press).

Dingwall, R. and J.M. Eekelaar (1979) 'Social and Legal Perceptions of Child Neglect: Some Preliminary Considerations', *Child Abuse and Neglect*, 3, pp.303-14.

Dingwall, R., G. Payne and J. Payne (1980) 'The Development of Ethnography in Britain', BSA Annual Conference, 1980, published as Centre for Socio-Legal Studies Occasional Paper.

Dock, L. (1949) 'The Relations of Training Schools to Hospitals', in I. Hampton and Others *Nursing of the Sick 1893* (New York: McGraw-Hill).

Dornbusch, S.M. (1955) 'The Military Academy as an Assimilating Institution', *Social Forces*, 32, pp.321-7.

Douglas, C. (1977) *The Houseman's Tale* (London: Fontana).

Douglas, C. (1980a) *The Greatest Breakthrough since Lunchtime* (London: Fontana).

Douglas, C. (1980b) *Bleeders Come First* (London: Fontana).

Duman, D. (1979) 'The Creation and Diffusion of a Professional Ideology in Nineteenth Century England', *Sociological Review*, 27, pp.113-38.

Elliott, P. (1972) *The Sociology of the Professions* (London: Macmillan).

Elston, M.A.C. (1980) 'Medicine' in R. Silverstone and A. Ward (eds), *Careers of Professional Women* (London: Croom Helm).

Elwyn-Jones, Lord (1974) 'The Lord Chancellor's Aims', *New Law Journal*, 124, p.282.

Elwyn-Jones, Lord (1975) 'The Office of Lord Chancellor', *Graya*, 79, pp.43-5.

Emshweiller, J.R. (1978) 'Using the Law's Delay, Myron Cherry Attacks Atomic-Power Projects', *Wall Street Journal*, 1, col 1, (10 Mar).

Engel, G.V. (1969) 'The Effect of Bureaucracy on the Professional Autonomy of the Physician', *Journal of Health and Social Behavior*, 10.

Engel, G.V. (1970) 'Professional Autonomy and Bureaucratic Organisation', *Administrative Science Quarterly*, 15.

Erlanger, H.S. and D.A. Klegon (1978) 'Socialisation Effects in Professional School', *Law and Society Review*, 13, pp.11-35.

Etzioni, A. (1964) *Modern Organisations* (Englewood Cliffs, N.J.: Prentice-Hall).

Faulks, Sir, N. (1977) *No Mitigating Circumstances* (London: William Kimber).

Faulks, Sir, N. (1978) *A Law Unto Myself* (London: William Kimber).

Fitzgerald, J.M. (1975) 'The Contract Buyers League and the Courts: A Case Study of Poverty Litigation', *Law and Society Review*, 9, pp.165-95.

Fitzpatrick, M.L. (1975) *The National Organisation for Public Health Nursing, 1912-1952: Development of a Practice Field* (New York: National League of Nursing).

Flexner, A. (1915) 'Is Social Work a Profession?' in *Studies in Social Work*, No.4, (New York: New York School of Philanthropy).

Flynn, C.A. and F. Gardner (1969) 'The Careers of Women from the Royal Free Hospital', *British Journal of Medical Education*, 3, pp.28-42.

Fogarty, M., R. Rapoport and R.M. Rapoport (1971) *Sex, Career and Family* (London: PEP/Allen and Unwin).

Fores, M. and I. Glover (1978) 'The British Disease: Professionalism', *The Times Higher Education Supplement* (24 Feb) p.15.

Foucault, M. (1977) 'Intellectuals and Power', in D.F. Bouchard (ed.), *Language Counter-Memory, Practice,* (Oxford: Basil Blackwell).

Fox, R. (1957) 'Training for Uncertainty', in R.K. Merton, *et al.* (eds), *The Student Physician* (Cambridge, Mass: Harvard University Press).

Fredericks, M.A. and P. Mundy (1976) *The Making of a Physician* (Chicago: Loyola University Press).

Freidson, E. (1970a) *Profession of Medicine: A Study of the Sociology of Applied Knowledge* (New York: Dodd, Mead and Co.).

Freidson, E. (1970b) *Professional Dominance: The Structure of Medical Care* (Chicago: Aldine-Atherton).

Freidson, E. (1973) 'Professionalisation and the Organisation of Middle-Class Labour in Post-industrial Society', in P. Halmos (ed.), *Professionalisation and Social Change* (Keele: Sociological Review Monograph. No. 20) pp.47-59.

Freidson, E. (1975) *Doctoring Together: A Study of Professional Social Control* (New York: Elsevier).

Freidson, E. (1977) 'The Futures of Professionalisation', in M. Stacey, M.E. Reid, R. Dingwall and C. Heath, (eds), *Health and the Division of Labour* (London: Croom Helm) pp.14-38.

Fried, C. (1976) 'The Lawyer as Friend: The Moral Foundations of the Lawyer-Client Relation', *Yale Law Journal,* 85, pp.1060-89.

Friedman, L.M. (1965) 'Freedom of Contract and Occupational Licensing, 1890-1910', *California Law Review,* 43, pp.481-534.

Friedman, L.M. and Z.L. Zile (1964) 'Soviet Legal Profession: Recent Developments in Law and Practice', *Wisconsin Law Review,* pp.32-77.

Friedman, M. (1962) *Capitalism and Freedom,* (Chicago: University of Chicago Press).

Friedman, M. and S. Kuznets (1945) *Income from Independent Professional Practice,* General Series no. 45, (New York: National Bureau of Economic Research).

Galanter, M. (1968-69) 'Introduction: The Study of the Indian Legal Profession', *Law and Society Review,* 3, pp.201-18.

Galanter, M. (1973) Untitled talk on some Bases for the Comparison of Legal Professions reported at *International Legal Center Newsletter,* 9 (Jul).

Galanter, M. (1974) 'Why the "Haves" Come Out Ahead: Speculations on the Limits of Legal Change', *Law and Society Review,* 9, pp.95-160.

Galanter, M. (1976) 'Delivering Legality: Some Proposals for the Direction of Research', *Law and Society Review,* 11, pp.226-46.

Galanter, M. (1979) 'Justice in Many Rooms', *Working Paper 1979 - 4, Disputes Processing Research Program* (University of Wisconsin Law School).

Galbraith, J. (1973) *Designing Complex Organisations* (Reading, Mass: Addison-Wesley).

Galuccio, N. (1978) 'The Rise of the Company Lawyer', *Forbes,* 123 (18 Sep), pp.168-81.

Gamarnikow, E. (1978) 'Sexual Division of Labour: the Case of Nursing', in A. Kuhn and A. Wolpe (eds), *Feminism and Materialism* (London: Routledge and Kegan Paul).

Gaskell, E. (1964) 'Bibliography of Hospital History', in F.N.L. Poynter (ed.), *The Evolution of Hospitals in Britain* (London: Pitman).

Gay, P. (1970) *Weimar Culture: the Outsider as Insider* (New York: Harper and Row).

Geer, B. (ed.) (1972) *Learning to Work*, (Beverly Hills: Sage).

Geer, B., J. Haas, C.V. Vona, S.J. Miller, C. Woods and H.S. Becker (1968) 'Learning the Ropes: Situational Learning in Four Occupational Training Programs', in L. Deutscher and E.J. Thompson (eds), *Among the People* (New York: Basic Books) pp.223-8.

Gella, A. (1976) 'An Introduction to the Sociology of the Intelligentsia', in A. Gella (ed.), *The Intelligentsia and the Intellectuals: Theory, Method and Case Study* (London: Sage).

Gellner, E. (1974) *Legitimation of Belief* (Cambridge: Cambridge University Press).

Gilb, C.L. (1966) *Hidden Hierarchies: The Professions and Government* (New York: Harper and Row).

Ginzberg, E. (1951) *Occupational Choice* (New York: Columbia University Press).

Glaser, B. and A.L. Strauss (1971) *Status Passage* (London: Routledge and Kegan Paul).

Goddard, L. (1959) 'Politics and the British Bench', *Judicature*, 43, p.131.

Goffman, E. (1959) *The Presentation of Self in Everyday Life* (New York: Doubleday).

Goffman, E. (1961) 'Fun-in-Games', in *Encounters* (Indianapolis: Bobbs-Merrill).

Goffman, E. (1968) *Asylums* (Harmondsworth, Penguin); first printed as *Asylums: Essays on the Social Situation of Mental Patients and Other Inmates* (New York: Anchor-Doubleday, 1961).

Goldman, S. and T.P. Jahnige (1976) *The Federal Courts as a Political System* (New York: Harper and Row, 2nd edn).

Goldner, F.H. and R.R. Ritti (1967) 'Professionalisation as Career Immobility' *American Journal of Sociology*, 72.

Goode, W.J. (1957) 'Community Within a Community: The Professions', *American Sociological Review*, 22, pp.194-200.

Goode, W.J. (1960) 'Encroachment, Charlatanism, and the Emerging Profession: Psychology, Sociology, and Medicine', *American Sociological Review*, 25, pp.902-14.

Goode, W.J. (1969) 'The Theoretical Limits of Professionalization', in A. Etzioni (ed.), *The Semi-Professions and their Organization* (New York: Free Press) pp.266-313.

Goode, W.J., R.K. Merton and M.J. Huntington (1956) *The Professions in Modern Society* (New York: Russell Sage Foundation, mimeo).

Goulden, J.C. (1972) *The Superlawyers: the Small and Powerful World of the Great Washington Law Firms* (New York: David McKay Co).

Gouldner, A.W. (1962) 'Anti-Minotaur: The Muth of a Value-free Sociology', *Social Problems*, 9, pp.199-212.

Gouldner, A.W. (1978) 'The New Class Project', *Theory and Society*, 6, pp.153-203 and 343-89.

Gramsci, A. (1971) *Selections from the Prison Notebooks* (London: Lawrence and Wishart).

Granvill, S. (1973) Vol. 123, *New Law Journal*, p.1144.

Green, M.J. (1975) *The Other Government: the Unseen Power of Washington Lawyers* (New York: Grossman/Viking).

Green, P. (1979) 'Review of J. Fonterose, *The Delphic Oracle*' (University of

California Press) in *New York Review of Books* (5 Apr) p.12.

Greenwood, E. (1957) 'Attributes of a Profession', *Social Work*, 2, pp.44-55.

Griffith, J. (1977) *The Politics of the Judiciary* (London: Fontana).

Gusfield, J. (1976) 'The Literary Rhetoric of Science, Comedy and Pathos in Drinking Driver Research', *American Sociological Review*, 41, pp.16-34.

Gyarmati, G. (1975) 'Ideologies, Roles and Aspirations. The Doctrine of the Professions: the Basis of a Power Structure', *International Social Science Journal*, 27, pp. 629-54.

Haas, J. and W. Shaffir (1977) 'The Professionalization of Medical Students: Developing Competence and a Cloak of Competence', *Symbolic Interaction*, 1, pp.71-88.

Hailsham, Lord (1971) 'The Lord Chancellor's Address', *New Law Journal*, 121, pp. 934-5.

Hailsham, Lord (1975) *The Door Wherein I Went* (London: Collins).

Hall, O. (1948) 'The Stages of a Medical Career', *American Journal of Sociology*, 53, pp.327-36.

Hall, R.H. (1968) 'Professionalisation and Bureaucratisation', *American Sociological Review*, 33.

Handler, J. (1967) *The Lawyer and his Community* (Wisconsin: University of Wisconsin Press).

Handler, J. (1978) *Social Movements and the Legal System: A Theory of Law Reform and Social Change* (New York: Academic Press).

Harris, C.M. (1974) 'Formation of Professional Attitudes in Medical Students', *British Journal of Medical Education*, 8, pp.241-5.

Harris, D.K. (1972) 'Correspondence', *Law Society Gazette*, 69, p.468.

Hart Jackson, R. de L. (1972) 'Correspondence', *Law Society Gazette*, 69.

Hazard, Jr., G.C. (1978) *Ethics in the Practice of Law* (New Haven: Yale University Press).

Hazell, R. (ed.) (1978) *The Bar on Trial* (London: Quartet Books).

Heidenheimer, A. *et al.* (1975) *Comparative Public Policy* (London: Macmillan).

Heinz, J.P. and E.O. Laumann (1978) 'The Legal Profession: Client Interests, Professional Roles and Social Hierarchies', *Michigan Law Review*, 76, pp.1111-42.

Henderson, L.J. (1935) 'Physician and Patient as a Social System', *New England Journal of Medicine*, 212, pp.819-23.

Hillyard, S. (1975) 'Providing Legal Services', *New Law Journal*, 25, pp.1044-7.

Hoffman, P. (1973) *Lions in the Street: The Inside Story of the Great Wall Street Law Firms* (New York: Saturday Review Press/E.P. Dutton).

Horobin, G.W. (1973) *Experience with Abortion: A Case Study of North-East Scotland* (Cambridge: Cambridge University Press).

Horobin, G.W. and J. McIntosh (1977) 'Responsibility in General Practice', in M. Stacey, M.E. Reid, R. Dingwall and C. Heath (eds), *Health and the Division of Labour* (London: Croom Helm) pp.88-111.

Horwitz, M.J. (1977) *The Transformation of American Law, 1780-1860*, (Cambridge: Mass: Harvard University Press).

Hughes, E.C. (1956) 'The Making of a Physician', *Human Organisation*, 14, pp.22-5.

Hughes, E.C. (1958) *Men and their Work* (Glencoe, Ill: Free Press).

Hughes, E.C. (1971) *The Sociological Eye* (Chicago: Aldine).

Hurst, J.W. (1950) *The Growth of American Law: The Law Makers* (Boston: Little, Brown).

Illich, I. (1975) *Medical Nemesis: The Expropriation of Health* (London: Calder and Boyars).

Illich, I. (1977) *Disabling Professions* (London: Marion Boyars).

Jacob, H. (1969) *Debtors in Court: The Consumption of Government Services* (Chicago: Rand-McNally).

Jamous, H. and B. Peloille (1970) 'Professions or Self-perpetuating Systems? Changes in the French University-hospital System', in J.A. Jackson (ed.), *Professions and Professionalisation* (Cambridge: Cambridge University Press) pp.111-52.

Jarman, F. (1980) 'The Development of Conceptions of Nursing Professionalism among General Hospital Nurses, 1860-1895', M.A. Thesis, University of Warwick.

Jewson, N.D. (1974) 'Medical Knowledge and the Patronage System in 18th Century England', *Sociology*, 8, pp.369-85.

Jewson, N.D. (1976) 'The Disappearance of the Sick-Man from Medical Cosmology, 1770-1870', *Sociology*, 10, pp.225-44.

Johnson, Jr., E., S. Bloch, A. Drew, W. Felstiner, E. Hansen and G. Sabagh (1979) 'Comparative Analysis of the Statistical Dimensions of the Justice System of Seven Industrial Democracies'. A report submitted to the National Institute for Law Enforcement and Criminal Justice.

Johnson, M.L. (1976) 'That was Your Life: A Biographical Approach to Later Life', in J.M.A. Munnichs and W.L.A. van den Hevval (eds). *Dependency and Interdependency in Old Age* (The Hague: Martinus Nijhoff). Reprinted in V. Carver and P- Liddiard (eds), *An Ageing Population: A Reader and Sourcebook* (London: Hodder and Stoughton/Open University Press 1978).

Johnson, M.L. (1978) 'Biographies and the Assessment of Needs in Older People', Paper presented at the 9th World Congress of Sociology, Uppsala.

Johnson, M.L. (1974) *Ageing in Society: Relations and Relationships*, Block 1, Unit 4 (Milton Keynes: Open University Press).

Johnson, M.L. and M.A.C. Elston (1979) 'Medical Careers, an end of grant report to the Social Science Research Council', (London).

Johnson, T.J. (1972) *Professions and Power* (London: Macmillan).

Johnson, T.J. (1977) 'The Professions in the Class Structure', in R. Scase (ed.), *Industrial Society: Class, Cleavage and Control* (London: Allen & Unwin) pp.93-110.

Johnstone, Q. and D. Hopson Jr. (1967) *Lawyers and their Work: An Analysis of the Legal Profession in the United States and England* (Indianapolis: Bobbs-Merrill).

Jowitt, Earl (1967) 'Message from Britain', *American Bar Association Journal*, 33.

Justice (1972) *The Judiciary* (London: Stevens).

Justice (1977) *Lawyers and the Legal System* (London: Justice).

Kaelble, H. (1978) 'Soziale Mobilität in Deutschland, 1900-1960', in H. Kaelble *et al.*, *Probleme der Modernisierung in Deutschland* (Opladen: Westdeutscher Verlag) pp.235-327.

Kakutani, M. (1980) 'Do Facts and Fiction Mix?', *New York Times Book Review*, (27 Jan) pp.28-9.

Katz, M.B. (1972) 'Occupational Classification in History', *Journal of Interdisciplinary History*, 3, pp.63-88.

Keating. P. (ed.) (1976) *Into Unknown England 1866-1913: a Selection from the Social Explorers* (London: Fontana).

Kendall, P.L. (1965) *The Relationships Between Medical Education and Medical Practitioners: Sources of Strain and Occasions for Cooperation* (Evanston: Association of American Medical Colleges).

Kennedy, H. (1978) 'Women at the Bar', in R. Hazell (ed.), *The Bar on Trial* (London: Quartet Books) pp.149-50.

Kennedy, H. (1978) *Women in the Legal Services*, Evidence of Equal Opportunities Commission to the Royal Commission on Legal Services.

Kervasdoué, J., de. and J. Kimberly (1978) 'Are Organisation Structures Culture-Free? The Case of Hospital Innovations in the U.S. and France', in A. Negandi and B. Wilpert (eds), *Cross Cultural Studies on Organisational Functioning* (Ohio: CARI Press).

Kessel, R.A. (1958) 'Price Discrimination in Medicine', *Journal of Law and Economics*, 1, pp.20-53.

Kilmuir, Lord (1964) *Political Adventure*, (London: Weidenfeld and Nicholson).

King, M. (1973) 'The Allocation of Criminal Legal Aid in Magistrates Courts - A Study in London Courts', *Law Society Gazette*, 70.

King, M. (1976) *The Effects of a Duty Solicitor Scheme* (London: Cobden Trust).

Klegon, D.A. (1978) 'The Sociology of Professions: an Emerging Perspective', *Sociology of Work and Occupations*, 5, pp.259-83.

Klerman, G.L. and D.J. Levinson (1969) 'Becoming the Director: Promotion as a Phase in Personal-Professional Development', *Psychiatry*, 32, pp.411-27.

Kocka, J. (1977) *Angestellte zwischen Faschismus and Demokratie* (Gottingen: Vandenhoeck and Ruprecht).

Kohlmeier, L.H. (1976) 'Antitrust Litigation: It's Big Business', *New York Times*, 111-12, col. 3, (21 Nov).

Kornhauser, W. (1962) *Scientists in Industry* (Berkeley: University of California Press).

Kosa, J. (1970) 'Entrepreneurship and Charisma in the Medical Profession', *Social Science and Medicine*, 4, pp.25-40.

Kuhn, T.S. (1961) 'The Function of Measurement in Modern Physical Science', in H. Woolf (ed.), *Quantification: A History of the Meaning of Measurement in the Natural and Social Sciences* (Indianapolis: Bobbs-Merrill).

Kuhn, T.S. (1970) *The Structure of Scientific Revolutions* (Chicago: Chicago University Press, revised edition).

Kumar, K. (1978) *Prophecy and Progress: the Sociology of Industrial and Post-Industrial Society* (Harmondsworth: Penguin).

Ladinsky, J. (1963) 'Career of Lawyers, Law Practice and Legal Institutions', *American Sociological Review*, 47.

Lahr, J. (1980) *Prick Up Your Ears: the Biography of Joe Orton* (Harmondsworth, Penguin).

Landauer, J. (1977) 'Braniff's Bitter Battle to Curb a Little Rival Probed by Grand Juries', *Wall Street Journal*, 1, col. 1, (23 Jun).

Lane, M. (1980) 'Brave New Weltanschauungen: the intellectual context of sociology in Britain', paper given at BSA Annual Conference, Lancaster.

Larson, M.S. (1977) *The Rise of Professionalism: a Sociological Analysis* (London: University of California Press).

Laski, H.L. (1931) 'The Limitations of the Expert', *Fabian Tract*, No. 235.

Last, J.M. *et al.* (1968) 'Survey of British Medical Students in their First and Final Years', Appendix 19 to *Report of the Royal Commission on Medical Education*, Cmnd. 3569 (London: HMSO).

Laumann, E.O. and J.P. Heinz (1977) 'Specialization and Prestige in the Legal Profession: The Structure of Deference', *American Bar Foundation Research Journal*, pp.155-216.

Laumann, E.O. and J.P. Heinz (1979) 'The Organization of Lawyers' Work: Size, Intensity and Co-Practice of the Fields of Law', *American Bar Foundation Research Journal*, pp.217-46.

Lavine, D. (1979) 'It's Harder to Make Partner', *National Law Journal*, 1, (1 Oct).

Law Society, see Council of the Law Society.

Lawrence, T. (1975) "Letter", *Law Society Gazette*, 72, p.525.

Lefcourt, R. (1971) *Law Against the People* (New York: Random House).

Legal Action Group (1977) Editorial, *Legal Action Group Bulletin*, p.98.

Lenski, G. (1966) *Power and Privilege* (New York: McGraw-Hill).

Levin, M.A. (1977) *Urban Politics and the Criminal Courts* (Chicago: University of Chicago Press).

Leys, S. (1978) *Chinese Shadows* (Harmondsworth: Penguin).

Lindsey, R. (1978) 'Tax-Exempt Foundations Formed to Help Business Fight Regulation', *New York Times*, 1, col. 4, (12 Feb).

Litwak, E. (1961) 'Models of Bureaucracy which Permit Conflict', *American Journal of Sociology*, 67.

Llewellyn, K. (1933) 'The Bar Specialises - with what Results?', *Annals of the American Academy of Political and Social Sciences*, 167, p.177.

Lortie, D.C. (1959) 'Laymen to Lawmen: Law Schools, Careers and Professional Socialization', *Harvard Educational Review*, 29, pp.352-69.

Lyden, F.J., H.J. Geiger and O. Peterson (1968) *The Training of Good Physicians: Critical Factors in Career Choices* (Cambridge, Mass.: Harvard University Press).

Lyle Belsley, G. (1937) 'Nursing and the Merit System', *American Journal of Nursing*, 37.

Macaulay, S. (1979) 'Lawyers and Consumer Protection Laws', *Law and Society Review*, 14, pp.115-71.

McCormick, J. (1979) *The Doctor: Father Figure or Plumber* (London: Croom Helm).

McIntosh, J. and G.W. Horobin (1978) 'General Practice in Remote Areas: attractions, expectations and experience', *Journal of the Royal College of General Practitioners*, 28, pp.227-32.

Macintyre, S. and D. Oldman (1977) 'Coping with Migraine', in A.G. Davis and G.W. Horobin (eds) *Medical Encounters. The Experience of Illness and Treatment* (London: Croom Helm) pp.55-71.

McIver, P. (1940) 'Public Health Nursing in the US Public Health Service'. *American Journal of Nursing*, 40.

Macmillan, Lord (1952) *A Man of Law's Tale* (London: Macmillan).

Malcolm, J. (1966) *Lets Make It Legal* (Reading: Educational Explorers Ltd).

Manson, T. (1976) 'Management, the Professions and the Unions: A Social Analysis of Change in the National Health Service', in M. Stacey, M.E. Reid, R. Dingwall and C. Heath (eds), *Health and the Division of Labour* (London: Croom Helm) pp.196-214.

Margolick, D.M. (1980) 'Wall Street's True Blue Chip', *National Law Journal*, 1 (14 Jan).

Marshall, T.H. 'The Recent History of Professionalism in Relation to Social Structure and Social Policy', *Canadian Journal of Economics and Political Science*, 5, pp.325-40.

Marx, K. (1953) 'The Eighteenth Brumaire of Louis Bonaparte', in *Marx and Engels: Selected Works*, Vol. 1 (London: Lawrence and Wishart; originally published 1855).

Marx, K. (1976) 'The German Ideology', in *Collected Works V*, (London: Lawrence and Wishart).

Maugham, Viscount (1954) *At the End of the Day* (London: Heinemann).

Maurice, M. (1972) 'Propos sur la Sociologie des Professions', *Sociologie du Travail*, 13, pp.213-25.

Maxwell, N. (1977) 'Southern Law Firm Fights Death Penalty With Tough Tactics', *Wall Street Journal*, 1, col. 4 (20 Jun).

Maynard, A. and A. Walker (1978) *Doctor Manpower 1975-2000: Alternative Forecasts and their Resource Implications* (London: HMSO).

Medcalf, L. (1978) *Law and Identity* (Beverly Hills: Sage).

Megarry, R. (1962) *Lawyer and Litigant in England* (London: Stevens).

Mercer, H. (1970) 'Occupational Choice among Law Students', unpublished Sociology Dissertation at Edinburgh University.

Merton, R.K. (1957) 'Manifest and Latent Functions', in *Social Theory and Social Structure*, revised edition (New York: Free Press) pp.19-84: first published 1949.

Merton, R.K. (1957) 'Some Preliminaries to a Sociology of Medical Education', in R.K. Merton, G. Reader and P.L. Kendall (eds), *The Student Physician* (Cambridge, Mass: Harvard University Press) pp.3-79.

Merton, R.K. (1960) *Some Thoughts on the Professions in American Society* (Providence: Brown University Papers, No. 37).

Merton, R.K. (1968) *Social Theory and Social Structure*, second revised edition (New York: Free Press); first published 1949; first revised edition 1957.

Miller, G.A. (1968) 'Professionals in Bureaucracy: Alienation among Industrial Scientists and Engineers', *American Sociological Review*, 32.

Miller, S.J. (1970) *Prescription for Leadership: Training for the Medical Élite* (Chicago: Aldine).

Millerson, G. (1964) *The Qualifying Associations* (London: Routledge and Kegan Paul).

Millman, M. (1976) *The Unkindest Cut: Life in the Backrooms of Medicine* (New York: M. Morrow) (paperback edition, 1978).

Mitchell, D. (1979) 'Synanon legal dept. - how legal is it?', *Point Reyes Light*, 1, (29 Mar).

Mnookin, R.H. and L. Kornhauser (1979) 'Bargaining in the Shadow of the Law: The Case of Divorce', *The Yale Law Journal*, 88, pp.950-97.

Moerman, M. (1974) 'Accomplishing Ethnicity', in R. Turner (ed.), *Ethnomethodology* (Harmondsworth: Penguin) pp.54-68.

Monopolies and Mergers Commission (1976a) *Barristers' Services: A Report on the Supply of Barristers' Services in Relation to Restrictions on Advertising*, Cmnd 559. (London: HMSO).

Monopolies and Mergers Commission (197b) *Services of Solicitors in England and*

Wales: A Report on the Supply of Services of Solicitors in England and Wales in Relation to Restrictions on Advertising Cmdn, 557. (London: HMSO).

Morris, P., R. White and P.S.C. Lewis (1973) *Social Needs and Legal Action* (London: Martin Robertson).

Morris, P. and M. Zander (1973) 'The Allocation of Criminal Legal Aid in Magistrates Courts - A Study in London Courts', *Law Society Gazette*, 70, p.2372.

Morton, J. (1977) Correspondence, *Justice of the Peace*, 141.

Mulkay, M. (1979) *Science and the Sociology of Knowledge* (London: Allen and Unwin).

Mullaney, T.E. (1977) 'Carter's Pledge to Help Cut Regulatory Complexity', *New York Times*, D-7, col. 1, (23 Dec).

Mumford, E. (1970) *Interns: From Students to Physicians* (Cambridge, Mass: Harvard University Press).

Mungham, G. and P.A. Thomas (1979) 'Advocacy and the Solicitor-Advocate in Magistrates' Courts in England and Wales', *International Journal of the Sociology of Law*, 7, pp.169-95.

Mungham, G. and P.A. Thomas 'Studying Lawyers, Aspects of the Theory, Method and Politics of Social Research', *British Journal of Law and Society* 8, pp.79-96.

Napley, D. (1977) *The Times* (12 Oct).

National Board For Prices And Incomes (1968) *Remuneration of Solicitors* Cmnd. 3529 (London: HMSO). (First Report Cmnd. 4217, 1969; Second Report Cmnd. 4624, 1971).

National Law Journal (1979) 'National Lawfirm Survey', *National Law Journal* (1 Oct and 8 Oct) pp.28ff and 30ff.

National Law Journal (1980) '1980 Corporate Law Department Survey', *National Law Journal*, 2, pp.26ff.

National Organisation For Public Health Nursing (NOPHN) (1932) *Principles and Practice of Public Health Nursing* (New York: NOPHN).

Navarro, V. (1976) *Medicine Under Capitalism* (London: Croom Helm).

Navarro, V. (1978) *Class Struggle, the State and Medicine* (London: Martin Robertson).

Newton, K. (1969) 'City Politics in Britain and the United States', *Political Studies*, 17.

Newton, K. (1974) 'Community Decision Makers and Community Decision-Making in England and the United States', in T.N. Clark, *Comparative Community Politics* (London: Wiley).

Newton, K. (1975) 'Community Politics and Decision-Making: the American Experience and its Lessons', in K. Young, *Essays on the Study of Urban Politics* (London: Macmillan).

O'Gorman, H.J. (1963) *Lawyers and Matrimonial Cases* (Glencoe, Ill: Free Press).

Ogston, D. and W.D. Ogston (1971) 'Honours Graduates in Medicine of the University of Aberdeen 1931-1960', *British Journal of Medical Education*, 5, pp.30-4.

Olesen, V. and E. Whittaker (1968) *The Silent Dialogue: The Social Psychology of Professional Socialization* (San Francisco: Jossey-Bass).

Olesen, V. and E. Whittaker (1970) 'Critical Notes on Sociological Studies of Professional Socialization', in J.A. Jackson (ed.), *Professions and*

Professionalization (Cambridge: Cambridge University Press) pp.181-221.

Pahl, J.M. and R.E. Pahl (1971) *Managers and their Wives* (London: Allen Lane).

Parkhouse, J. (1977) 'A Simple Model for Medical Manpower Studies', *British Medical Journal*, (20 Aug) p.6085.

Parkhouse, J. (1978a) 'Medical Manpower in Britain I: The Background', *Medical Education*, 12, pp.40-53.

Parkhouse, J. (1978b) 'Medical Manpower in Britain 2: The Career Structure', *Medical Education*, 12, pp.54-62.

Parkhouse, J. (1979) *Medical Manpower in Britain* (London: Churchill Livingstone).

Parkin, F. (1979) *Marxism and Class Theory* (New York: Columbia University Press).

Parsons, T. (1939) 'The Professions and Social Structure', *Social Forces*, 17, pp. 457-67.

Parsons, T. (1947) see Weber (1964).

Parsons, T. (1951) *The Social System* (London: Routledge and Kegan Paul; Glencoe, Ill.: Free Press).

Parsons, T. (1954) 'A Sociologist looks at the Legal Profession', in *Essays in Sociological Theory* (Glencoe, Ill: The Free Press) pp.370-85.

Parsons, T. (1962) 'The Legal Profession', in W. Evan (ed.), *Law and Sociology* (Glencoe: Ill: Free Press).

Parsons, T. (1968) *The Structure of Social Action* (New York: Free Press; first published 1937).

Parsons, T. (1968) 'Professions', in D. Sills (ed.), *International Encyclopedia of the Social Sciences*, XII, (New York: Macmillan and The Free Press) pp.536-47.

Paterson, A. (1974) 'Judges: A Political Élite?', *British Journal of Law and Society*, 1 pp.118-35.

Payne, G., R. Dingwall, J. Payne, and M.P. Carter (1981) *Sociology and Social Research* (London: Routledge and Kegan Paul).

Perrow, C. (1963) 'Goals and Power Structures: a Historical Case Study', in E. Freidson (ed.), *The Hospital in Modern Society* (Glencoe, Ill: Free Press).

Peterson, M.J. (1978) *The Medical Profession in Mid-Victorian London* (London: University of California Press).

Podmore, D. (1980a) *Solicitors and the Wider Community* (London: Heinemann).

Podmore, D. (1980b) 'Bucher and Strauss Revisited - The Case of the Solicitors' Profession', *British Journal of Law and Society*, 7, pp.1-21.

Pound, R. (1953) *The Lawyer from Antiquity to Modern Times* (St. Paul, Minn: West Publishing Co.).

Powell, A. (1951-75) *A Dance to the Music of Time* (London: Heinemann).

Powell, A. (1980) *John Aubrey and his Friends* (London: Heinemann).

Poynter, F.N.L. (ed.), (1964) *The Evolution of Hospitals in Britain* (London: Pitman).

Pugh, D. and D. Hickson (eds), (1976) *Organisational Structure in its Context: the Aston Programme I* (Farnborough, Hants: Saxon House).

Pugh, D. and C.R. Hinings (eds), (1976) *Organisational Structure: Extensions and Replications: the Aston Programme II* (Farnborough: Saxon House).

Pugh, D. and R. Payne (eds), (1977) *Organisational Behaviour in its Context: the Aston Programme III* (Farnborough: Saxon House).

Rabin, R.L. (1976) 'Lawyers for Social Change: Perspectives on Public Interest

Law', *Stanford Law Review*, 28, pp.207-63.

Radcliffe, V. (1968) *Not in Feather Beds* (London: Hamish Hamilton).

Reader, W.J. (1967) *Professional Men: The Rise of the Professional Classes in Nineteenth Century England* (New York: Basic Books).

Reck, A. (1964) *Recent American Philosophy: Studies of Representative Thinkers* (New York: Pantheon).

Rees, W.M. (1975) 'Clinical Legal Education: An Analysis of the University of Kent Model', *The Law Teacher*, 9, pp.125-40.

Reid, M.E. (1980) 'The Development of Academic General Practice in Scotland: a Sociological Analysis', unpublished Ph.D thesis, University of Glasgow.

Rhyne, C.S. (1978) *Law and Judicial Systems of Nations* (Washington: World Peace Through Law Center, 3rd ed.).

Ringer, F.K. (1979) 'The German Academic Community', in A. Oleson and J. Voss (eds), *The Organization of Knowledge in Modern America 1860-1920* (Baltimore: Johns Hopkins University Press).

Roberts, M.M. (1954) *American Nursing: History and Interpretation* (New York: Macmillan).

Robson, J. (1973) 'The NHS Company Inc? The Social Consequences of Professional Dominance in the National Health Service', *International Journal of Health Services*, 3, pp. 413-26.

Rock, P. (1979) *The Making of Symbolic Interactionism* (London: Macmillan).

Rodabaugh, J.H. and M.J. Rodabaugh (1951) *Nursing in Ohio: a History* (Columbus, Ohio: The Ohio State Nurses' Association).

Rosen, G. (1963) 'The Hospital: Historical Sociology of a Community Institution', in E. Freidson (ed.), *The Hospital in Modern Society* (Glencoe: Ill: Free Press).

Rosenberg, C.E. (1967) 'The Practice of Medicine in New York a Century Ago', *Bulletin of the History of Medicine*, 41, pp.223-53.

Rosenberg, C.E. (1977) 'And Heal the Sick: the Hospital and the Patient in 19th Century America', *Journal of Social History*, 10, pp.428-77.

Rosenberg, C.E. (1979) 'Florence Nightingale on Contagion: the Hospital as a Moral Universe', in C.E. Rosenberg (ed.), *Healing and History* (New York: Dawson).

Rosenthal, D. (1974) *Lawyer and Client: Who's in Charge?* (New York: Russell Sage).

Ross, H.L. (1970) *Settled Out of Court: The Social Process of Insurance Claims Adjustment* (Chicago: Aldine).

Roth, J. (1963) *Timetables: Structuring the Passage of Time in Hospital and Other Careers* (Indianapolis: Bobbs-Merrill).

Roth, J. (1974) 'Professionalism: the Sociologist's Decoy', *Sociology of Work and Occupations*, 1, pp.6-23.

Rottenberg, D. (1979) 'The Pinstripe Revolution', *Chicago*, 28, pp.98-124.

Royal College of General Practitioners (1977) 'Trends in General Practice', *British Medical Journal* (London) pp.10-11.

Royal Commission On Legal Services (1974) Final Report (2 volumes), (London: HMSO) Cmnd. 7648.

Rueschemeyer, D (1964) 'Doctors and Lawyers: A Comment on the Theory of the Professions', *Canadian Review of Sociology and Anthropology*, 1, pp.17-30.

Rueschemeyer, D. (1973a) 'Professions, Historisch and Kulturell Vergleichende Überlegungen', in G. Albrecht, H. Daheim and F. Sack (eds), *Soziologie: René König zum 65. Geburtstag* (Opladen: Westdeutscher Verlag) pp.250-60.

Rueschemeyer, D. (1973b) *Lawyers and their Society. A Comparative Study of the Legal Profession in Germany and in the United States* (Cambridge, Mass: Harvard University Press).

Rueschemeyer, D. (1977) 'Structural Differentiation, Efficiency, and Power', *American Journal of Sociology*, 83, pp.1-25.

Rueschemeyer, D. (1980) 'Professionalisierung. Theoretische Probleme für die vergleichende Geschichtsforschung', *Geschichte und Gesellschaft*, 6.

Runciman, G. (1970) 'Sociology in its Place', in G. Runciman, *Sociology in its Place, and Other Essays* (Cambridge: Cambridge University Press).

Sahlins, M. (1979) *New York Review of Books* (22 Mar) p.47.

Scheingold, S. (1974) *The Politics of Rights* (New Haven: Yale University Press).

Schell, O.N. (1974) 'The Development of National Law Firms', *The Business Lawyer*, 34, pp.963-8.

Schudson, M. (1977) 'Public, Private and Professional Lives: The Correspondence of David Dudley Field and Samuel Bowles', *American Journal of Legal History*, 21, pp.191-211.

Schutz, A. (1964) 'The Well Informed Citizen: An Essay on the Social Distribution of Knowledge', in A. Broderson (ed.), *Collected Papers 2*, (The Hague: Martinus Nijhoff) pp.120-34.

Scott, W.R. (1965) 'Reactions to Supervision in a Heteronomous Professional Organisation', *Administrative Science Quarterly*, 10.

Scott, W.R. (1966) 'Professionals in Bureaucracies: Areas of Conflict', in H. Vollmer and D. Mills (eds), *Professionalisation* (Englewood Cliffs, N.J.: Prentice Hall).

Scott, W.R. (1969) 'Professional Employees in a Bureaucratic Structure: Social Work', in A. Etzioni (ed.), *The Semi-Professions and their Organisation* (New York: Free Press).

Scoville, J.G. (1965) 'The Development and Relevance of U.S. Occupational Data', *Industrial and Labour Relations*, 19, pp.70-9.

Sharlin, A. (1979) 'From the Study of Social Mobility to the Study of Society', *American Journal of Sociology*, 85, pp.338-60.

Sharpe, L.J. (1973) 'American Democracy Reconsidered (Part One)', *British Journal of Political Science*, 3.

Shaw, H. (1979) 'The Careers of Women Graduates of St. Mary's Hospital Medical School, London, 1961-72', *Medical Education*, 13, pp.275-83.

Sheldrake, P.F. and S. Berry (1976) *Looking at Innovation* (Windsor: National Foundation for Educational Research).

Shelley, P.B. (1923) *A Defence of Poetry*, in H.F.B. Brett-Smith (ed.), *Peacock's Four Ages of Poetry* (Oxford: Blackwell).

Shem, S. (1980) *House of God* (London: Corgi).

Shetreet, S. (1976) *Judges on Trial* (Amsterdam: North-Holland).

Shils, E. (1980) 'Tradition, Ecology and Institution in the History of Sociology', in E. Shils, *The Calling of Sociology* (Chicago: University of Chicago Press) pp.165-258.

Shuval, J. (1975a) 'From "Boy" to "Colleague": Processes of Role

Transformation in Professional Socialization', *Social Science and Medicine*, 9, pp.413-20.

Shuval, J. (1975b) 'Socialisation of Health Professionals in Israel: Early Sources of Congruence and Differentiation', *Journal of Medical Education*, 50, pp.443-57.

Simmel, G. (1964) 'The Secret and the Secret Society', in K.H. Wolff (ed.), *The Sociology of Georg Simmel* (New York: Free Press); first published 1950.

Smigel, E. (1964) *The Wall Street Lawyer* (Bloomington: Indiana University Press; revised edition 1969).

Smith, P. and P.A. Thomas (1978) *The Duty Solicitor Scheme as Operated at Cardiff's Central Charge Unit 1977* (Cardiff: University College Law Department).

Snowise, A.W. (1972) Letter: 24 Hours, *Law Society Gazette*, 69, 8.

Sorensen, J. and J. Sorensen (1974) 'The Conflict of Professionals in Bureaucratic Organisations' *Administrative Science Quarterly*, 19

Spencer, H. (1914) *The Principle of Sociology*, Vol. III, part 7 (New York: Appleton).

Spurling, H. (1977) *Handbook to Anthony Powell's Music of Time* (London: Heinemann).

Stacey, M. (ed.) (1976) *The Sociology of the NHS* (Keele, Sociological Review Monograph 22).

Stacey, M., M.E. Reid, C. Heath, and R. Dingwall (eds), (1977) *Health and the Division of Labour* (London: Croom Helm; New York: Prodist).

Stebbins, R.A. (1970) 'Careers: The Subjective Approach', *Sociological Quarterly*, pp.32-49.

Steiner, G. (1971) *Bluebeard's Castle: Some Notes Towards the Redefinition of Culture* (London: Faber and Faber).

Steiner, G. (1978) 'The Distribution of Discourse', in G. Steiner, *On Difficulty* (London: Oxford University Press) pp.61-94.

Stephen, W.J. (1979) *An Analysis of Primary Medical Care: An Interactional Study* (London: Cambridge University Press).

Stevenson, A. (1975) 'Duty Solicitors', *Law Society Gazette*, 72, p.317.

Stevenson, Adlai (1978) 'Reform and Judicial Selection', *American Bar Association Journal*, 64.

Steward, J. (1979) 'Pulitzer Prize Weekly in a Hurricane's Eye', *Madison Press Connection*, 1, (25 April).

Stewart, R.B. (1975) 'The Reformation of American Administrative Law', *Harvard Law Review*, 88, pp.1667-813.

Stinchcombe, A. (1965) 'Social Structure and Organisations', in J.G. March (ed.), *Handbook of Organisations* (Chicago: Rand McNally).

Stinchcombe, A.L. (1968) *Constructing Social Theories* (New York: Harcourt, Brace and World).

Straus, R. (1957) 'The Nature and Status of Medical Sociology', *American Sociological Review*, 22, pp.200-9.

Strauss, A.L. (1978) *Negotiations: Varieties, Contexts, Processes and Social Order* (San Francisco: Jossey-Bass).

Strauss, A.L., L. Schatzman, R. Bucher, D. Ehrlich, and M. Sabshin (1963) 'The Hospital and its Negotiated Order' in E. Freidson (ed.), *The Hospital in Modern Society* (Glencoe, Ill.: Free Press).

Strauss, A.L., L. Schatzman, R. Bucher, D. Ehrlich and M. Sabshin (1964)

Psychiatric Ideologies and Institutions (New York: Free Press).

Strong, P.M. (1979a) *The Ceremonial Order of the Clinic* (London: Routledge and Kegan Paul).

Strong, P.M. (1979b) 'Sociological Imperialism and the Profession of Medicine', *Social Science and Medicine*, 13A, pp.199-215.

Strong, P.M. and A.G. Davis (1977) 'Roles, Role Formats and Medical Encounters: A Cross Cultural Analysis of Staff-Patient Relationships in Children's Clinics', *Sociological Review*, 25, pp.775-800.

Strong, P.M. and G.W. Horobin (1978) 'Politeness is All - The Forms, Causes and Consequences of Medical Gentility', (Institute of Medical Sociology, University of Aberdeen: Unpublished Mimeo).

Stumpf, H.P. and R.J. Janowitz (1971) 'Judges and the Poor: Bench Response to Federally Financed Legal Services', *Stanford Law Review*, 21.

Tate, C.N. (1975) 'Paths to the Bench in Britain', *Western Political Quarterly*, 28.

Thielens, W. (1957) 'Some Comparisons of Entrants to Medical and Law School', in R.K. Merton, G. Reader and P. Kendall (eds), *The Student Physician* (Cambridge, Mass: Harvard University Press).

Thomas, P.A. (1978) 'Plea Bargaining in England', *Journal of Criminal Law and Criminology*, 69, p.170.

Thomas, P.A. and G. Mungham (1973) 'Cardiff Duty Solicitor Scheme', *Law Society Gazette*, 70, p.2395.

Thomas, P.A. and G. Mungham (1976) 'A Report on the Duty Solicitor Scheme Operating in Cardiff Magistrates Courts 1973-4', (Cardiff: University College Law Department).

Thomas, P.A. and G. Mungham (1977) 'Duty Solicitor Schemes: In Whose Interest?', *New Law Journal*, 127, pp.180-1.

Thomas, P.A. and P. Smith (1978) 'Distribution of Criminal Work', *New Law Journal*, 128, pp.324-6.

Thompson, E.P. (1967) 'Time, Work Discipline, and Industrial Capitalism', *Past and Present*, 38.

Timasheff, N.S. (1940) 'Business and the Professions in Liberal, Fascist and Communist Society', *American Journal of Sociology*, 45, pp.363-9.

Tinnin, D.B. (1973) *Just About Everybody vs. Howard Hughes* (New York, Garden City: Doubleday).

Tooley, S.A. (1906) *The History of Nursing in the British Empire* (London: Bousfield).

Towers, R. (1979) 'Review of *Birdy*, by William Wharton and *The Cement Garden* by Ian McEwan', *New York Review of Books*, (8 May) p.8.

Trilling, L. (1972) *Sincerity and Authority* (London: Oxford University Press).

Turner, C. and M.N. Hodge (1970) 'Occupations and Professions', in J.A. Jackson (ed.), *Professions and Professionalisation* (Cambridge: Cambridge University Press).

Twiss, B. (1942) *Lawyers and the Constitution* (Princeton: Princeton University Press).

Tybor, J.R. (1978) 'Ouster in Chicago; It Ain't Cheap', *National Law Journal* (7 Aug). 18.

United States Bureau of Census (1958) *County Business Patterns 1956* (Washington: Government Printing Office).

United States Bureau of Census (1967a) *County Business Patterns 1966*

(Washington: Government Printing Office).

United States Bureau of Census (1967b) *1967 Census of Selected Service Industries, Legal Services Report*, SC 67-5-4, (Washington: Government Printing Office).

United States Bureau of Census (1972) *1972 Census of Selected Service Industries, Legal Services Report*, SC 72-5-4 (Washington: Government Printing Office).

United States Bureau of Census (1974) *County Business Patterns 1973* (Washington: Government Printing Office).

United States Bureau of Census (1975) *Historical Statistics of the United States, Colonial Times to 1970. Bicentennial Ed.* (Washington: Government Printing Office).

United States Bureau of Census (1979) *Statistical Abstract of the United States 1978 (100th edn)* (Washington: Government Printing Office).

United States Department of Commerce (1968) *Survey of Current Business, Jul-Dec. 1968*, (Washington).

United States Department of Commerce (1978) *Survey of Current Business, Jul-Dec. 1978*, (Washington).

Vogel, M.J. (1978) 'Patrons, Practitioners and Patients: the Voluntary Hospital in Mid-Victorian Boston', in J.W. Leavit and R.L. Numbers (eds), *Sickness and Health in America* (Madison, Wis: University of Wisconsin Press).

Vollmer, H.W. and D.J. Mills (eds) (1966) *Professionalization* (Englewood Cliffs, N.J.: Prentice-Hall).

Waddington, I. (1973) 'The Role of the Hospital in the Development of Modern Medicine: a Sociological Analysis', *Sociology*, 7, pp.211-24.

Waddington, I. (1977) 'General Practitioners and Consultants in Early 19th Century England: The Sociology of an Intra-professional Conflict', in J. Woodward and D. Richards, (eds), *Health Care and Popular Medicine in 19th Century England* (London: Croom Helm).

Walker, A.H. and J.W. Lorsch (1970) 'Organisation Choice: Product versus Function', in J.W. Lorsch and P. Lawrence, *Studies in Organisational Design* (Homewood, Ill: Irwin Dorsey).

Warkov, S. and J.Zelan (1965) *Lawyers in the Making* (Chicago: Aldine).

Weber, M. (1954) (translated M. Rheinstein, ed.) *On Law in Economy and Society* (Cambridge, Mass.: Harvard University Press).

Weber, M. (1964) (translated T. Parsons) *The Theory of Social and Economic Organisation* (New York: Free Press; first published 1947).

Wegg-Prosser (1964-5) *Law Society Annual Report*.

Weinstein, H. (1975) 'Defending What? The Corporation's Public Interest', *Juris Doctor*, 6, p.39.

Wiebe, R.H. (1967) *The Search for Order: 1877-1920*, (New York: Hill and Wang).

Wilensky, H.L. (1960) 'Work Careers and Social Integration', *International Social Science Journal*, pp.543-60.

Wilensky, H.L. (1964) 'The Professionalization of Everyone?', *American Journal of Sociology*, 70, pp.142-6.

Williams, E.A. (1973) The Solicitor and his Social Conscience', *Solicitor's Journal*, 117, p.199.

Willock, I. (1969) 'Scottish Judges Scrutinised', *Juridical Review*.

Wilson, J.Q. (1968) *Varieties of Police Behavior: The Management of Law and Order in Eight Communities* (Cambridge, Mass.: Harvard University Press).

Wolfe, T. (1975) *The New Journalism* (London: Picador).

Wolfe, T. (1977) 'The Truest Sport: Jousting with Sam and Charlie', in T. Wolfe, *Mauve Gloves and Madmen, Clutter and Vine* (New York: Corgi).

Woodward, E.S. (1937) 'The WPA and Nursing', *American Journal of Nursing*, 37.

Working Party on Judicial Studies and Information (1978) (London: HMSO).

Young, H. (1978) 'Talking about the Law', *Listener*, (17 Aug).

Young, M.F.D. (ed.), (1971) *Knowledge and Control: New Directions for the Sociology of Education* (London: Collier-Macmillan).

Zander, M. (1969) 'Unrepresented Defendants in the Criminal Courts', *Criminal Law Review*, p.632.

Zander, M. (1972) 'Unrepresented Defendants in Magistrates Courts, 1972', *New Law Journal*, 122, pp.1041-2.

Zola, I. (1972) 'Medicine as an Institution of Social Control', *Sociological Review*, 20, 4.

Author Index

Subject Index